D1200264

The Rhetoric of Empiricism

The Rhetoric of Empiricism

Language and Perception from Locke to I. A. Richards

JULES DAVID LAW

CORNELL UNIVERSITY PRESS
Ithaca and London

First published 1993 by Cornell University Press.

Library of Congress Cataloging-in-Publication Data

Law, Jules David, 1957—
   The rhetoric of empiricism : language and perception : from Locke to I.A. Richards / Jules David Law.
      p.   cm.
   Includes bibliographical references and index.
   ISBN 0-8014-2706-1 (alk. paper)
   1. Empiricism—History.   2. Rhetoric—Philosophy.   I. Title.
B816.L39   1993
146'.44'09—dc20   92-44276

Printed in the United States of America

⊗The paper in this book meets the minimum requirements
of the American National Standard for Information Sciences—
Permanence of Paper for Printed Library Materials, ANSI Z39.48-1984.

THIS BOOK IS FOR MY PARENTS,

Harriet Law and Charles Law

Contents

PREFACE ix

INTRODUCTION 1

1. "Beside the Design of Language": Molyneux's Question
   and the Empiricist Construction of Rhetoric 19

2. Locke's Grammar of Reflection 51

3. Toward the Surface and Back Again: Berkeley's
   Reflections on Language 93

4. Empiricist Aesthetics: Burke's "Analogy"
   of the Senses 131

5. The "Character" of Reflection: Hazlitt
   on Depth and Superficiality 165

6. Ruskin's "Truth of Space": The Technique of Surface
   and the Ethics of Depth in *Modern Painters* 204

EPILOGUE. From Ruskin to I. A. Richards: The End
   of Empiricism and the Beginning of Empiricist
   Literary Criticism 235

APPENDIX. Empiricism among the Isms 245

WORKS CITED 249

INDEX 257

Preface

To MANY, A "rhetoric of empiricism" must seem a contradiction in terms. British empiricism, according to the common view, is a stridently antirhetorical philosophy that emphasizes the epistemological primacy of our sense data and (ideally) the reliability of our reports on them. Yet the status of rhetorical—and particularly figurative—language in empiricism is far more contested than we commonly suppose. Perhaps the simplest way of stating the argument of this book is to suggest that our understanding of the British empiricist tradition has suffered because we have stressed Locke's "ideas of sensation" at the expense of his more ambiguous "ideas of reflection" and have assumed his account of perception to be the restrictive and determining basis for his ideas about language.

In this book I begin with the "classical" empiricism of Locke and attempt to construct a tradition of empiricist writing defined by a paradigmatic dramatic scene—the blind man returned to sight—and a particular set of rhetorical figures—reflection, surface, and depth. Empiricism, I argue, is concerned with the rhetoric of perception—that is, with the point at which characterizations of linguistic propriety and characterizations of sensory perception intersect, producing a mutually defining relationship between language and image. The trajectory of my argument—from Locke and Berkeley, through Burke and Hazlitt, to Ruskin—moves gradually away from "philosophy" and toward "literary" and "art" criticism. The canon of empiricist writers developed here is thus a polemical one, a strategic compromise between "empiricism" as it has been defined by historians of philosophy and "empiricism" as it has been identified and criticized by literary critics, historians, and theorists.

This book is less a reconstruction of the philosophical aims of early British empiricism than an attempt to trace the consequences for literary theory of taking a classical empiricist stance. To scholars in literature departments, empiricism connotes both a way of reading texts and a philosophical tradition that literary writers—from Richardson to Wordsworth to Beckett—have variously aligned themselves with and repudiated. Empiricism has thus come down to us both as a methodological imperative and as a trope in literary historiography, each with its own theoretical consequences. It is my belief that much contemporary literary theory has defined itself inaccurately and unnecessarily in opposition to empiricism. Empiricism is accused of privileging the visual over the discursive, the literal over the rhetorical, the static over the temporal, and totalizing explanations over dialectical processes. It is my goal to unsettle these binary oppositions and to argue that at the heart of empiricism lies a sophisticated, dynamic, and dialectical account of the relationship between language and visual perception that has been—and may continue to be—fruitful for literary study.

Many heterogeneous kinds of encouragement and criticism went into the making of this book. I would like in particular to thank four teachers who helped shape my intellectual interests long before this project was conceived: Lee Patterson, Stanley Fish, Jerome McGann, and Patricia Parker. Later, Jerome Christensen, Michael Fried, and Neil Hertz all provided clues that steered me toward rewarding problems in Ruskin and Burke. Over the years, intellectual friendships with Reed Way Dasenbrock, Deborah Esch, David Bromwich, and Michal Ginsburg have supported and challenged me in ways that extend beyond this book.

Several friends and colleagues have read portions of the manuscript, not only criticizing and correcting it but providing new directions for the book as it developed. At Princeton, David Bromwich, Hans Aarsleff, and Ian Balfour provided invaluable readings of individual chapters, while at Northwestern University, John Brenkman, Michal Ginsburg, Helen Deutsch, Paul Breslin, Christopher Herbert, Martin Mueller, and John McCumber all offered important advice and encouragement. Larry Lipking and Sharon Achinstein provided close and cogent readings of the early chapters, sharpening my sense of important problems in Locke and Berkeley. Gerry Graff read countless versions of introductory sections and helped me with the special problem of situating the work within specific intellectual and disciplinary debates.

At Cornell University Press I was fortunate to receive valuable encouragement and advice from Bernhard Kendler, and readers' reports of great intelligence, generosity, and breadth from Richard Kroll and David Marshall. This book would not have been the same without their contributions, and I regret only not being able to realize all the extended possibilities for the project that they envisioned.

I owe a special debt to John Brenkman, who read the manuscript in its most critical stages and helped me turn the most important corners. As both colleague and friend, he has demonstrated a clarity, courage, and insight that have been a constant source of inspiration for me. I also owe a special debt to Amy Kight-Law, who whose love and encouragement over the years helped make it possible to write this book. My final thanks are to Wendy Wall, who has sustained, challenged, and inspired me, as colleague, friend, and partner.

Chapters 3 through 6 were drafted during a year's leave from Princeton University, aided by a fellowship from the American Council of Learned Scholars. I am immensely grateful for the support of both institutions.

JULES DAVID LAW

Evanston, Illinois

The Rhetoric of Empiricism

Introduction

EMPIRICISM DOES NOT stand in very high repute among literary theorists these days. Regarded generally as a discredited philosophical paradigm characterized by its naive positivism, its highly normative account of "common sense" and its hostility to rhetoric, empiricism is nonetheless suspected of being the philosophical attitude persisting at the heart of most Anglo-American criticism and critical theory.[1] Empiricism, according to Catherine Belsey's polemical account, is the distinguishing and disenabling feature of Anglo-American critical theory.[2] The empiricist critic, writes Belsey, "urg[es]" us "to get on with the reading process, to respond directly to the text without worrying about niceties of theory" (4) and justifies this procedure through an appeal to the "transparency of language" (4). This ideal of linguistic transparency in turn presupposes a world of preconstituted entities (objects, thoughts, and meanings) that precludes any genuinely critical thinking about the mediating roles of history and culture. "The vice of Anglo-American empiricism," concludes Fredric Jameson, "lies indeed in its stubborn will to isolate the object in question from everything else."[3]

---

[1] On the antirhetorical bias of classical empiricism, see Hans Aarsleff, *From Locke to Saussure: Essays on the Study of Language and Intellectual History* (Minneapolis: University of Minnesota Press, 1982), 25–26, 43–44.

[2] Catherine Belsey, *Critical Practice* (London: Methuen, 1980), chap. 1, passim.

[3] Fredric Jameson, *The Prison-House of Language: A Critical Account of Structuralism and Russian Formalism* (Princeton: Princeton University Press, 1972), 23. Jameson comments generally, and critically, on empiricism throughout his first chapter (e.g., 4, 23–24, 31–32). This negative estimate of empiricism is echoed at numerous other points in Jameson's work. See, e.g., *Marxism and Form: Twentieth-Century Dialectical Theories of Literature* (Princeton: Princeton University Press, 1971), 367–68. Jameson's criticisms would be more appropriately addressed to the positivistic impulse that forms one strand in the history of modern British philosophy but that cannot be confused with classical empiricism. It is worth noting that Lukács, whom Jameson invokes as a critic of Lockean empiricism (*Prison-House*, 23–24), explicitly distinguishes the "irrational" and "tradition"-bound character of classical empiricism from the "rational systematization" of modern capitalism. See "Reification and the Consciousness of the Proletariat," in *History and Class Consciousness: Studies in Marxist Dialectics*, trans. Rodney Livingstone (Cambridge: MIT Press, 1971), 96–97.

Belsey suggests that empiricism has persisted in Anglo-American criticism even in cases where the ethos of "common sense" has been adequately demystified.[4] Ironically, theorists more temperamentally sympathetic to empiricism than Belsey have proceeded in quite the opposite direction and sought to defend a "common sense" purged of empiricism's more positivist trappings. Thus E. D. Hirsch and Wayne Booth have both criticized modern positivism and attempted to construct complex accounts of the "common sense" or "communal" processes of "validation" that constrain interpretation, while recognizing that the ideals of "objective" validation and corrigibility originate historically in an empiricist philosophy that still has some claims on our interest.[5]

The central point on which all these theorists agree is that traditional empiricist inquiry is limited by its schematic reliance on *optical* models of cognition and judgment, a reliance that leads to highly problematic analogies between language and visual perception and to the mistaken belief that interpreting a text is like "seeing" an "object."[6] Hirsch regards empiricism's foundational optical metaphorics as an empirical liability,

[4] E.g., in the New Critics and in Northrop Frye. See Belsey, *Critical Practice*, 3–4, 20.

[5] See E. D. Hirsch, Jr., *The Aims of Interpretation* (Chicago: University of Chicago Press, 1976), 27–36, 45–49, 96, and *Validity in Interpretation* (New Haven: Yale University Press, 1967), 224–44; and Wayne Booth, *Modern Dogma and the Rhetoric of Assent* (Chicago: University of Chicago Press, 1974), xiii, 62–64, 100–101, and chap. 4, passim. See similar attempts to preserve the communal, scientific spirit of empiricism within a less foundational framework in Karl Popper, *Conjectures and Refutations: The Growth of Scientific Knowledge* (London: Routledge and Kegan Paul, 1963), 13–14, 22–23, 49–54; W.V.O. Quine, "Two Dogmas of Empiricism," in *From a Logical Point of View* (Cambridge: Harvard University Press, 1953), 41–44; Ian Hacking, *Why Does Language Matter to Philosophy?* (Cambridge: Cambridge University Press, 1975), 187; and Michael Williams, *Groundless Belief: An Essay on the Possibility of Epistemology* (Oxford: Basil Blackwell, 1977), 178–81.

[6] See Belsey's repeated references to the empiricist "illusion" of "the transparency of language" and to the empiricist ideal of responding directly to "bare" facts (*Critical Practice*, 4, 8–9, 38). See also Hirsch's critique of the "analogy of visual perspective" in *The Aims of Interpretation*, 27–31, 45–49; and related remarks on empiricism, positivism, and phenomenology by Paul de Man in "Form and Intent in the New American Criticism" and "The Dead-End of Formalist Criticism" (*Blindness and Insight: Essays in the Rhetoric of Contemporary Criticism*, rev. ed. [Minneapolis: University of Minnesota Press, 1983], especially 33–34, 231–45).

The critique of empiricism as a philosophy crippled by its model of visual evidence and insufficiently attuned to the complexities of temporal, linguistic meanings, is echoed in recent historiographical theory. See Joan W. Scott's critique of the use of "experience" in revisionist cultural history ("The Evidence of Experience," *Critical Inquiry* 17 [Summer 1991]: 773–97). Scott argues that the invocation of "experience" by cultural historians as a strategy for disrupting the normative-empiricist-positivist model of inquiry is self-defeating,

whereas Belsey regards it as an ideological smoke screen; but in both cases there is an assumption that empiricism moves systematically and reductively from accounts of visual sensation to accounts of language.[7] In this book, however, we shall see that the empiricist concern with language goes far beyond the specular ideals of plain-speaking and definitional clarity and of the accompanying suspicion of rhetoric as a kind of distorting medium. For in that confrontation with the sensory world that constitutes the central drama of empiricist writing, language and sensation (particularly visual perception) are inextricably, in fact *dialectically*, related. It is not simply that empiricist claims are necessarily expressed in language, or even that they are unavoidably rhetorical—but that the empiricist characterization of perceptual knowledge is articulated explicitly in terms of linguistic distinctions: between signifier and signified, proper and improper, true and false analogy, literal and metaphorical, voice and print, character and word, and so on. As we shall see in Chapter 1 when we turn to the successive attempts to resolve the "Molyneux Question" (the question of how a man born blind and restored to sight might describe his first visual impressions), the empiricist account of *what we see* is inseparable from an account of *what we say*.

One of the central claims of empiricism (and, when supplemented by a particular rhetoric, one of its central *myths*) is that the world as we "see" it is actually flat: that what we really see when we look at the world is a two-dimensional arrangement of color, light, and figure, which only inference, habit, or association can convert into an impression of three-

---

since it continues to model the *observation* of experience along visual and static rather than discursive and dialectical lines.

7 A more recent study of Lockean rhetoric, Cathy Caruth's *Empirical Truths and Critical Fictions: Locke, Wordsworth, Kant, Freud* (Baltimore: Johns Hopkins University Press, 1991), brilliantly reverses the critiques of empiricism outlined above and argues that Locke consistently moves away from visual models and toward discursive ones. Though the official doctrine of Locke's *Essay* is that "reflection" is structured like visual perception, argues Caruth, "in the *Essay*'s own reflections on the two sources of knowledge . . . the principles that govern the self-presentation of knowledge are closer to the conventions of literary writing than to the laws of visual perception" (18). Caruth sees a continual "slippage" in Locke's argument: Locke's assumption that "reflection is structured like sensation" is consistently undermined by his reliance on "narrative and figure" (27, 16, 18). I agree wholeheartedly with Caruth that Lockean empiricism "is neither simply a reductive doctrine of experience, nor even simply a doctrine at all, but a complex text that raises many questions about the interpretation of its own vocabulary" (20). However, as the remainder of this book will show, I believe that the movement between the visual and the discursive in empiricism is a dialectical one rather than a unilinear regression in *either* direction.

dimensional space.[8] This optical empiricism, or optical constructivism, is central to all the writers discussed in this book. Empiricists tend to describe the constructive process, somewhat figuratively, as the conversion of surfaces into depth through a *pre*reflective act of judgment, recognized, ironically, only through reflection.

To reflect is to remember, to review, to note, to attend, to meditate, to introspect, to deduce, to analogize, and to analyze. Reflection thus ranges from the most passive to the most active of mental processes, from the most mechanical and material to the most intellectual of phenomena, and from the activity that most confirms and supports common sense to the skeptical and critical energy most destructive of it. Reflecting on our sensory impressions, we note how unreflectingly we proceed in the normal course of things, though reflection also proves this *un*reflection to be rather the condensation or sedimentation of previous acts of reflection. Habit and custom, in the empiricist view, are built up out of successive stages of recalling and forgetting, successive shifts of focus, a complex, deliberate structure of attention and inattention.[9]

It is, ironically, from empiricism's dramatic account of perception in terms of reflections, surfaces, and depths that we get our familar, reductive view of empiricism as a philosophy concerned primarily with the surfaces of things—whether the rock-solid surfaces of Locke and Johnson, or the chimerical surfaces of Berkeley. This popular view is not all wrong, nor could it be, proceeding as it does from intuitions about the *rhetoric* of empiricism. But it is hardly the whole story. One of the distinc-

---

[8] Not all twentieth-century empiricists hold this position, and it is in fact one of the important distinctions between classical and twentieth-century empiricism. The differences between the two on the topic of perceptual inference (and, as well, the differences among the major twentieth-century positions) are summarized by Roderick Firth. See "Sense-Data and the Percept Theory," in *Perceiving, Sensing, and Knowing: A Book of Readings from Twentieth-Century Sources in the Philosophy of Perception*, ed. Robert J. Swartz (Berkeley and Los Angeles: University of California Press, 1965), 204–70.

[9] For an excellent discussion of the important role played by the concept of "attention"—and the emphasis on diversified attention—in eighteenth-century literary criticism and theory, see Ralph Cohen, *The Art of Discrimination: Thomson's "The Seasons" and the Language of Criticism* (Berkeley and Los Angeles: University of California Press, 1964), 97–98. See also David Hume's famous statement concerning the importance of "inattention" as an antidote to skeptical "reflection," in *A Treatise of Human Nature*, ed. L. A. Selby-Bigge, rev. P. H. Nidditch (Oxford: Clarendon Press, 1978), chap. 1, part 2, sec. 4, p. 218. Hereafter cited as *Treatise*, with chapter, part, and section numbers from this edition.

tive features of empiricism, in fact, is that it treats these figures as at once the most literal and the most metaphorical of terms; hence our difficulty in deciding whether—or in what way—we object to many of empiricism's claims. In the empiricist analysis of perception—that complex drama of surfaces, depths, and reflections—there is a circular argument that leads us from a consideration of the world as we perceive it to a consideration of the world as we commonly talk about it, and back again. To what extent this is a metaphoric or analogical argument, and to what extent it is rather a psycho-physiological model for the linguistic categories we call metaphor and analogy, is a question upon which empiricism constantly meditates. The answers to this question—and the thoughts that various empiricists have had about it—have important consequences for the way we talk about visual objects and written texts, and for the constant comparisons between the two in art, literature, criticism, and philosophy.

Empiricism is not an uncontested term among historians of philosophy, and much recent revisionist work in the historiography of philosophy has attempted to call to our attention the highly contingent nature of our philosophical canons and narratives.[10] Does "classical" empiricism begin with Bacon, Hobbes, or Locke? Does it really include Berkeley? Does it reach its apogee in the skeptical Hume or the stone-kicking Johnson? Does it end with Mill or William James, with Ayer or Popper? Part of the problem here has to do with distinguishing between classical empiricism and more modern, positivist philosophical movements. (In the Appendix, I outline briefly the chief differences among empiricism, positivism, realism, logical analysis, and phenomenalism). As Ian Hacking and Michael Williams in particular have emphasized, there is a considerable disjunction between twentieth-century empiricism and its classical predeces-

---

[10] Locke's reputation in particular has shifted over time, in response as much to the cultural, religious, and political requirements of successive historical eras as to shifting configurations and alliances in the history of philosophy more narrowly understood. On the revisionist historiography of philosophy, see the introduction and essays by Richard Rorty and Bruce Kuklick in *Philosophy in History: Essays on the Historiography of Philosophy*, ed. Richard Rorty, J. B. Schneewind, and Quentin Skinner (Cambridge: Cambridge University Press, 1984). On the shifting reputation of empiricism in general and Locke in specific, see Aarsleff (*From Locke to Saussure*, particularly the introduction and the chapters "Leibniz on Locke and Language," "The History of Linguistics and Professor Chomsky," and "Locke's Reputation in Nineteenth-Century England").

sors.[11] Philosophical empiricism in the twentieth century is verification-ist, foundationalist, and concerned above all with theories of *meaning*—that is, with theories about the criteria for establishing the meaningful-ness of propositions. All this is very foreign to classical empiricism, whose concern with "objects" (as opposed to propositions)[12] and whose catego-ries of "judgment," "sensation," and "reflection" are not only rhetori-cally but philosophically alien to the mathematical, logical, and semantic preoccupations of positivist and analytic philosophy. One need only browse through a few pages of Locke, Berkeley, or Hume, and then Canarp, Ayer, or Popper to sense the ways in which classical empiricism is very much a part of a larger literary and philosophical culture in a way that modern empiricism is not.[13]

We might illustrate this distinction by comparing remarks made by Karl Popper and W. K. Wimsatt, Jr., concerning the methods of empiri-cism. Popper chastises traditional empiricism—which he characterizes as "observationalist" and "foundationalist"—for ignoring common sense in its pursuit of justifiable knowledge:

> The programme of tracing back all knowledge to its ultimate source in observation is logically impossible to carry through . . .
>
> The most striking thing about the observationalist programme of asking for sources—apart from its tediousness—is its stark violation of common sense. For if we are doubtful about an assertion, then the normal procedure is to test it, rather than to ask for its sources; and if we find independent corroboration, then we shall often accept the assertion without bothering at all about sources.[14]

[11] Hacking, *Why Does Language Matter to Philosophy?* 15–25, 33, 50–53, and chap. 13, passim; and Michael Williams, "Hume's Criterion of Significance," *Canadian Journal of Philosophy* 15 (June 1985): 284, 302.

[12] See Richard Rorty on the distinction between "objects" and "propositions" as subjects of analysis (*Philosophy and the Mirror of Nature* [Princeton: Princeton University Press, 1979], 141–42). See also Quine on a related distinction between the traditional empiricist focus on individual words and the analytic emphasis on statements ("Two Dog-mas of Empiricism," 38–42).

[13] On the centrality of literary culture generally and rhetoric specifically (the latter both as a theory of persuasion and as a theory of tropes) to enlightenment philosophy and in particular to empiricist writing, see Aarsleff, *From Locke to Saussure*, 24–26, 123; Caruth, *Empirical Truths and Critical Fictions*, 2–4, and chap. 1, passim; Carol Kay, *Political Constructions: Defoe, Richardson, and Sterne in Relation to Hobbes, Hume, and Burke* (Ithaca: Cornell University Press, 1988), 1–2, 14–15, 21–24, 33–38; and Richard W. F. Kroll, *The Material Word: Literate Culture in the Restoration and Early Eighteenth Centu-ry* (Baltimore: Johns Hopkins University Press, 1991), 2–3, 22, 55, 65–77.

[14] Popper, *Conjectures and Refutations*, 23.

For Popper, a model empiricist by contemporary standards, traditional empiricism fails because it looks for "sources" instead of engaging in testing and experimentation. In short, the "authority" of introspection provides a false alternative to the "authority" of received wisdom. Yet according to Wimsatt, it was precisely the ready and easy experimental methods of traditional empiricism that made it so attractive and accessible. The experiments that characterized seventeenth-century science and underlay empiricism, writes Wimsatt, were "experiments which almost anybody might be expected to understand . . . and they were experiments which many might be expected to emulate. . . . The diction of such a science necessarily had an average generality and easiness of meaning."[15]

Both Popper and Wimsatt are right. Classical empiricism is not experimental—let alone verificationist—by modern standards.[16] Yet it *does* seem to offer "experiments which many might be expected to emulate," in the sense that it consistently illustrates its claims about perception and knowledge by appealing to simple examples and analogies from common experience. "Look at an object in your room, and then pay attention to what it is you really *see*," empiricism counsels, adding, "It is just like what happens as you read the words printed on this page." We might say, then, that empiricism does not proceed so much by experiment as by examples and analogies *presented as reproducible experiments*. Thus classical empiricism offers us example and analogy (and thus rhetoric) precisely in the places where modern empiricism would expect experimental procedures.

If the lines of continuity between classical and modern empiricism are highly problematic, there can be little dispute about the strong influence of empiricism on English literature of the eighteenth, nineteenth, and even twentieth centuries. An entire literary historiography has been con-

---

[15] W. K. Wimsatt, Jr., *Philosophic Words: A Study of Style and Meaning in the "Rambler" and "Dictionary" of Samuel Johnson* (New Haven: Yale University Press, 1948), 10.

[16] It should be noted that Popper has been a prominent critic of the "verification" theory of meaning; but what he offers in its place is "the criterion" of "falsifiability, or refutability, or testability." Although Popper's conception of "corroborability" has considerable significance and value (E. H. Gombrich's *Art and Illusion* is a testimony to this), I do not think it distinguishes him from verificationism as strongly as it distinguishes him from classical empiricism. The idea of "testing" underlies both "verifiability" and "corroborability" in a way that it does not underlie empiricist "reflection." See *Conjectures and Refutations*, 35–37. For Gombrich's debt to Popper, see E. H. Gombrich, *Art and Illusion: A Study in the Psychology of Pictorial Representation* (Princeton: Princeton University Press, 1969), 28–29, 272.

structed around Ian Watt's reading of the eighteenth-century English novel as an expression of empiricist individualism and sensationism, and
M. H. Abrams's reading of British romanticism as a reaction against
Lockean materialism.[17] More detailed versions of these general narratives
have focused on empiricism's privileging of visual sensation, and the
resulting turn toward—and eventual reaction against—literary "pictorialism" over the course of the eighteenth century.[18] Still other critics have

[17] See Ian Watt, *The Rise of the Novel: Studies in Defoe, Richardson, and Fielding*
(Harmondsworth: Penguin, 1972), chap. 1, passim; and M. H. Abrams, *The Mirror and the
Lamp: Romantic Theory and the Critical Tradition* (Oxford: Oxford University Press,
1953), 57–69, 159–67. An equally influential work has been Perry Miller's "The Rhetoric
of Sensation," in *Errand into the Wilderness* (Cambridge: Harvard University Press, 1956),
167–83, which argues for Locke's and Berkeley's influence on Jonathan Edwards. See also
Murray Cohen's account of the mid-eighteenth-century reaction against Locke, in *Sensible
Words: Linguistic Practice in England, 1640–1785* (Baltimore: Johns Hopkins University
Press, 1977), 44–74; Ernest Lee Tuveson's account of Locke's influence on romanticism, in
The Imagination as a Means of Grace: Locke and the Aesthetics of Romanticism (Berkeley
and Los Angeles: University of California Press, 1960), 18, 25–30; and A. D. Nuttall's
argument concerning the influence of empiricism's "rational solipsism" on the "tempera-
mental solipsism" of romantic and modernist writers such as Wordsworth and T. S. Eliot, in
A Common Sky: Philosophy and the Literary Imagination (Berkeley and Los Angeles:
University of California Press, 1974), 11–23, 246–61.

There is in addition a considerable critical literature concerning the influence of Locke
on specific writers, most notably Sterne and Dr. Johnson. On Sterne, the classic critical statement is John Traugott's *Tristram Shandy's World: Sterne's Philosophical Rhetoric* (Berkeley
and Los Angeles: University of California Press, 1954), chap. 1, passim; see also Wolfgang
Iser's more recent and equally extensive analysis in *Laurence Sterne: Tristram Shandy*, trans.
David Henry Wilson (Cambridge: Cambridge University Press, 1988), 1–54. On Johnson,
see Wimsatt (*Philosophic Words*, 1–19, 94–121) and Jean Hagstrum, *Samuel Johnson's
Literary Criticism* (Chicago: University of Chicago Press, 1967), chap. 1, passim.

[18] See, e.g., Tuveson, *The Imagination as a Means of Grace*, 72–75; George P. Land-
ow, *The Aesthetic and Critical Theories of John Ruskin* (Princeton: Princeton University
Press, 1971), 75–78; and Stephen K. Land, *From Signs to Propositions: The Concept of
Form in Eighteenth-Century Semantic Theory* (London: Longman, 1974), 22–24, 40–48.
All three emphasize the privileging of visual sensation in Lockean empiricism, and the
congeniality of Lockean epistemology to the literary doctrine of *ut pictura poesis*. Both
Ernst Cassirer and Jean Hagstrum, however, remind us that Lessing's *Laokoon*—often seen
as the exemplary critique of *ut pictura poesis*—was neither dogmatic nor categorical in its
rejection of poetic imagery, and that the idea of a definitive mid-eighteenth-century shift
away from literary pictorialism is misleading. See Cassirer, *The Philosophy of the Enlightenment*, trans. Fritz C. A. Koelln and James P. Pettegrove (Boston: Beacon Press, 1951), 350–
60; and Hagstrum, *The Sister Arts: The Tradition of Literary Pictorialism and English
Poetry from Dryden to Gray* (Chicago: University of Chicago Press, 1958), 155–56.

Alternative versions of this general literary historiography assign to Shaftesbury and
Addison the credit for modifying Lockean epistemology so as to provide accounts of the
imagination and aesthetic intuition—accounts that arguably had more influence on
eighteenth-century aesthetic and moral philosophy than did Locke's own starker sensation-

argued that the very debate over the nature of literary pictorialism and literary imagery can be traced back to a tension in empiricism itself between pictorialist and antipictorialist descriptions of language and mind. According to these accounts there are contradictions from the beginning in the Cartesian-Lockean model of the mind's eye: the mind is required to be at once spectator and spectacle; to mirror the world passively and yet actively to produce ideal reflections; and to "clarify" its ideas without proceeding to confuse them with "images."[19]

All these narratives treat empiricism as the philosophical source for models and metaphors of mind that then crop up in art, literature, and criticism. Artists and critics are seen as "working with" or "reacting against" certain pictures of the mind and its operations—as embracing or rejecting certain pictures of the relationship between language and physical sensation, including the picture of "picturing" itself. More recently, however, a number of studies have begun to investigate empiricism as a *genre* rather than as a source of figurative models and analogies.[20] This shift from figure to genre also signals a shift in interest: away from empiri-

---

ism. On Shaftesbury's influence, see Cassirer, *Philosophy of the Enlightenment*, 312–38; René Wellek, *A History of Modern Criticism: 1750–1950*, 7 vols. (New Haven: Yale University Press, 1955–86), vol. 1, 106–7; and Tuveson, *The Imagination as a Means of Grace*, 42–55. See also David Marshall's fascinating reading of Shaftesbury in *The Figure of Theater: Shaftesbury, Defoe, Adam Smith, and George Eliot* (New York: Columbia University Press, 1986), 14–70. On Addison's influence, see Hagstrum, *The Sister Arts*, 136–37; W. K. Wimsatt, Jr., and Cleanth Brooks, *Literary Criticism: A Short History* (New York: Knopf, 1959), 254–55, 262; and W.J.T. Mitchell, *Iconology: Image, Text, Ideology* (Chicago: University of Chicago Press, 1986), 23–24.

[19] See particularly Mitchell, *Iconology*, 23–25; 121–25. See also passing remarks in Cohen's *The Art of Discrimination*, chap. 4, passim; and John Richetti, *Philosophical Writing: Locke, Berkeley, Hume* (Cambridge: Harvard University Press, 1983), 24–25. In *The Sister Arts*, Hagstrum discusses the conflicting implications of the "mirror" analogy in empiricist writing—the "mirror" representing, on the one hand, the reflection of an "ideal" and, on the other hand, the reflection of mere visual particulars—and argues that this ambiguity allowed empiricism to be invoked on behalf of both pictorialist and antipictorialist literary doctrines throughout the eighteenth century (135–39, 151).

[20] This shift has been inspired at the most general level by the work of two very different historians of philosophy and culture: Michel Foucault and Richard Rorty. Foucault's rewriting of European history in terms of its discursive models and practices (particularly in his early study *The Order of Things*) and Rorty's rewriting(s) of the history of Western philosophy in terms of style and genre (particularly in his *Philosophy and the Mirror of Nature*) have contributed greatly to the renewed interest in philosophical rhetoric that informs both my own work and the studies I discuss in the following few pages. See Foucault, *The Order of Things: An Archaeology of the Human Sciences*, a translation of *Les mots et les choses* (New York: Random House, 1973).

cist epistemology, narrowly conceived, and toward the articulation of empiricism's broader cultural aims. In different ways, John Richetti, Michael McKeon, Carol Kay, and Richard Kroll have all suggested that empiricist philosophy epitomizes a particular narrative itinerary that is cultural in the broadest sense: literary, moral, social, and political. Richetti's *Philosophical Writing* demonstrates how Locke, Berkeley, and Hume employ techniques of irony and literalization in order to reconnect the moral wisdom and social vision embodied in literary practice with the discursive techniques of philosophy and natural science.[21] Michael McKeon's *The Origins of the English Novel* outlines a "formal posture of naive empiricism" whose stylistic values—for example, historicity, verisimilitude, plain speaking, and documentary authenticity—constitute a genre of reportage that is profoundly ideological in content and aim.[22] Carol Kay's *Political Constructions* argues that seventeenth- and eighteenth-century empiricists—fictional writers and political philosophers alike—share the goal of constructing an "audience," a project that is rhetorical and political rather than narrowly epistemological in aim.[23] And in *The Material Word*, Richard W. F. Kroll has pointed to the fundamental relationship in neoclassical discourse between a stress on the materiality of language and a stress on language's social function.[24]

Accompanying the reevaluation of empiricism's broader aims and

[21] Richetti writes that the "lingering hope" of "philosopher-writers" in the empiricist tradition "is to close the emerging gap between technical or philosophic truth and a wisdom embodied in literary practice" (*Philosophical Writing*, 18). Richetti frequently refers to the latter as a "moral-literary tradition" (32) and argues that Locke's, Berkeley's, and Hume's "problem as writers . . . is to balance a profoundly individualistic epistemology with a cultural and literary habit of mind that suspects individuality and self-definition and insists upon the presence of an audience for meaningful discourse" (29).

[22] Michael McKeon, *The Origins of the English Novel, 1600–1740* (Baltimore: Johns Hopkins University Press, 1986), 105–9. In McKeon's scheme, "naive empiricism" is a reaction against "romance idealism" and is superceded by the "extreme skepticism" that empiricism itself generates (21).

[23] Kay, *Political Constructions*. For Kay, political problems and stylistic problems inform one another in the writings of empiricist philosophers: "The problem of identifying the audience for philosophy, and along with that decision the appropriate rhetoric and form, affects the history of discourse. Difficulties in making these choices shape the careers of such authors as Locke, Shaftesbury, Berkeley, and Hume. The collected works by any one of these authors resemble a kind of debate among forms: the formal, extended arguments of the scientific treatise or the philosophical history confront the shorter, more casually connected, more conversational forms of essays, letters, and dialogues" (37).

[24] Kroll, *The Material Word*, 1–3, 22, 55, 66–79. Neoclassical culture, writes Kroll, is a "culture of contingency . . . defined by a nexus of linguistic and behavioral cues awaiting constant reenactment by its participants or readers" (55). The rhetoric of neoclassicism and

methods has been a renewed inquiry into the alleged rejection and eclipse of neoclassicism by romanticism at the turn of the nineteenth century. In various ways Hans Aarsleff, David Bromwich, Richard Kroll, and Cathy Caruth have all pointed to the endurance of empiricism's guiding questions well into the nineteenth century and to the difficulties this causes for our traditional characterizations of the neoclassical-romantic divide.[25] All these critics recognize in empiricism's rhetorical strategies and epistemological problems a continuous intellectual tradition that survives romanticism intact and cannot be reduced to the nineteenth century's schematic opposition of empiricism to rationalism or to the late twentieth century's schematic opposition of British to continental temperaments. Empiricism shares with continental rationalism a complicated blend of historicist and structuralist conceptions of language; and it shares with romanticism a fascination with the figures of reflection, surface, and depth.

The overall effect of this recent work has been to direct our attention to the social, moral, and political dimension of empiricist rhetoric, a dimension perhaps most fully grasped only when we look beyond local figures and tropes—eye, mirror, reflection, impression, imprint—and fo-

---

empiricism is "illocutionary . . . language as social action" (72): "A rhetoric of empiricism, then, can be said to support an ideology of contingency" (76).

[25] Bromwich sees Locke's chapter "Power" as the source of many of the most important romantic insights into the nature of the imagination. Bromwich reads Hazlitt's career as a continuation and critique of empiricist concerns rather than as a categorical rejection of them and identifies Hazlitt as at once the critic and exemplary spirit of the romantic generation. See David Bromwich, *Hazlitt: The Mind of a Critic* (New York: Oxford University Press, 1983), 24–34, 46–57, 68–77. Aarsleff criticizes the nineteenth-century distinction between empiricism and rationalism, arguing that it overlooks the constant overlapping, convergence, and divergence of philosophical ideas in the eighteenth century and the continually shifting and even contradictory appropriations of Locke. Aarsleff's critique of our rage for historical periodization is one of the guiding themes of *From Locke to Saussure*, particularly the introduction, "Locke's Reputation in Nineteenth-Century England," and "An Outline of Language-Origins Theory since the Renaissance." Kroll takes issue with the "poststructuralist critique of language," which he sees as driven by a false distinction between an antirhetorical neoclassicism and a revisionary romanticism that celebrates figural language (*The Material Word*, 2–5, 15, 60–72). Caruth suggests that the critical tendency to identify empiricism as an excessively literal discourse has led to a reading of romantic poetry that mistakenly reads the tropes of "perception" and "eye" along the lines of a mechanical, physiological process (*Empirical Truths and Critical Fictions*, 2–3). Caruth also points out that "the fiction of a single derivation of eighteenth-century associationism from Locke is as elaborate a (Lockean) associationist fiction as any Romantic story." Revising this fiction "would certainly change the way in which we conceive of the genres and periods of empiricism and Romanticism" (43).

cus on the larger rhetorical patterns and choices that constitute narrative form and, ultimately, genre. The consequence of these two shifts in focus—from metaphor to narrative strategy, and from theories of language to social issues—has been to help us reconceive the goals and character of early British empiricism. Instead of a dry, plodding effort at squaring the physiology of sense perception with the aphorisms of common sense, empiricism now appears as a highly rhetorical cultural enterprise, concerned with persuasion as much as demonstration, with social vision as much as scientific inquiry, and with "coherence" as much as "correspondence." The popular conception of empiricism as a naively dogmatic, stone-kicking positivism, hostile at all points to rhetoric, is beginning to be questioned, which can only help us understand empiricism more accurately.

Yet is it only by shifting our interest beyond rhetorical figures and epistemological questions concerning perception that we can begin to rethink the character of empiricism? Are empiricism's privileged metaphors of perception truly obstacles to any genuine reevaluation of the empiricist tradition? In this book I intend to remain focused on the metaphorics of "reflection" in the belief that empiricism's rhetorical figures have a more complicated story to tell about the itinerary of that intellectual tradition than we have yet recognized. My interest is in the inevitable rhetorical dimension of theories of perception. Perception, according to empiricism, is a rhetorical affair, but not simply because we must eventually have recourse to language (and ultimately to figurative language) in order to communicate perceptual sensations. Such a formulation—while indeed outlining the initial, minimal way in which our perceptions engage language—only gets us as far as the complementary truisms of postanalytic philosophy: that all knowledge is rhetorical and that reality must be encountered under some description. But empiricism's fascination with the rhetorical dimension of sensory perception goes far beyond that, because empiricist accounts of perception are inevitably intertwined with *accounts* of language and of linguistic usage. When, as in Locke's or Berkeley's work, visual perception is consistently explained with reference to the structure of linguistic signs (including distinctions between proper, figurative, and analogical signification) and linguistic meaning is explained in terms of what we "see," we are presented with an account of perception and knowledge that is *inseparable from language* on at least two counts.

Language and perception are connected, first, because we treat our optical sensations as "signs," precisely in the same way that we treat words as signs. Sensory and verbal signifiers alike have a referential function. This argument is most clearly articulated in Berkeley's work. Second, perception and language are connected because in "seeing" we convert raw optical sensations into normative perceptions, and language is not only an exemplary but in fact the *chief* normalizing factor in human experience. We "see" the world as it is described by ordinary language; not as mere shapes and colors but as nameable objects. Both these accounts posit a strong connection between language and perception, yet both are complicated by the fact that empiricist theories of language tend to be antipictorial—and thus to resist translation into a theory of images, imagery, and imagination—while empiricist theories of perception tend to explain the relationship among sensations as a kind of "language" and thus to require the very categories of figurative language, analogy, metaphor, and nonarbitrary signification that the theory of language paradoxically is intended to suppress. And beyond the general analogy, a further problem arises: is the identification of perception with language a "literal" identity (so that our perceptions are ultimately nothing *but* language)? Or is it rather an "analogy" grounded in structurally similar but nonetheless distinct processes? Or is it perhaps only a speculative "metaphoric" identity, a postulated connection between two postulated, inaccessible, unverifiable mental processes (e.g., "sensing" and "signifying")?

I outline this potentially endless regress of questions concerning the role of language only to emphasize how thoroughly and technically rhetorical are the questions that preoccupy empiricism. At every turn, the tension between rhetorical and expository discourse shapes empiricism's most basic claims concerning what can and cannot be *experienced*. Yet to see these questions as exclusively, or even principally, linguistic ones would be very unempiricist indeed. If, as empiricism clearly suggests, language and perception operate as normative constraints upon one another, then any truly critical activity—any act of "reflection"—will inevitably have to proceed in both of two directions, remaining attentive both to the sensory, material context of language and to the linguistic, rhetorical component in sensation. In the discourse of empiricism we are presented not simply with a case of sensory or visual terms functioning as metaphors for mental and linguistic processes but also with the case of linguistic terms functioning as metaphors for sensory perception.[26] The

---

[26] Cf. a similar observation by Ian Hacking, in *Why Does Language Matter to Philosophy?* concerning the relationship between "visual perception" and "mental perception" in

point in articulating this reversibility is not to privilege language but to emphasize the continual alternation between *criteria* and *symptoms*: linguistic functions are sometimes invoked as criteria by which we may judge or distinguish the true from the chimerical sensation; whereas at other times language is seen simply as an expressive function of sensation.

As an experiential theory of knowledge, empiricism has an interest in demystifying or falsifying all knowledge claims that cannot be traced to discrete experiences. This requires that some criteria be established for determining what can and what *cannot* be experienced. But the category of "that which cannot be experienced" quickly resolves into "what cannot be said," and this in turn resolves into "what cannot be said in propriety of common usage." Thus empiricism is notoriously suspicious of knowledge claims that cannot be expressed in terms of ordinary language. The empiricist investigation of accounts of perception, then, proceeds simultaneously along two lines: testing interpretations of sensation against the judgments embedded in "custom" (the latter both embodied and constituted by language); and testing verbal expression against experience, and in particular against sensation.

Empiricist reflection is a self-critical procedure, in which perpetual correction and revision (of impressions, of language, and of judgments) are more important than the establishing of permanent categories or conditions of knowledge. This is, unfortunately, one of the aspects of empiricist reflection that gives Anglo-American philosophy and criticism its distinctively moralistic bearing. Gaining a critical distance from this moralistic dimension requires that we come to recognize empiricism's techniques for identifying and describing "error." My argument, accordingly, centers not only on the complex and various uses of "reflection" in empiricist texts but also on the tendency of those texts to assign the explanation for our errors of judgment alternately to the *philosophical* and to the *common* employment of figures of speech.

This vacillation about the source and origins of mistaken judgments is central to the texts of empiricism, and it can be seen most acutely in the kinds of things these texts say about "reflection." Here is where an understanding of empiricism can have an important role, in terms not only of

---

the Cartesian worldview. Hacking writes that "visual perceptions are referred to in terms of mental perception, often with little or no consciousness of metaphor. This is true even in the case of the most concrete experience, anatomical dissection, or observation with a microscope" (31–33). (Hacking writes in a footnote: "These remarks paraphrase Michel Foucault, *The Birth of the Clinic* [London: Tavistock, 1973], xiii.")

how it helps us reevaluate the influence of Locke and Berkeley on the history of literature but also of how we conceive the relative dogmatism or corrigibility of our own work as literary critics in an Anglo-American academy, with all that that entails. Fredric Jameson, as I noted earlier, has criticized "Anglo-American empirical realism" for its implacable hostility to "all dialectical thinking."[27] This is a serious charge, and if proven against the texts of classical empiricism, it would certainly compromise their value for contemporary critical theory. But if this book can illustrate the complex interweaving of the sensory with the linguistic, of "attention" with "inattention," of "common sense" with "philosophy," and of fact and value in the texts of empiricism, then it may help to begin questioning the too-common view of empiricism as a dogmatic philosophy immune to anything but the most sterile and predictable forms of self-criticism.

The chapters that follow chart a trajectory from empiricist "philosophy" proper to empiricist writing on the verbal and visual arts. The trajectory is not arbitrary: the abiding problems of classical empiricism are ones that gradually became central to our ways of thinking about the arts, and these problems are condensed in the philosophical question of what the eye really "sees." A traditional history of philosophy would not recognize the Molyneux Question as the central problem of empiricism (though the question's continued relevance for philosophers well into the twentieth century is testimony to its "philosophical" importance in the narrow sense), but it is my contention that the historical development of the Molyneux Question took empiricism beyond a strict philosophical orbit precisely because the question necessarily raised complicated issues of rhetoric and of representation—issues that required working out on the terrain of literary and art criticism.

In Chapter 1 I discuss the origin, stakes, and development of the Molyneux Question, its bearing on empiricist attitudes toward rhetoric, and its relation to the specific figures of reflection, surface, and depth. The second half of the chapter places these issues in the context of Locke's influential account of the origins of figurative language. Chapter 2 continues with a reading of Locke's *An Essay Concerning Human Understanding* and discusses the double sense of Lockean "reflection" as both a kind of self-seeing and a kind of self-reading. The distinction between the two

---

[27] Jameson, *Marxism and Form*, 367.

turns out to be crucial since Locke believes that images can exist unnoticed in the mind, but that words, characters, and imprints cannot. The analogy linking language to the act of noticing is extended and complicated in Berkeley's work, and in Chapter 3 I examine the relation of two myths concerning that work: the literary myth that Berkeley presents us with a world entirely of surfaces and the philosophical myth that he presents us with a world entirely of language.

Chapter 4 is an essay on Burke's *A Philosophical Enquiry into the Origin of Our Ideas of the Sublime and Beautiful* and discusses the implications for empiricist aesthetics of a world articulated in terms of the figures reflection, surface, and depth—a world inherited directly from empiricist philosophy. Burke initially attempts to align the sublime and the beautiful with qualities of depth and of surface, respectively—the latter two distinguished by differences in their relation to reflection. Yet he eventually comes to recognize that uncertainties about whether reflection is a linguistic operation or not render ambiguous the very distinction he seeks to establish between sublimity and beauty. Chapter 5 pursues the thematic shift from issues of perception to issues of representation and examines Hazlitt's theories of deep and superficial "character." Character, in Hazlitt's view, is largely a matter of rhetorical self-presentation; but whether it is most accurately interpreted by spontaneous or by reflective reading is uncertain. Hazlitt's solution is an ironic one: we must learn to regard the distinction between surface and depth as a schematic abstraction, but one inevitably imposed by our rhetorical habits.

Chapter 6, on Ruskin, completes the transition from empiricist epistemology to empiricist aesthetics. Ruskin's work is full of painstakingly detailed accounts of the physiology and psychology of perception. Yet it is never entirely clear just when Ruskin is talking about nature, when he is talking about the mind, and when he is talking about painting. His "surfaces" are ambiguously both the surfaces of landscape and those of the canvas; his "depths" are ambiguously both depth of field and depth of meaning; his "reflections" are both the reflections of light on visible surfaces and the reflections of the mind that sorts them out.

Ruskin takes the rhetoric of empiricism as far as it can go without becoming entirely metaphorical and speculative. In the Epilogue I argue that the rhetoric of empiricism can still be recognized in attenuated form in I. A. Richards's *Principles of Literary Criticism*, particularly in the analogy he draws between sensations and "signs." But Richards's work also represents too many of the postempiricist trends of modern criticism and philosophy (e.g., Coleridgean organicism, positivist verificationism, gestalt psychology) to fit comfortably into the tradition that links Locke and Ruskin. Richards is perhaps a little too confident in his distinctions between literal and figurative discourse, a distinction that classical empiricism preaches but does not practice. It is the ability of empiricist rhetoric to clarify and render meaningful the drama of perception through a terminology at once speculative and literal that gives empiricism its particular characteristics and strength and allows it to avoid the reductive identification of experience with perception. And it is the incipient blurring of the speculative and the literal in Ruskin's work that prefigures the end of empiricism.

"Beside the Design of Language": Molyneux's Question and the Empiricist Construction of Rhetoric

> The perception of solid Form is entirely a matter of experience. We *see* nothing but flat colours; and it is only by a series of experiments that we find out that a stain of black or grey indicates the dark side of a solid substance, or that a faint hue indicates that the object in which it appears is far away. The whole technical power of painting depends on our recovery of what may be called the *innocence of the eye*; that is to say, of a sort of childish perception of these flat stains of colour, merely as such, without consciousness of what they signify,—as a blind man would see them if suddenly gifted with sight. . . .
>
> Strive, therefore, first of all, to convince yourself of this great fact about sight. This, in your hand, which you know by experience and touch to be a book, is to your eye nothing but a patch of white, variously gradated and spotted.
>
> —JOHN RUSKIN, *The Elements of Drawing*

FROM MOLYNEUX'S QUESTION TO THE "INNOCENT EYE"

EMERGING INTO THE sunlight in book 7 of the *Republic*, Plato's allegorical cave-dweller dramatizes the principal speculative—and specular—metaphor that has dominated the history of Western philosophy and art. Thinking, according to this allegory, is a kind of seeing, and clear seeing is true knowledge.[1] Yet if the metaphor of the "mind's eye" links even the

---

[1] The most influential contemporary account of Western philosophy's reliance on, and derivation from, the metaphor of the "mind's eye" is Rorty's *Philosophy and the Mirror of Nature*. Rorty sees his own work as extending a critique of philosophy's ocular metaphors, a critique both implicit and explicit in the work of other post- (or anti-) analytic philosophers such as Wittgenstein, Heidegger, Ryle, and Derrida.

most disparate of Western epistemologies (as numerous postanalytic philosophers have pointed out),[2] and if it thereby provides the guiding trope for a certain master narrative of intellectual history, the fascination with the actual mechanics of optical perception—and its attendant style of reportage—must still form a distinctive chapter within that narrative. It did not answer Plato's purpose to consider precisely how his cave dweller would describe his new optical sensations; Socrates poses chiefly rhetorical questions about the cave dweller's new experiences, and in any case his interest is in the general categories of "illusion" and "reality" rather than in the question of how specific objects might appear and be described.[3] Yet it is just that question that preoccupies the philosophical tradition we know as classical empiricism.

Toward the end of the seventeenth century the trope of *restored sight*—of the abrupt confrontation with optical sensation—began to function as something both more and less than a speculative metaphor. During the eighteenth and nineteenth centuries philosophers and scientists became fascinated with Molyneux's Question, the quite literal question of what the "born blind" would see if their sight were restored.[4] Yet the ideal of a direct confrontation with optical sensations becomes, in the unfolding of this philosophical tradition in Britain, increasingly difficult to disengage from questions of language; even as investigations of language became increasingly concerned with the visual, pictorial, and material nature of verbal signification. To understand how the question of *what the formerly blind would see* could be the locus for a set of distinctive meditations upon the relationship of sight to language, and to glimpse the stakes of this question for a philosophical and literary cul-

---

[2] See, for instance, Rorty's point about the contrasting schematic uses made of "mirror" and "eye" metaphors in the Aristotelean and Cartesian traditions, respectively (*Philosophy and the Mirror of Nature*, 45ff.).

[3] Plato, *Republic*, trans. Francis MacDonald Cornford (Oxford: Oxford University Press, 1941), chap. 25 (VII. 514 A-521 B). Cf. Wimsatt and Brooks on the difference between neo-Platonism and Addison's Lockean privileging of "sight" (*Literary Criticism*, 257).

[4] The fullest historical account of the Molyneux Question is Michael Morgan's *Molyneux's Question: Vision, Touch, and the Philosophy of Perception* (Cambridge: Cambridge University Press, 1977). For discussions of the neoclassical fascination with—and privileging of—experimental optics in general, and questions concerning the "born blind" in particular, see John MacLean, *John Locke and English Literature of the Eighteenth Century* (New Haven: Yale University Press, 1936), 106ff.; and Marjorie Hope Nicolson, *Newton Demands the Muse: Newton's "Opticks" and the Eighteenth-Century Poets* (Princeton: Princeton University Press, 1946), 81–89.

ture, we might turn to the single most famous phrase associated with this tradition: Ruskin's "innocence of the eye."

Ruskin was perhaps the last major writer seriously to believe in the "innocence of the eye," that is, in the existence and representability of optical sensations untutored by convention, custom, inference, suggestion, or judgment. As the epigraph to this chapter shows, Ruskin considered this optical "innocence" to be equivalent not only to the sensations of early childhood but also to the first visual experiences of the formerly blind. Ruskin urges the aspiring artist to rediscover the visual world in all its glorious "flatness"—to rediscover the world as it ostensibly appears before judgment and habit make it leap into the stereoscopic depth of "solid" form. Not long after Ruskin wrote this famous note to his *Elements of Drawing*,[5] however, the terms of perceptual psychology were altered permanently by the ambiguous legacy of impressionist painting, the increasing emphasis of modernist painting and literature on "surfaces," the phenomenological psychology of William James and the gestalt school, and the increasingly Kantian and Hegelian assumptions of modern philosophy of perception.[6] All these presented challenges to— and by many accounts overthrew—an empiricist tradition in which the

[5] John Ruskin, *The Elements of Drawing*, in *The Works of John Ruskin*, 39 vols., ed. E. T. Cook and Alexander Wedderburn (London: George Allen, 1903–12), vol. 15, 27–28. The quotation used as the epigraph to this chapter appears in an extended footnote to section 5. All subsequent references to Ruskin's works will cite volume and page numbers from this edition.

[6] E. H. Gombrich stresses that impressionist painting—which Ruskin ostensibly advocated—turned out to be at best an ambiguous confirmation of Ruskin's theories concerning the "unadulterated truth of natural optics" (*Art and Illusion*, 14–15, 297–99). And William James, while sympathizing with Ruskin's empiricist impulses, concludes that Ruskin's ideal of unconceptualized optical sensations mistakes the normative for the natural. See William James, *The Principles of Psychology*, 2 vols. (New York: Dover, 1950). James cites with approval Ruskin's advice to the "young draughtsman" to "recover . . . the 'innocence of the eye'" (2.179) but then has to concede the hypothetical and normative status of that innocence: "'Don't draw the thing as it *is*, but as it *looks!*' is the endless advice of every teacher to his pupil; forgetting that what it 'is' is what it would also 'look,' provided it were placed in what we have called the 'normal' situation for vision" (2.243). As the following discussion will show, the particular phrase of Ruskin that James quotes—the "innocence of the eye"—is taken from a passage in which Ruskin characterizes the unconceptualized optical world as *two-dimensional* ("flat" rather than "solid"); this is the central and enduring error of empiricist optical theory, according to James, and is directly attributable to Berkeley (2.212–16, 240–43, 270–82).

The second-wave influence of Kantian and Hegelian thought on English culture toward the end of the nineteenth century (the first wave arriving via Coleridge at the beginning of the century) is too large a topic to pursue or even satisfactorily condense here. For our purposes it is adequate to note that I. A. Richards characterizes the "reaction against

world as it appears to common sense is interpreted as a combination of sensory impressions and inferential judgments, transformed into habits and spontaneous associations that escape our attention. Such an account stresses a distinction between sensing and *noticing*. And in such a tradition, the conversion of raw sensory impressions into the world of common sense through the mediation of judgment is consistently figured as "reflection" acting upon "surfaces" to produce "depth." The empirical investigation of the physical world and the psychological investigation of interior processes thus share a common vocabulary, and even a common mythological mechanism.

According to William James, E. H. Gombrich, and others, Ruskin's impressionist theory of perception is the culmination—the perverse and yet unimpeachable conclusion—of a tradition that starts with Locke and Berkeley.[7] This general narrative is correct, but for more reasons than Gombrich or James acknowledge. What links Locke and Berkeley (and later, as we shall see, Burke and Hazlitt) with Ruskin is not only the empiricist pursuit of "visual truth" ("what we really see" as opposed to "what we merely know")[8] but a number of other distinctive philosophical gestures as well. First is the tendency to describe both the world of appearances and the mechanisms of the mind in terms of a common set of figures: reflection, surface, and depth. This raises, among other issues, the problem of distinguishing literal from metaphoric usages. Second is the constant analogizing of optical sensations and verbal language in terms of one another—to the extent that we are inevitably challenged by empiri-

---

Ruskin" as part of a historical moment that also includes "the influence, rather suddenly encountered, of Continental and German aesthetics upon the English mind," resulting in the hypostatization of an autonomous "aesthetic experience" and a correlative depreciation of the empirical, scientific analysis of aesthetic perception. See Richards, *Principles of Literary Criticism* (New York: Harcourt Brace Jovanovich, 1925), 72–73.

[7] Given Berkeley's theory of vision "which was accepted by nearly all nineteenth-century psychologists," writes Gombrich, "Ruskin's conclusions appear to be unimpeachable" (*Art and Illusion*, 297). I stress the perversity of the "conclusion," since Berkeley was by no means recommending the virtues of unconceptualized retinal sensations, and by some accounts—even those sympathetic to Gombrich's—Berkeley in fact *denied* the coherence or availability of the "innocent eye." See, for instance, Nelson Goodman, *Ways of Worldmaking* (Indianapolis: Hackett, 1978), 6. James's view of the relationship between Berkeley and Ruskin is outlined in n. 6. For a more general discussion of the relationship between British empiricism and impressionism, which does not mention Ruskin specifically, see Ian Watt, *Conrad in the Nineteenth Century* (Berkeley and Los Angeles: University of California Press, 1979), 169–72.

[8] The phrases are all Gombrich's, paraphrasing Ruskin (*Art and Illusion*, 14).

cist writers to "reflect" on the fact that our immediate object of attention while reading their texts is, paradoxically, not an argument or an idea but a printed page. This gesture of self-referentiality ironizes empiricist writing and in so doing foregrounds its constitutive tension between "common sense" and the destruction of the same through "reflection." Finally, there is the rhetorical nature of empiricist characterizations of the relationship between visual perception and language—between seeing and saying.

We shall see a particularly concise example of this last problem in the continuing discussion of the Molyneux Question throughout empiricist writing. Here, considerations of what the formerly blind man would say are hedged about with counterarguments concerning what he *could not say*, and these arguments in turn are defended not by reference to documentary evidence but to wholly rhetorical arguments about the nature and decorum of linguistic signification—about what could possibly be said or meant, "in propriety of language."[9] Molyneux's Question in each of its successive incarnations is framed, and to a great extent shaped, by the particular kind of speech-act it asks for in response: it is, variously, a question about what the blind man might "tell," "distinguish," "say with certainty," "denominate," "name," or "recognize"—and it raises further the question of whether any of this would be "proper" or "metaphorical" speaking. What such an array of possibilities illustrates is not only the intimate connection between visual and verbal operations but the empiricist tendency to make propriety of speech as much a criterion for the clarity and dependability of sensations as vice versa. Perception is always rhetorically mediated, but rhetorical mediation can only be conceived along the lines of perception.

Tracing the history of these three general problems may help us eventually to see how the empiricist tradition could culminate in Ruskin's odd combination of rhetorical extravagance with an almost obsessive attentiveness to the details and mechanics of visual perception and representation (just as Ruskin saw landscape painting culminating in Turner's "heartsight deep as eyesight").[10] Ruskin's highly figurative prose and

---

[9] George Berkeley, *An Essay towards a New Theory of Vision* §96, in *The Works of George Berkeley*, 3 vols., ed. Alexander Campbell Fraser (Oxford: Clarendon Press, 1871), vol. 1, 80. Hereafter cited as *Essay*, along with paragraph numbers from this edition.

[10] Ruskin, *Works*, 7.377. See René Wellek's remarks on Ruskin's odd combination of an almost scientific observationism with an almost mystical "impressionism," in *History of Modern Criticism*, 5.140–44.

empirically rigorous observations bring to a pitch the tensions implicit in empiricism's vocabulary of reflections, surfaces, and depths; a set of figures describing not only the exterior world of appearances and the interior world of mental processes and mechanisms but the very logic controlling the relationship between the two. As we move from Locke and Berkeley through Burke and Hazlitt to Ruskin, there is an increasing emphasis on the role of judgment and language in our mediations of sensory impressions *and* an increasing attention to the details and mechanics of optical perception. This leads ultimately to a stress on the rhetoric that joins all these phenomena, and above all, as we shall see, to a stress on the concept of reflection.

What, exactly, was Molyneux's Question? In order to answer this we need to turn back to a passage added to the second edition of *An Essay Concerning Human Understanding* (1694), where Locke first outlined the question and its stakes.[11] Locke's purpose in rehearsing the problem was to emphasize the role of judgment or inference—of "habitual custom"—in our perceptions. The purpose of this emphasis, in turn, was to acknowledge the existence of prereflective experience while demonstrating that such experience could not be coherent enough to imply the existence of "innate" ideas. If our "first sensations" were not recognizable, there could hardly be any "first ideas" in the strong sense intended by idealism. Locke's discussion of this issue begins with a classic empiricist statement concerning the "flatness" of the preconceptualized visual world: "When we set before our Eyes a round Globe, of any uniform colour . . . 'tis certain, that the *Idea* thereby imprinted in our Mind, is of a flat Circle variously shadow'd," which "Judgment presently, by an habitual custom, alters" into a three-dimensional image (a "convex Body") (2.9.8).[12] This narrative of the passage from prereflective to habit-

[11] See John Locke, *An Essay Concerning Human Understanding*, ed. Peter H. Nidditch (Oxford: Clarendon Press, 1975). All subsequent references to Locke will cite book, chapter, and paragraph numbers from this edition. Molyneux's relationship with Locke is touched on briefly by Morgan (*Molyneux's Question*, 6).

[12] Cf. a similar passage in Hume's *Treatise*, in which our construction of a three-dimensional visual field from optical sensations that "appear as if painted on a plain surface" is attributed to "reason" rather than "sense." It requires "reflexion," writes Hume, to "correct" this "most natural and familiar way of thinking," i.e., the common belief that we have actual sensations of "pure extension." Hume supports his argument by reference to the absence of any sensations of pure extension in "a blind man" (1.2.5). William James challenges this, arguing that "the blind . . . multiply mentally the amount of a distinctly felt freedom to move, and gain the *immediate sense* of a vaster freedom still" (*Principles of Psychology*, 2.204, my emphasis).

ual impressions—dramatized as the construction of a three-dimensional world from essentially two-dimensional optical sensations—is then followed by an even more speculative anecdote:

> I shall here insert a Problem of that very Ingenious and Studious promoter of real Knowedge, the Learned and Worthy Mr. *Molineux*, which he was pleased to send me in a Letter some Months since; and it is this: *Suppose a Man born blind, and now adult, and taught by his touch to distinguish between a Cube, and a Sphere of the same metal, and nighly of the same bigness, so as to tell, when he felt one and t'other, which is the Cube, which the Sphere. Suppose then the Cube and Sphere placed on a Table, and the Blind Man to be made to see. Quære, Whether by his sight, before he touch'd them, he could now distinguish, and tell, which is the Globe, which the Cube.* To which the acute and judicious Proposer answers: *Not. For though he has obtain'd the experience of, how a Globe, how a Cube affects his touch; yet he has not yet attained the Experience, that what affects his touch so or so, must affect his sight so or so; . . .* I agree with this thinking Gent. whom I am proud to call my Friend, in his answer to this his Problem; and am of opinion, that the Blind Man, at first sight, would not be able with certainty to say, which was the Globe, which the Cube, whilst he only saw them: though he could unerringly name them by his touch, and certainly distinguish them by the difference of their Figures felt. This I have set down, and leave with my Reader, as an occasion for him to consider, how much he may be beholding to experience, improvement, and acquired notions, where he thinks, he has not the least use of, or help from them. (2.9.8)

Molyneux's Question concerns not simply what the blind man would see but what he would say: what he could "tell" or "name."[13] And the assimilation of questions concerning vision to questions concerning language becomes even more pronounced in the following paragraphs, as Locke proceeds to elaborate a systematic analogy between the operations of sight and those of language. (Our "Sensation" is converted spontaneously into an "idea" of "judgment," writes Locke, "and is scarce taken notice of it self; as a Man who reads or hears with attention and understanding, takes little notice of the Characters, or Sounds, but of the *Ideas*, that are excited in him by them" [§9]).

An anecdote that begins by staging the starkest possible version of a

[13] Morgan makes this point in *Molyneux's Question* and in fact chastises contemporary psychologists for interpreting Molyneux's problem simply as the question of whether the "blind man, on recovering his sight, would *see* or not" (7).

confrontation with sense data concludes by conceding not only the necessary mediation of "experience" and "judgment," and not only the necessary mediation of language but the *reflection* necessary for comparing the structure of vision with the structure of verbal behavior (an analogy that Locke says we shall notice only if we "take the pains to reflect" [§10]). From local questions concerning what could or would be said about particular sensations, Locke moves to the larger question of how seeing is indeed like reading, speaking, and hearing.

When Berkeley comes to consider the Molyneux Question, in his *Essay Towards a New Theory of Vision* (1709), its link to issues of linguistic propriety becomes even more pronounced. Berkeley's reasons for addressing the problem are somewhat different from Locke's. Whereas Locke intends to disprove the existence of innate complex sensations, Berkeley's concern is to deny that there can be a single or unitary *object* of sensation. In Locke's and Molyneux's accounts the blind man eventually comes to realize that his new optical sensations *refer to the same object* as those tactile sensations with which he was previously familiar, that is, that they are transmitted from a common source: his task, as we have seen, is to learn by experience that "what affects his touch so or so, must affect his sight so or so." But Berkeley denies that any single "what" can cause these two distinct species of "affect." "What" the blind man senses by touch, according to Berkeley, cannot be the same thing as "what" he eventually senses by sight—the two impressions are not "of the same sort" (§133).[14] What Molyneux's anecdote demonstrates, in Berkeley's interpretation, is that perceptual judgment does not *reassemble* an external world that has been refracted by our various senses, but rather that a certain economy of language creates the fiction of a unitary external world.

From the very beginning, Berkeley's discussion of this process aligns distinctions of sensory categories with distinctions of linguistic propriety. Even more than in Locke's account the focus of interest is on what we can *say*. A blind man's vocabulary of space relations, argues Berkeley, "properly" denominates only tactile sensations; its application to anything else would be "metaphorical":

---

[14] Cf. Jorge Luis Borges's ironic rendering of this scene in "Funes the Memorious." See Borges, *Labyrinths: Selected Stories and Other Writings*, ed. Donald A. Yates and James E. Irby (New York: New Directions, 1964), 62–65.

It is certain that a man actually blind, and who had continued so from his birth, would, by the sense of feeling, attain to have ideas of upper and lower. By the motion of his hand, he might discern the situation of any tangible object placed within his reach. That part on which he felt himself supported, or towards which he perceived his body to gravitate, he would term "lower," and the contrary to this "upper;" and accordingly denominate whatsoever objects he touched.

But then, whatever judgments he makes concerning the situation of objects are confined to those only that are perceiveable by touch. All those things that are intangible, and of a spiritual nature—his thoughts and desires, his passions, and in general all the modifications of his soul—to these he would never apply the terms upper and lower, except only in a metaphorical sense. He may perhaps, by way of allusion, speak of high or low thoughts: but those terms, in their proper signification, would never be applied to anything that was not conceived to exist without the mind. (§§93–94)

The immediate distinction Berkeley proposes here—between the literal description of tactile sensations and the metaphorical or allusive description of mental processes—is perhaps surprisingly uncontroversial. In fact *the issue of blindness would seem to be beside the point.* That the description of "thoughts," "desire," and "passions" in terms of space-relations is metaphorical goes for anyone, blind or not. But Berkeley's point in establishing a strong proper/metaphorical distinction here is to prepare for his subsequent suggestion that *all things* other than tactile sensations—not only thoughts, desires, and passions but visual sensations as well—can be described only allusively by our space-relations vocabulary. Though Berkeley does not repeat the word "metaphorical" in the following paragraphs, it seems clear that he thinks the restoration of sight would provide for the blind man only a new set of impressions requiring metaphoric description:

> Whence it plainly follows, that such a one, if we suppose him made to see, would not at first sight think that anything he saw was high or low, erect or inverted. For, it hath been already demonstrated, in sect. 41, that he would not think the things he perceived by sight to be at any distance from him, or without his mind. . . . the proper objects of vision make a new set of ideas, perfectly distinct and different from the former, and which can in no sort make themselves perceived by touch. There is, therefore, nothing at all that could induce him to think those terms applicable to them. (§95)

It is not simply that the blind man would not know which space-relations words to apply to which optical sensations but also that the application of his space-relations vocabulary to anything other than tactile sensations could only strike him as a departure from proper speech: "never having known those terms applied to any other save tangible things, or which existed in the space without him, and what he sees neither being tangible, nor perceived as existing without, he could not know that, in propriety of language, they were applicable to it" (§96). In short, optical impressions would appear to be of more or less the same nature as "thoughts," "desires," and "passions"—a set of internal sensations in reference to which the vocabulary of tactile space relations could be applied only metaphorically. Accordingly Berkeley agrees with the most general "solution of Mr. Molyneux's problem, published by Locke" (§132), while dissenting from Locke's reasoning on the question. The blind man's initial inability to assimilate new visual impressions to an old vocabulary of tactile impressions indicates a category difference, not merely a lack of experience.

Berkeley begins his final "reflection" on the Molyneux Question by converting it explicitly into a linguistic issue: "it has been made evident that a man blind from his birth, would not, at first sight, denominate anything he saw, by the names he had been used to appropriate to ideas of touch" (§135). Yet what is it that prompts the eventual—and in Berkeley's eyes "metaphorical"—application of names to our optical impressions? Why do we use a vocabulary "appropriate to ideas of touch" for our optical sensations, thus giving the illusion of a three-dimensional visual world when our optical sensations in fact lack any dimension of depth? Berkeley's answer sidesteps the question: the relation of words to the ideas they signify is arbitrary, and thus we should not expect any natural logic of naming to apply in the first place. In short, the denomination of visual impressions in terms of our vocabulary for tactile qualities implies nothing about the relationship of visual to tactile sensations, since words—mere collections of alphabetic letters—have nothing in common with the properties of the ideas they signify:

> *First*, therefore, it will be demanded how visible extension and figures come to be called by the same name with tangible extension and figures, if they are not of the same kind with them? It must be something more than humour or accident that could occasion a custom so constant and universal as this. . . .

To which I answer, we can no more argue a visible and tangible square to be of the same species, from their being called by the same name, than we can that a tangible square, and the monosyllable consisting of six letters whereby it is marked, are of the same species, because they are both called by the same name. It is customary to call written words, and the things they signify, by the same name: for, words not being regarded in their own nature, or otherwise than as they are marks of things, it had been superfluous, and *beside the design of language*, to have given them names distinct from those of the things marked by them. The same reason holds here also. Visible figures are the marks of tangible figures . . . hence it is that in all times and places visible figures are called by the same names as the respective tangible figures suggested by them; and not because they are alike, or of the same sort with them. (§§139–40, my emphasis)

Berkeley is in fact pursuing two separate arguments here: first, that words are arbitrarily related to ideas; second, that the sharing of a name does not imply the identity of two ideas but is rather the function of a certain economy intrinsic to "the design of language." Either of these arguments could stand without the other, but the two arguments are combined into one, and in fact complement each other in Berkeley's philosophical agenda. Berkeley's treatment of the Molyneux Question thus opens up into a much larger discussion of language and perception, involving, at the very least, questions concerning the relationship of signification to "suggestion" and "allusion," of language to writing, and of ideas to words (§§132–60). We shall examine Berkeley's treatment of these questions later (in Chapter 3), but here it is sufficient to indicate that Berkeley's contribution to the Molyneux problem pushes the issue even farther in the direction of an account of language's "design" while at the same time specifying far more fully than Locke the logic and interrelation of sense impressions that produce our commonsense perception of a three-dimensional visual world.

Burke's *A Philosophical Enquiry into the Origin of Our Ideas of the Sublime and Beautiful* (1757) does not take up the Molyneux Question directly, but Burke does address the question of what a blind person could say or write with "propriety." Though the Molyneux Question asks us to consider what the *formerly* blind might say, both Locke and Berkeley had premised their solutions on assumptions about the status of the blind man's speech *prior* to the recovery of sight. Berkeley, as we have seen, first establishes the metaphorical character of the blind man's space-relations vocabulary when applied to anything other than tactile sensations.

Locke, in a passage from the *Essay* that we have not yet considered, implies much the same thing about the language of the blind. Locke's characterization of a blind man's visual understanding occurs in a passage that attempts to illustrate the concept of a "simple idea." Simple ideas, argues Locke, are not capable of verbal definition or explanation; they must be obtained directly through experience. Color and light are examples of such simple ideas, and it follows, then, that a blind man cannot attain to ideas of color:

> A studious blind Man, who had mightily beat his Head about visible Objects, and made use of the explication of his Books and Friends, to understand those names of Light, and Colours, which often came in his way; bragg'd one day, That he now understood what *Scarlet* signified. Upon which his Friend demanding, what *Scarlet* was? the blind Man answered, It was like the Sound of a Trumpet. Just such an Understanding of the name of any other simple *Idea* will he have, who hopes to get it only from a Definition, or other Words made use of to explain it. (3.4.11)[15]

When Locke writes "just such an Understanding . . . will he have," he insinuates that this is little or no understanding at all; that the blind man's statement is merely rhetorical or metaphorical, a verbal exercise.[16] Like Berkeley's, then, Locke's arguments about what can or cannot be said resolve into determinations about the propriety of what *might be said*. It is clear, though, that both Locke and Berkeley think of the argu-

---

[15] The importance of this anecdote for Locke is emphasized by his earlier references to it in the *Essay* (2.6.5–6).

[16] That Locke's remark was recognized as a critique of rhetoric is confirmed by Dr. Johnson's reference to the anecdote in *The Rambler*, nos. 92 and 94, which examine synesthesia in poetry. Though admitting in a qualified way the existence of something like onomatopoeia, Johnson appears to take an ironic view of exaggerated claims about the synaesthetic power of great poets: "Many beauties of this kind [onomatopoeia], which the moderns, and perhaps the ancients, have observed, seem to be the product of blind reverence acting upon fancy. Dionysius himself tells us, that the sound of Homer's verses sometimes exhibits the idea of corporeal bulk: is not this a discovery nearly approaching to that of the blind man, who after long enquiry into the nature of the scarlet colour, found that it represented nothing so much as the clangor of a trumpet?" Johnson's allusion to Locke here is an ironic criticism of Dionysius's claim concerning the "corporeal bulk" of Homer's verse. Johnson suggests that the synesthetic effects that Dionysius claims to have identified have about as much epistemological validity as the Lockean blind man's claim to have discovered the natural relationship between a particular color and particular sound—in other words, none whatsoever. See "The Rambler," in *The Yale Edition of the Works of Samuel Johnson*, 16 vols., ed. W. J. Bate and Albrecht B. Strauss (New Haven: Yale University Press, 1958), vol. 4, 121–30, 135–43.

ment from linguistic propriety as secondary to the argument from the logic of sense impressions. It is because the sense impressions are organized in such and such a way that the line distinguishing proper from improper speaking is established where it is.

From Berkeley's formulation in particular, it is but a short step to reversing the equation and making propriety of speech a criterion for determining the status and relationship of the sense faculties. It is here that Burke contributes so distinctively to the tradition of Locke, Berkeley, and Hume, bringing the investigation of the senses and passions most openly into conflict with the official antirhetorical doctrine of empiricism. For Burke shares with Locke and Berkeley a number of central beliefs about linguistic propriety: that our terms must be carefully and simply defined; that language does not operate by eliciting visual images or even through a one-to-one correspondence of individual words to individual ideas; that "figurative" terms are "not extremely accurate" ("Introduction on Taste," 12); that introspection is the only true test for the validity or existence of particular ideas, and that this introspection takes impressions as its object: "When we go but one step beyond the immediately sensible qualities of things, we go out of our depth" (4.1.129–30). Yet despite all this, Burke acknowledges a category virtually foreign to Locke and Berkeley: the propriety of rhetoric.

When Burke comes to consider how the blind may be limited in their use of language, it does not seem to him unthinkable that someone who had never had optical sensations might be capable of using the vocabulary of visual sensations *with propriety*, even though such use would clearly be rhetorical:

> Since I wrote these papers I found two very striking instances of the possibility there is, that a man may hear words without having any idea of the things which they represent, and yet afterwards be capable of returning them to others, combined in a new way, and with great propriety, energy and instruction. The first instance, is that of Mr. Blacklock, a poet blind from his birth. Few men blessed with the most perfect sight can describe visual objects with more spirit and justness than this blind man. (5.5.168)

As if in response to Locke's ironic assertion, "just such an Understanding will he have," Burke declares that the blind man's understanding of visual terms is indeed rhetorical, and not at all lacking in "propriety" or descriptive power for all that. The blind man's use of visual terms becomes for Burke an exemplary instance of rhetoric, and, even further, of "common discourse." The example of the blind poet is followed by that of the blind "professor of mathematics" who "gave excellent lectures upon light and colours." This "learned man," according to Burke, "did nothing but what we do every day in common discourse. When I wrote this last sentence, and used the words *every day* and *common discourse*, I had no images in my mind of any succession of time; nor of men in conference with each other; nor do I imagine that the reader will have any such ideas on reading it" (169–70). Burke's antipictorialist theory of language does not require him at all to abandon the criterion of linguistic propriety or to make rhetorical speech the evidence of a category error. Burke in fact constantly highlights the rhetorical and descriptive problems of empiricism, pointing out that what we say is an unavoidable criterion for determining how and what we see.

Despite Burke's virtually wholesale assimilation of optics to rhetoric he remains in some ways wed to the empiricist fascination with the responses of the formerly blind, and in some of the more disturbing sections of the *Enquiry* he appears quite willing to treat accounts of such responses as a special glimpse into the character of unmediated sense impressions—of impressions prior to any "reflection" on them (2.5.65). (His chapters on "darkness" and "blackness," where he recounts an anecdote of Cheselden's concerning a formerly blind patient who reportedly "was struck with great Horror" at his first "Sight" of a "Negroe Woman" [4.15.144n.], are an example.) Whereas Berkeley and Locke had alternated between accounts of verbal signification and accounts of visual perception, Burke alternates between a fully *rhetorical* view of the world and an ostensibly prereflective one, which nonetheless incorporates the rhetoric and the myths of the constructed, "reflected" world. The line distinguishing reflective judgment from prereflective sensations becomes ever harder to determine, even though Burke's *Enquiry* in many ways pursues an empirical investigation of the senses in far more detail than does Locke's famous "*physiology* of the human understanding."[17] Burke's contribution to the empiricist tradition, then, consists not so much in his turning its attention to the "passions" (something Hume had already done in book 2 of his *Treatise*) as in turning empiricism's increasing reliance on accounts of language back on itself (as dramatized, iron-

[17] The phrase is Kant's, from *Critique of Pure Reason*, trans. Norman Kemp Smith (New York: St. Martin's Press, 1965), 8 (A.ix).

ically, in the phrase "when I wrote this last sentence") and in rhetoricizing empiricism more thoroughly than any other writer in the tradition up to that point.

Like Burke, Hazlitt considers himself an empiricist—a philosopher of "experience" and "common sense"—though he effectively denies this title to most of his philosophical predecessors. The "material or *modern* philosophy," he argues in his *Lectures on English Philosophy* (1812), "first rose at the suggestion of Lord Bacon, on the ruins of the school-philosophy, [and] has been gradually growing up to its present height ever since, from a wrong interpretation of the word *experience*." Hazlitt intends to counter this wayward tradition with "a system more conformable to reason and experience, and, in its practical results at least, approaching nearer to the common sense of mankind."[18] He complains that empiricism has tended to reduce "All thought . . . into *sensation*" and he denies that anything like our commonsense view of the world could ever have been constructed from "sensation" alone. Some capacity for abstract reasoning must be present; and Hazlitt insists that Locke's and Berkeley's solutions to the Molyneux Question either ignore or deny the necessary role of "abstraction" in our experience of sensory data.

One way or another, argues Hazlitt, both Locke and Berkeley attribute the construction of our commonsense view of the world to the mere accumulation of sensory experiences and thus leave us to conclude that judgment could only be the consequence of a sufficient number of repeated impressions. Both appear to deny, for instance, that any spontaneous act of reasoning alone could enable us to identify the optical and tactile impressions of a cube's "sharp angles." After quoting Locke's account of Molyneux's Question at length, Hazlitt challenges Locke's conclusion that the blind man could not immediately coordinate his new optical sensations with his inherited vocabulary of tactile sensations:

> It appears to me that the mind must recognise a certain similarity between the impressions of different senses in this case. For instance, the sudden change or discontinuity of the sensation, produced by the sharp angles of the cube, is something common to both ideas [the visual and the tactile], and if so, must afford a means of comparing them together. Berkeley, in his "Essay

[18] William Hazlitt, *The Complete Works of William Hazlitt*, 21 vols., ed. P. P. Howe, after the edition of A. R. Waller and Arnold Glover (London: J. M. Dent, 1930–34), vol. 2, 124. All subsequent references to Hazlitt's work will cite volume and page numbers from this edition.

on Vision," goes so far as to deny that there is any intuitive analogy between the ideas of number as conveyed by different senses, and asserts that the distinction between the two legs of a statue, for instance, as perceived by the touch or by the sight, would not imply any idea of like or same. I grant this consequence to be true, on the principle maintained by him that there are no abstract ideas in the mind, for on this principle there can be no idea answering to the words *same* or *different*, but then this argument would destroy all kind of coincidence not only between ideas of different senses, but between repeated impressions of the same sense. (184)

Hazlitt believes that Berkeley's critique of Locke is justified only if we are willing to renounce the idea of an external world of which we have impressions—impressions that we can intuitively sort into (at the very least) the categories of "same" and "different." Once we acknowledge an ability to sort impressions according to these minimal categories—and Hazlitt cannot imagine a world without them—we have acknowledged an innate, primitive capacity for abstraction, and Berkeley's denial of any possible resemblance between visual and tactile sensations is accordingly undermined.[19]

Hazlitt's brief discussion of the Molyneux problem is lodged in the middle of an extended critique of Locke, which is itself part of a larger series of "lectures" on British empiricism, from Hobbes to Horne Tooke. Hazlitt's most interesting ideas concerning the relationship between perception and language are not, in fact, developed in these early lectures (delivered in 1812), but in a number of later, shorter, and more miscellaneous essays on character, style, judgment, and rhetoric, which we shall discuss in Chapter 5. However, Hazlitt's response to the question is important, not only because he dissents from the received wisdom concerning the problem—whose most general solution even Locke and Berkeley had agreed upon—but because he does so in the name of the phenomenon most antipathetic to orthodox empiricism: "abstraction." When writing the *Lectures*, Hazlitt had not yet fully developed his ideas con-

---

[19] Hazlitt's critique here points toward more modern criticisms of empiricism, themselves also empiricist in spirit. See for instance, Karl Popper's remarks in *Conjectures and Refutations*: "Without waiting, passively, for repetitions to impress or impose regularities upon us, we actively try to impose regularities upon the world. We try to discover similarities in it, and to interpret it in terms of laws invented by us. Without waiting for premises we jump to conclusions. They may have to be discarded later, should observation show that they are wrong" (46). See also similar remarks by Williams in *Groundless Belief*, 79–80, 143.

cerning "abstraction," but as we shall see in Chapter 5, that process eventually becomes inextricably linked in his mind with our capacity to comprehend the world rhetorically: that is, our ability to see our judgments as shaped by figures of speech, and furthermore to imagine the consequences of changing those figures.[20] As we shall also see, Hazlitt directs the attention of empiricism away from questions concerning the impressions of the natural world and toward questions concerning "character," to which he ironically—and yet quite seriously—applies the empiricist rhetoric of surfaces and depth.

This brings us back to Ruskin and the "innocent eye" of the "blind man . . . suddenly gifted with sight." Like Burke, Ruskin is interested in the full range of the (formerly) blind man's representational skills: not only what he can "tell" but what impressions and effects he can produce with paint or pen. And like Hazlitt, Ruskin is concerned to discover the "character" that inheres in all representations, whether of the self or of the natural world. But Ruskin's rhetoric goes well beyond the controlled ironies of Hazlitt's prose. Whereas Hazlitt argues for the superior value of "superficial" knowledge, and cannily mixes evidence from the discourses of sensory perception and of moral judgment, Ruskin quite intentionally assimilates the sensory to the moral in his conception of the "innocent eye."

The discursive figures of empiricism—rhetoricized by Burke and ironized by Hazlitt—are finally mythologized by Ruskin. One can go no further than Ruskin in the investigation of optical phenomena and representational techniques without abandoning the organizing metaphors of empiricism and shifting to some new vocabulary. Ruskin pursues empirical detail as far as it can be pursued while retaining the conventional figuration of the mind as a reflective mechanism. The triumph of empiricism lies in its ability to sustain a double vocabulary; or better, a vocabulary performing double service, as discursive account of the "world" and metaphorical account of the "mind." But Ruskin's rhetoric grafts the two accounts together so closely that they no longer function as mutually illustrating analogies. When Ruskin's rhetoric reaches its highest pitch, as we shall see, mind and world simply mimic one another.

After Ruskin, the figure of depth begins to lose its distinctive double

---

[20] Cf. Popper on the possibility of a "critical attitude, which shares with the dogmatic attitude the quick adoption of a schema of expectations—a myth, perhaps, or a conjecture or hypothesis—but which is ready to modify it, to correct it, and even to give it up" (*Conjectures and Refutations*, 49). See also Williams, *Groundless Belief*, 161–62, 180.

character as both literal and metaphoric sign mediating between a directly intuited world and a world of judgment and sensation. This shift in the
character of depth is related to developments in optical theory and is
epitomized by William James's rejection of "the so-called English empiricist position" in favor of his own "sensationalism."[21] Though James
agrees with the empiricist solution to the Molyneux Question (210), his
reasoning brings him directly into conflict with the tradition of Locke and
Berkeley. Habitual inferences based on associations and experience are
necessary to lend order and measurement to our visual sensations, agrees
James, and to that extent our visual sensations are indeed "signs." But
James differs from the empiricists on a critical point: according to James
our visual sensations are intrinsically three-dimensional. The "depth-
sensation" is thus an immediate, directly intuited, and irreducible component of visual experience (213). Though "Berkeleyans unanimously assume that no retinal sensation can primitively be of volume," writes
James, it is nevertheless a fact that "all objects of sensation are volumi-
nous in three dimensions": "It is impossible to lie on one's back on a hill,
to let the empty abyss of blue fill one's whole visual field, and to sink
deeper and deeper into the merely sensational mode of consciousness
regarding it, without feeling that an indeterminate, palpitating, circling
depth is as indefeasibly one of its attributes as its breadth" (212–13). The
sensation of depth is not a construct out of optical signs that possess
merely two-dimensional extension, James argues; optical signs are always
already three-dimensional in character. Depth, he implies, is signified
quite literally by our optical sensations. Gone is the empiricist oscillation
between literal and figurative signs, and gone is the running analogy
linking perception to a language structured through the opposition of
different kinds of signs (literal and figurative, visible and phonic, etc.).[22]

Even I. A. Richards's subsequent empiricism—which we shall discuss

---

[21] James, *The Principles of Psychology*, 2.211–22, 270–82.

[22] James does employ an analogy with language later in his chapter, but only to
indicate that both language and perception observe the general economy of the type/token
distinction: "The selection of the several 'normal' appearances from out of the jungle of our
optical experiences, to serve as the real sights of which we shall think, is psychologically a
parallel phenomenon to the habit of thinking in words, and has a like use. Both are
substitutions of terms few and fixed for terms manifold and vague" (*Principles of Psychology*, 2.240). James's interest in language is simply in the fact that a language allows signs to
take on generalized reference; the issue of different kinds of reference or different kinds of
signs does not arise.

in the Epilogue—is qualified by James's literalizing of depths. Whereas Ruskin had followed the classical empiricists in denying that color possessed intrinsic qualities of spatial depth; Richards argues that "Colours as signs . . . have certain very marked spatial characters of their own," including volume, saturation, and depth of field.[23] Furthermore when Richards does discuss the construction of depth he assumes that it is at issue only in the *representation* of space. Instead of the Molyneux Question, it is the painter's canvas that interests Richards. He is fascinated by the instant in which visual space leaps into three dimensional focus, but only insofar as this is a *re*constructed phenomenon:

> An impression which, if interpreted in one way (e.g. by a person measuring the pigmented areas of a canvas), is correctly counted as a sign of a flat coloured surface, becomes, when differently interpreted, an intricately divided three-dimensional space— (150)

> A perfectly flat, meticulously detailed depiction of conventionally conceived objects, such as is so often praised in the Academy for its "finish", may be very nearly the same from its first impression on the retina to the last effort which vision can make upon it. At the other extreme a Cézanne, for example, which to the eye of a person quite unfamiliar with such a manner of painting may at first seem only a field or area of varied light, may, as the response develops, through repeated glances, become first an assemblage of blots and patches of colour, and then as these recede and advance, tilt and spread relatively to one another and become articulated, a system of volumes. Finally, as the distances and stresses of their volumes become more definitely imagined, it becomes an organisation of the entire "picture-space" into a three-dimensional whole. . . . With familiarity the response is of course shortened. The retinal impression, the sign, that is, for the response, contains actually but a small part of the whole final product. (149–50)

While Richards's interest centers on the ways in which judgment constructs three-dimensional space, and while he retains the empiricist interest in the analogy between impressions and signs, he is less interested in the innocent than in the trained eye. Whereas Ruskin remains poised between problems of perception and problems of representation, Richards seems interested primarily in representation. Since for Richards visual signs already possess intrinsic depth, the questions that preoccupy him

[23] Richards, *Principles of Literary Criticism*, 153.

concern simply degrees of economy in the arrangement of signs. Depth is no longer, as it was for the classical empiricists, an entirely constructed affair.

LOCKE AND THE "ORIGINS" OF FIGURATIVE LANGUAGE

The double valence of reflection, surface, and depth—as terms referring both to optical and to mental phenomena—broaches a central question in our understanding of texts in the classical empiricist tradition: to what extent are empiricist descriptions of the mind's operations intended as literal accounts of a physiological process, and to what extent are they figurative or analogical accounts of an inaccessible mechanism? It is tempting to opt for some sophisticated form of the latter alternative; this is, for instance, largely the reading given to Berkeley's theory of mind by Colin Turbayne, who resolves some of the more notorious shifts and inconsistencies in Berkeley's philosophy by positing "language" itself (with its attendant distinctions between writing and reading, between sign and signified, and between literal and figurative) as the "model" for all Berkeley's descriptions of phenomenal relations. Some minor reservations aside, I agree with Turbayne's account of Berkeley (see Chapter 3). But the more we redescribe psychological and epistemological theories as theories of language, the more we find ourselves relying on an unexamined distinction between the literal and the figurative. The danger of a reliance on the category of the figurative as the model for imponderable or intuitively sensed relationships is not so much that it dispenses with any sort of verification, as that it ignores the tremendous diversity of tropes. Similitude, analogy, metaphor, synecdoche, example, and allegory—to name but a few—are all modes of the figurative, and all bear different relations to that heuristic construct called the literal. To say that Locke's description of ideas as "impressions" on the mind is figurative is not yet to specify the nature of the relationship (particularly in the absence of any clear-cut Lockean reference to *literal* impressions in the mind, from which his figurative use of "impressions" would have to be distinguished); and if we proceed to say that his description of reasoning as something "deep" is also figurative, we now need to determine whether we are speaking of the same kind of figure in both cases.

Turbayne's redescription of Berkeley's immaterialism as a theory of language is perhaps not so much an explanation, then, as a twist. Paul de

Man suggests much the same relationship while emphasizing its potential for inversion when he writes of Locke's figurative language that "one may wonder whether the metaphors illustrate a cognition or if the cognition is not perhaps shaped by the metaphors."[24] De Man casts the problem in the form of a quite serious rhetorical question; we are reminded that a writer's epistemology has as much claim to explaining the central terms of his theory of language as that theory has a claim to explaining the terms of the epistemology.

The traditional empiricist—and indeed commonsense—rejoinder to this rhetoricizing of epistemological questions is entered by Berkeley, who denies that there are any philosophical issues at stake in our habitual figures of speech concerning the mind:

> *Phil.* Look you, *Hylas,* when I speak of objects as existing in the mind, or imprinted on the senses, I would not be understood in the gross literal sense—as when bodies are said to exist in a place, or a seal to make an impression upon wax. My meaning is only that the mind comprehends or perceives them; and that it is affected from without, or by some being distinct from itself.
> . . . Nor is there anything in this but what is conformable to the general analogy of language; most part of the mental operations being signified by words borrowed from sensible things; as is plain in the terms *comprehend, reflect, discourse, &c.,* which, being applied to the mind, must not be taken in their gross, original sense.[25]

Here we have an attitude toward philosophical rhetoric whose import is difficult to gauge and equally difficult not to underestimate. Despite the covert value judgments embedded in words such as "borrowed" and "gross," Berkeley cannot be interpreted as entering simple objections either to the literal or to the metaphorical employment of words. Berkeley's criticism concerns the philosophical tendency to hypostatize ordinary figures of speech. It further concerns any attempt to analyze such hypostatizations. In other words, Berkeley does not believe that any purpose is served by analyzing philosophical rhetoric in order to establish either its categorical distinction from or essential identity with the meanings embedded in ordinary discourse. The target of Berkeley's criticism

24 Paul de Man, "The Epistemology of Metaphor," *Critical Inquiry* 5 (Autumn 1978): 16.

25 Berkeley, *Three Dialogues between Hylas and Philonous,* in *Works,* 1.346–47. Hereafter cited as *Dialogues,* with page numbers from this edition.

here is the literal/figurative distinction itself; and what Berkeley offers implicitly as an alternative is the idea of *common figures of speech*, which are *proper* or *ordinary* even if not *literal*. Berkeley does not wish his own terminology to be understood as extending beyond this realm of the "proper." In short, he does not believe that philosophy's figures of speech can be investigated for meanings that might complicate, undo, or run counter to its most obvious, expository claims. Our question, then, is whether recasting the literal/figurative distinction as a distinction between "philosophical" and "ordinary" discourse exempts philosophical texts from questions concerning the difference between literal and figurative interpretations of their most basic terminology.

To begin answering this question, let us note that a concern with the literal/figurative distinction is hardly one imposed on the seventeenth-century text. It is invoked over and over again in Locke's *Essay* and is at issue in almost every passage where Locke attempts to explain relationships of occurrences "in the mind" to events and objects "outside the mind"—whether this relationship be one of physiological induction, logical extension, natural resemblance, or arbitrary convention, and whether it involve words, objects, sensations, or "reflections." Locke's philosophy is at crucial points grounded on assumptions about the *analogy* between mental and physical operations, the analogy among sense faculties, and the figurative manner in which human concepts signify the divine. This means that at the most basic level of explaining the knowledge acquisition of the individual subject, Locke has recourse to a literal/figurative distinction (e.g., mental operations are not *literally* material actions but are *like* them; the objects of sight are not literally the same as the objects of touch, but the two sets of objects are analogous and commensurable; God's "wisdom" is not literally, but rather figuratively "infinite" [2.17.1]).[26] The question of how Locke understands the literal/figurative distinction,

[26] Even our intuitions of God, in Locke's scheme, are figurative in varying ways. When Locke refers, in the phrase just cited, to our figurative ascription of infinite goodness to God, the rhetorical figure he has in mind is metonymy. I.e., we may rightly consider God's spatial extension to be literally infinite, but in order to imagine the boundlessness of his "goodness" we must "reflect" on the "Number or Extent of the Acts or Objects" of that "goodness." When it comes to conceiving the idea of "spirit," however, Locke suggests that our figurative ascription is more along the lines of "analogy" and "reflection": "For bating some very few, and those, if I may so call them, superficial *Ideas* of Spirit, which by reflection we get of our own, and from thence, the best we can, collect, of the Father of all Spirits . . . we have no certain information, so much as of the Existence of other Spirits, but by revelation" (*Essay*, 4.3.27).

then, is central to an understanding of his accounts of experience and knowledge acquisition. Yet when one turns to his account of the literal/figurative distinction, one finds it tied to a completely speculative —if not unfamiliar—historical account of the emergence of figurative from literal language, an account that both assumes and reproduces the initial distinctions of mind and body, interior and exterior, human and divine, sight and insight—all of which the "language analogy" was intended to explain:[27]

> It may also lead us a little towards the Original of all our Notions and Knowledge, if we remark, how great a dependance our *Words* have on common sensible *Ideas*; and how those, which are made use of to stand for Actions and Notions quite removed from sense, *have their rise from thence, and from obvious sensible* Ideas *are transferred to more abstruse significations*, and made to stand for *Ideas* that come not under the cognizance of our senses; *v.g.* to *Imagine, Apprehend, Comprehend, Adhere, Conceive, Instill, Disgust, Disturbance, Tranquillity*, etc. are all Words taken from the Operations of sensible Things, and applied to certain Modes of Thinking. *Spirit*, in its primary signification, is Breath; *Angel*, a Messenger: And I doubt not, but if we could trace them to their sources, we should find, in all Languages, the names, which stand for Things that fall not under our Senses, to have had their first rise from sensible *Ideas*. By which we may give some kind of guess, that kind of Notions they were, and whence derived, which filled their Minds, who were the first Beginners of Languages; and how Nature, even in the naming of Things, unawares suggested to Men the Originals and Principles of all their Knowledge; whilst, to give Names, that might make known to others any Operations they felt in themselves, or any other *Ideas*, that came not under their Senses, they were fain to borrow Words from ordinary known *Ideas* of Sensation, by that means to make others the more easily to conceive those Operations they experimented in themselves, which made no outward sensible appearances; (3.1.5)

---

[27] The locus classicus for the articulation of these mutually constituting relationships is chap. 25 of Plato's *Phaedrus*, trans. R. Hackforth (Cambridge: Cambridge University Press, 1952), 274B-278B. The finest account of its significance for Western philosophy is in Jacques Derrida's *Of Grammatology*, trans. Gayatri Chakravorty Spivak (Baltimore: Johns Hopkins University Press, 1976), particularly chaps. 1 and 2, "The End of the Book and the Beginning of Writing" and "Linguistics and Grammatology"; see also Derrida's "Plato's Pharmacy," in *Dissemination*, trans. Barbara Johnson (Chicago: University of Chicago Press, 1981), 61–171; and "White Mythology: Metaphor in the Text of Philosophy" in *Margins of Philosophy*, trans. Alan Bass (Chicago: University of Chicago Press, 1982), 207–72.

According to this account, figurative language consists in the extended application of "original," "sensible" terms for the specific and limited purpose of denoting things "quite removed from sense." But what principle guides the "borrowing" of particular "sensible ideas" to stand for particular nonsensible ones? And what does the etymological reversal of such borrowing (the revivification of dead metaphors) teach us about the "Notions" that "filled" the minds of our ancestors?[28]

Before answering these questions, posed by Locke's mytho-historical account of the emergence of figurative language—what Richetti calls Locke's primal "anthropological scene"[29]—we need to look briefly at the most influential seventeenth-century account of rhetoric in order to see how radical, how *ambiguous*, Locke's position really is. When we turn to the seventeenth-century account of rhetoric that has the greatest affinity to Locke's own work, we find not only the semantic-cognitive functions of the figure firmly established but a renewed emphasis as well on its historical-anthropological significance. Bernard Lamy's Port-Royalist rhetorical treatise, *The Art of Speaking* (1676),[30] begins by reimagining the historical development of language in a hypothetical utopian community: "Let us see how Men would form their Language, and make themselves intelligible one to another, should they be brought together from strange and remote places. Let us make use of the liberty of the Poets, and fetch either out of the Earth or the Heavens a Troop of new Men, alto-

[28] Foucault, Aarsleff, and Kroll have all observed that the neoclassical interest in the origins of language was more speculative and theoretical than historicist. According to Foucault, the Renaissance interest in the chronology of languages gives way in the neoclassical period to an interest in the typology of languages (*The Order of Things*, 89–90): "The guiding thread used for such [neoclassical] investigations was not the material transformations undergone by the word, but the constancy of its significations" (109). Aarsleff argues that Locke's comments on etymology were intended only to make a point about the necessarily pragmatic principles of language development, but were misinterpreted by the eighteenth century as a literal—and potentially heretical—argument for the exclusively material origins of knowledge (*From Locke to Saussure*, 68–69). And Kroll points out that Lockean arguments about language were prescriptive rather than descriptive (*The Material Word*, 60–61).

[29] Richetti, *Philosophical Writing*, 92–93. See also Land, *From Signs to Propositions*. Land describes Locke's account in the *Essay* (3.1.5) as "a conceptually isolated but historically important passage" concerning "the genesis of language," and suggests that the passage inspired "a number of anthropological and etymological speculations" in the mid-eighteenth century (18–19).

[30] Wilbur Samuel Howell, in *Eighteenth-Century British Logic and Rhetoric* (Princeton: Princeton University Press, 1971), points out that Lamy's *De l'Art de Parler* was "attributed erroneously to the Port-Royalists" but is "properly to be linked with the reforms proposed in *The Port Royal Logic*" (91–92).

gether ignorant of the benefit of Words.[31] Such a "troop of men," according to Lamy, would begin by inventing names for each of "The Objects of our Perceptions" but eventually would begin to use words in extended, figurative senses as an alternative to inventing new ones:

> Doubtless if these new Men would make it their business to find out Words that might be signs of all these Idea's which are the Objects of our perception (which, according to the Philosophers, is the first operation of the Mind) in the infinite variety of Words, it would not be difficult to find particular signs to mark every Idea, and give it a particular Name. In as much as we naturally make use of these primitive Notions, we may believe, that if other things should present themselves to their Minds, bearing any resemblance or conformity to those things which they had denominated before, they would not take the pains to invent new words, but (with some little variation) make use of the first Names to denote the difference of the things to which they would apply them. Experience persuades me, that where a proper Word does not occur immediately to our Tongue, we should make use of the Name of some other thing bearing some kind of resemblance to it. (1.1.3 [11])

Lamy does not call the new words "metaphors" in this passage, but he has already established that words whose reference is extended on the principle of "resemblance" are to be called "tropes" (preface, A4 verso), and later he will explain how metaphor is in fact the exemplary trope.[32] What is of particular interest to us here is Lamy's assumption that figurative language is founded on our perception of resemblances, and that tropes are called upon to name something *other* than "objects of percep-

---

[31] Preface to *The Art of Speaking: Written in French by Messieurs du Port Royal In pursuance of a former Treatise, Intituled, The Art of Thinking* (London, 1676), part 1, chap. 1, sec. 3, p. 9. All subsequent citations will refer to part, chapter, section, and page numbers from this edition. I have modernized the orthography, but not the spelling, in all citations.

[32] "Tropes are words transported from their proper significations, and applied to things that they signifie but obliquely. So that all Tropes are *Metaphors* or Translations, according to the Etymology of the Word. And yet by the Figure *Antonomasia* we give the name of *Metaphor* to a particular Trope, and according to that definition, a *Metaphor* is a Trope by which we put a strange and remote word for a proper word, by reason of its resemblance with the thing of which we speak" (2.1.2 [75]). Lamy is well aware of the irony that "tropes"—which he imagines were introduced to prevent the rank of proper names from swelling to infinity—are themselves infinite in their possibilities: "we may reckon, there are as many sort of Tropes, as there are different references; but it has pleased the Masters of this Art [rhetoric] to establish but few" (2.1.1 [71]). Thus it is that the relationship between "metaphor" and the entire class of "tropes" is itself given a tropic name: "antonomasia."

tion" (i.e., language *would* be capable of producing a new word for each "object" of perception, says Lamy; it is only "if *other* things should present themselves to the mind" that we would need to begin recycling the "first names").[33] Those "other things" that require tropes for their description are not objects of perception but rather products of the mind (though this may include the mind's imaginative *re*presentation of what is given immediately to the senses—what Hume will later describe as reflection, and Burke as imagination): "The Mind of Man is so fertile, all the Languages in the World are too barren to express its fecundity. It turns things so many ways, and represents things with so many different faces, that 'tis impossible to contrive words for all the forms of our thoughts" (2.1.1 [69–70]). Figurative language, then, represents things produced (or "turned" or troped) by the "fecund" mind, and it gives names to these ideas on the basis of their resemblance to ideas (presumably derived from objects of perception) that we have already encountered.

Locke's account of the emergence of figurative language (cited on p. 41) would at first glance seem to be quite similar to Lamy's. Literal language—the language used to name "ideas of sensation"—comes first; later these "original" words are recirculated to name "other *Ideas*, that [come] not under [the] Senses." Figurative language thus supplements knowledge by bringing new objects into the field of language. The reversal of this process—the discovery, in Locke's words, of the "sensible ideas" buried in "the names, which stand for Things that fall not under our Senses"—also produces knowledge, but of what *order* it is not clear. What is it that we learn by noting the original sensory figure?

Locke's most significant departure from Lamy, and in fact from the assumptions of the entire classical and neo-Ciceronian tradition, lies in the fact that he posits no essential *resemblance* between the original sensible idea and the extended figurative sense that are joined in one and the same word. The motive for metaphor is only general and not specific; the historical account is almost tautological. By noting "how great a dependance our *Words* have on common sensible *Ideas*," writes Locke, we learn simply that the "Notions . . . which filled [the] Minds" of our

---

[33] I follow Lamy here in observing no schematic distinction between "tropes" and "figurative" language. Lamy writes: "When to express a thing, we make use of an improper word, which Custom has applied to another Subject, that way of explaining our selves is figurative; and the words so transported from their proper signification, and applied to other things than what they naturally mean, are called *Tropes*, or *Changes* of Custom" (2.1.1 [71]).

ancestors were primarily "*Ideas* of Sensation" and that the names for these ideas were subsequently "borrowed" to provide names for "Notions quite removed from sense." We do not learn anything about particular kinds or classes of words or ideas, beyond the simple opposition of sensory to nonsensory experiences, and original to extended ("borrowed," "transferred") applications.

Nonetheless, the anthropological account has all the appearances of an explanatory model pointing the way to some more fundamental, simple strata of experience and meaning. The resonance of such Lockean phrases as "the Originals of all our Notions and Knowledge" seems to suggest that the genetic account of figurative language will play a critical role in the sorting out of knowledge claims. Derrida has described this kind of account—the belief, in his words, that "abstract notions always hide a sensory figure"—as "a classical motif, a commonplace of the eighteenth century." Such an account, writes Derrida, assumes "that a purity of sensory language could have been in circulation at the origin of language, and that the *etymon* of a primitive sense always remains determinable." Derrida refers to this primitive sense as the "sensory and material figure . . . equivalent to a literal meaning (*sens propre*)," which, according to the classical account, "becomes a metaphor when philosophical discourse puts it into circulation."[34]

One of Derrida's most important points is that the distinction between proper and metaphorical meanings—and the project of reversing or retracing the historical derivation of one from the other—is itself a metaphorical representation, a picture with its own history.[35] But it is unclear whether Locke is offering a genuinely historical thesis. Let us return to Locke and to the exceptional feature of his otherwise "classical" account. As we have seen, the astounding thing about Locke's primal linguistic scene is that it seems to make no assumption that the "original" and "borrowed" senses of words are linked by an underlying resemblance of ideas. The borrowing of sensory figures to designate the "internal Operations" of the mind is explained simply in terms of the need to make invisible things manifest. Locke gives a motive, but no principle, for the

---

[34] Derrida, "White Mythology," 210–11.

[35] This is but one of several complex theses in "White Mythology"; it is perhaps the foregrounded thesis, however, in the first two sections of that essay, "Exergue" and "Plus de métaphore" (209–29). Kenneth Burke makes a similar point concerning figurative projections of language's history in his appendix to *A Grammar of Motives* (Berkeley and Los Angeles: University of California Press, 1945), 506.

borrowing of terms. And correspondingly, the claim Locke makes for the "knowledge" that etymological reversal may yield concerns only the *historical* origin of abstract ideas,[36] not the principle upon which individual words were borrowed:

> We may give some kind of guess, what kind of Notions they were, and whence derived, which filled their Minds, who were the first Beginners of Languages; and how Nature, even in the naming of Things, unawares suggested to Men the Originals and Principles of all their Knowledge: whilst, to give Names, that might make known to others any Operations they felt in themselves, or any other *Ideas*, that came not under their Senses, they were fain to borrow Words from ordinary known *Ideas* of Sensation, by that means to make others the more easily to conceive those Operations . . . which made no outward sensible appearances.

What this passage says is simply that etymology will reveal to us the general class of things with which the "beginners of language" were concerned, that is, physical objects and sensations.[37] Locke does *not* say that etymology will reveal the resemblance, perception, or specific motivation underlying the historical choice of a particular sensory figure to represent a particular abstract idea. There is no Cratylic or Adamic nostalgia motivating either Locke's defense or his criticism of figurative language.

The two best modern accounts of rhetoric in Locke's *Essay* both pay respect to the enlightenment rewriting of Locke's advice by remaining alert to the sensory figures of his epistemological discourse. For Paul de

---

[36] For the sake of convenience I use the term "abstract" to describe what Locke refers to in this passage as "abstruse significations" and "Ideas that come not under the cognizance of the senses; v.g. to Imagine, Apprehend . . ." In this sense the abstract is simply distinct from the sensible. I preserve this commonsense usage because it is consistent with the terminology adopted by other commentators on these issues, e.g. Derrida and Richetti. However, it is important to note that Locke himself does not use the term "abstract" to designate the nonsensory or nonmaterial but rather to designate "general ideas" (*Essay*, 2.12.1). Thus "substance" is for Locke an abstraction, whereas "power" is not. When Derrida and Richetti speak of recovering the literal sense or sensory figure located in an abstract term, they are not referring to Locke's "abstractions" but to his "Ideas that come not under the cognizance of our Senses" and "which [make] no outward sensible appearances." Since I will not concern myself in this chapter with the vexed question of Locke's notion of "abstract ideas," I will use the term "abstract" in its current rather than in its Lockean sense.

[37] Aarsleff goes even further, suggesting that Locke "was merely illustrating that we grasp the less familiar by the more familiar" (*From Locke to Saussure*, 69).

Man, it is Locke's notion of "simple ideas" (2.2–9; 3.4) that brings the figurative and the literal into close—even indistinguishable—contact. For Locke, simple ideas like "light" or "power" are pure shocks of sensation or reflection. They cannot be analyzed into constituent parts, and thus no description of them can be built up out of other ideas or words. We "simply" name them. And our names for them represent, in de Man's words, the ideal "coincidence" of "nominal and real essence" and thus an ideal of literality; as de Man points out, "there can be no room for play or ambivalence between the word and the entity" in Locke's conception of simple ideas. Yet this makes the names of simple ideas uniquely susceptible to figurative distortion, since such ideas can never be given a definition and must settle instead for endless translation. De Man concludes that "the discourse of simple ideas is figural discourse or translation and, as such, creates the fallacious illusion of definition."[38] Tracing the sensory figure in Locke's work—the "light" in "idea" or the "passage" in "translation," to use de Man's examples—thus becomes an endless process of rhetorical figuration.

Like de Man, John Richetti emphasizes the sensory figures in Locke's *Essay*. Richetti, however, describes the trajectory from abstract word to sensory figure as something inspired by "the recurrent force of a literal view of things" in the *Essay*.[39] Locke's attempt to present the process of understanding in the form of a temporal drama rather than a hypostatized image becomes, in Richetti's view, an opposition of the literal to the metaphorical.[40] But for Richetti, the return to the literal—Locke's

---

[38] De Man, "The Epistemology of Metaphor," 15. This part of de Man's argument reaches its climax when he rephrases Locke's adjuration to "understand the idea of light" as "to light the light of light" (16). De Man's sense that an etymological "stutter of tautology" lurks just beneath the surface of Locke's text is shared by Berkeley, who notes in *Three Dialogues between Hylas and Philonous* that the implicitly Lockean discourse of "impressions" reduces to "talk of ideas imprinted in an idea causing that same idea, which is absurd" (*Works*, 1.302).

[39] Richetti, *Philosophical Writing*, 75–76.

[40] Richetti's references to Locke's "dynamic" and "dramatic" rhetorical strategy are too numerous to cite; he refers on p. 57 to Locke's rejection of "a hypostatized image of truth." Richetti summarizes this tension in his concluding section as "the literalizing and antimetaphoric drift of Locke's rhetoric" (112). Ironically, Richetti notes, a "literal" view of things focuses our attention at once *on* and *beyond* language. In discussing a passage from the *Essay* (4.2.15) in which Locke chooses "an image from reading to illustrate the swiftness of . . . intuitive knowledge," Richetti notes that Locke's emphasis on the materiality of language is *anti*textual: "Knowledge here is not actually like reading, but simply and literally the perceptual act that precedes reading, distinguishing black letters on a white field. . . . Intuitive knowledge . . . is a sudden seeing, a vision that in its momentary quality

revivification of the "half-dead metaphors of common speech"[41]—is a return to heterogeneous material instances, to concrete examples that defy generalizability, and not simply to an underlying and privileged metaphorics of "seeing" or "feeling."[42] The conception of the "literal" upon which the argument (and the rhetorical strategy) of the *Essay* turns is, in Richetti's view, not a naive belief in the stability or schematizability of the sensory world but an emphasis on the heterogeneous, local conditions of knowledge.

Despite the exceedingly subtle, productive, conceptions of "figurality" and "literality" that de Man and Richetti respectively present us with, we cannot avoid noting an irony in the fact that two critics who both purport to stay close to the sensory figures of Locke's prose describe the overall rhetorical effect of the *Essay* in quite opposite ways—one as an endless figurality, the other as a recurrent literalization.[43] Both writers recognize the existence of the "sensory figure" at the heart of philosophical discourse, but they choose to describe its characteristics in different ways. Richetti sees Locke's concrete figures as endlessly complex and variegated, but in every instance their effect is to distract us from the conventionality of the text. In Richetti's reading, the sensory figures in Locke's rhetoric are a bulwark against the hegemonizing impulse of textual philosophy. We accept the "bullion" of sensory figures in exchange for consistency of expository statement, since expository statement is the

---

excludes the long sequences of writing and reading and for the moment insists on the phenomenal qualities of the text in front of us and thereby diminishes it as a text. Reading and writing are clearly associated with a discredited merely verbal philosophy" (112–13). Thus, in Richetti's view, the literal/metaphoric distinction ultimately becomes a speech/text distinction.

[41] Ibid., 79.

[42] Locke, in Richetti's view, wishes to replace the philosophical discourse of innate ideas with "a language backed by the solid bullion of experience. But experience as the *Essay* elaborates it turns out to be so varied and individualized that such a substitution has to be ironically qualified" (*Philosophical Writing*, 103).

[43] It is worth noting that de Man and Richetti also present us with opposed views on the status of the "example" in Locke. For de Man it is an axiom that "examples used in logical arguments have a distressing way of lingering on with a life of their own" ("The Epistemology of Metaphor," 18n); examples always have a capacity for being extended beyond their intended application. For Richetti, however, "Locke's generalizations retain such dense and persistent qualification that in reading them we do not travel very far from the specific examples of experience" (*Philosophical Writing*, 61). Richetti prefers to read Locke's examples as less resonant, but more stable, than de Man would allow.

property of a discredited philosophical tradition indissociably linked to the classificatory impulse of rhetoric.[44]

Richetti uses the term "literal" to suggest, variously, qualities of sensory immediacy, of commonsensicality, and of antischolasticism. But it would be a mistake, I believe, to interpret Richetti's "literalization" in the light of formal distinctions between literal and figurative usage. The "literal," here, refers more to a general style and ethos, a trope of empiricist discourse, not a technical term from rhetoric or grammatic.

De Man interprets the sensory figures of Locke's text as symptoms of the fact that we have to describe our simple ideas rhetorically, for example, through analogy, metonymy, example, metaphor, synecdoche, and catachresis. Thus for de Man there can be no essential distinction between the primary alphabet of our ideas (to use Locke's analogy [2.7.10]) and the more schematic, "philosophical," or "rhetorical" systems we construct from that alphabet. De Man's decision to call all these phenomena "figuration" is thus as rhetorical as Richetti's, since it does not recognize the existence of any meaningful countercategory. De Man's "figural" is no more distinct from some articulated notion of the literal than Richetti's "literal" is distinct from some formal notion of the figurative.

Neither de Man nor Richetti is insensitive to the essential inconsistency that characterizes the deployment of figurative language; both are careful to demonstrate the radical contingency of all Locke's figures and to avoid privileging or thematizing any particular figure. And both are careful to observe the irreducibly complicated relationship of figurative language to expository statement in the *Essay*. But each emphasizes one particular direction that figurative language may take. De Man sees the rhetorical motions of Locke's text being driven by the radical, potentially endless combinatory power of words (which the classificatory impulse of stylistic rhetoric can never fully manage). Figures of speech lead to other figures of speech. Richetti, on the other hand, sees Locke's strategy as a continual attempt to dislodge us from customary forms of language by using figures of speech in a controlled way against themselves (e.g., the optical metaphors of traditional philosophy are countered by Locke's emphasis on sensory and material figures; the "half-dead metaphors of common speech" are at first literalized and then ironized; the metaphor of "seeing" is exemplified by, and then reduced to, the purely physical

---

[44] "Bullion" is Richetti's term; see n. 42.

aspects of "reading" and "writing"). The result is to dislodge us from language in order to let us "see" for ourselves.

In contrast to Richetti and de Man, I would like to suggest that there is a strategic tension between figurative and literal usages in empiricist writing, a tension related—though not reducible—to the tension between verbal and visual models of experience. In the chapters that follow we shall pay attention not just to what empiricist writers have to say about figurative language, nor simply to what philosophical operations they carry out under the cover of rhetoric, but more importantly to the ways in which the very idea of rhetoric—and of the line dividing the rhetorical from the nonrhetorical—is manipulated to illustrate the basic relations of experience. In particular this will lead us to see complexities in the empiricist use of the figure of "reflection," complexities that far exceed any simple binary understanding of the relationship between the literal and the figurative, and which point to the distinctive empiricist understanding of "experience" as a paradoxical structure of attention and inattention.

2

Locke's Grammar of Reflection

In his *language*, Locke is, of all philosophers, the most figurative, ambiguous, vacillating, various, and even contradictory; . . . The opinions of such a writer are not, therefore, to be assumed from isolated and casual expressions, which themselves require to be interpreted on the general analogy of his system.

—SIR WILLIAM HAMILTON, 1830

When Locke . . . develops his own theory of words and language, what he constructs turns out to be in fact a theory of tropes. Of course, he would be the last man in the world to realize and to acknowledge this. One has to read him, to some extent, against or regardless of his own explicit statements; . . . [H]e has to be read not in terms of explicit statements (especially explicit statements about statements) but in terms of the rhetorical motions of his own text.

—PAUL DE MAN

SEEING AND TALKING

OBSCURED BY THE more famous distinction between "sensation" and "reflection" in Locke's *An Essay Concerning Human Understanding* is a division perhaps even more fundamental for the tradition of empiricist writing. For Locke's account of knowledge and experience relies alternately on two radically different accounts of cognition: one modeled on visual perception and the other on the structure and effects of verbal language. The distinction is not an openly acknowledged, let alone a systematic, one in the *Essay*, but the reasons for this ambiguity are instructive. For Locke uses one and the same metaphor, "reflection," to refer indifferently to mental faculties modeled on the mechanics of vision and to those modeled on the processes of verbal meaning. Since Locke allows images, but not words, to exist unnoticed in the mind, the distinction is a crucial one. The consequences of Locke's shift between alternative models is an intentional blurring of the line that distinguishes attention from inattention, self-consciousness from habit or custom, and ultimately "common sense" from "philosophical" postures of the mind. The existence of this particular set of oppositions within empiricism has been explicit ever since Hume declared the inescapable tension between skeptical reflection and the ostensibly natural tendency to form habits.[1] My interests here, however, are less in Hume's closely reasoned account of this paradox than in the set of rhetorical and philosophical habits that generate such a set of oppositions from the single and distinctive trope of reflection, allowing empiricism to remain poised so delicately between accounts of what we see and what we say.

In the pages that follow I trace Locke's account of the inextricable relationship between seeing and talking. In the first section I examine a paradigmatic instance of Locke's shift from issues of visual perception to those of verbal meaning and then discuss the general relationship of "reflection" to these two processes. In the second section I outline the peculiar combination of philosophical and antiphilosophical attitudes condensed in the figure of "reflection." The third and fourth sections address Locke's intentional complication of the apparently simple materialist model in which the durability of ideas is equated metaphorically with the depth of impressions on the mind's surface. Whereas the first of these two sections focuses specifically on ambiguities in Locke's figure of "depth," the latter examines in greater detail the ambiguities of "reflection"—specifically, the fact that the development of our ideas, much like the activity of reading, requires a paradoxical combination of reflective and unreflective behavior.

To begin with we may look briefly at a passage from Locke's *Essay* that illustrates in exemplary fashion the shift in empiricist writing from optical to linguistic analogies. The passage unfolds over the course of three sections in the chapter "Perception" from book 2 (2.9.8–10). Not coincidentally these are the sections into which Locke inserted (in the second edition) his account of the Molyneux Question, which we have already discussed, and to which we shall return in Chapter 4. Locke's concern in this particular passage is with the apparently constitutive role of judgments and assumptions in sensory perception—the phenomenon we would now describe as "unconscious inference" or "perceptual judg-

---

[1] For Hume's famous account, see *A Treatise of Human Nature*, 1.4.2 ("Of scepticism with regard to the senses") and 1.4.7 ("Conclusion of this book"). Hume, of course, considers *both* skepticism and habit to be natural tendencies.

ment."[2] Upon introspection we discover that the pure act of visual perception is almost always supplemented—spontaneously, invisibly—by an act of judgment that rearranges raw sensations into signs of a recognizable world:

§8. We are farther to consider concerning Perception, that the *Ideas we receive by sensation, are often* in grown People *alter'd by the Judgment,* without our taking notice of it. When we set before our Eyes a round Globe, of any uniform colour, *v.g.* Gold, Alabaster, or Jet, 'tis certain, that the *Idea* thereby imprinted in our Mind, is of a flat Circle variously shadow'd, with several degrees of Light and Brightness coming to our Eyes. But we having by use been accustomed to perceive, what kind of appearance convex Bodies are wont to make in us; what alterations are made in the reflections of Light, by the difference of the sensible Figures of Bodies, the Judgment presently, by an habitual custom, alters the Appearances into their Causes: So that from that, which truly is variety of shadow or colour, collecting the Figure, it makes it pass for a mark of Figure, and frames to it self the perception of a convex Figure, and an uniform Colour; when the *Idea* we receive from thence, is only a Plain variously colour'd, as is evident in Painting.

Contrary to Locke's later and more celebrated definition of "judgment" as that analytic faculty opposed to wit, similitude, metaphor, and allusion (2.11.2), judgment here is represented as a spontaneous synthesizing power, allied with habit and custom, and altering sensation in the interest of common sense.

But Locke does not rest content with this single example drawn from our experience of visual perception. After attesting to the uniqueness of perceptual judgment in the field of vision (it is not "usual in any of our *Ideas*, but those received by *Sight*," he writes, that we "judge" certain sensory impressions by means of others), Locke feels compelled to provide a further analogy to explain this "habit":

This in many cases, by a settled habit, in things whereof we have frequent experience, is performed so constantly, and so quick, that we take that for the Perception of our Sensation, which is an *Idea* formed by our Judgment; so that one, *viz.* that of Sensation, serves only to excite the other, and is scarce taken notice of it self; as a Man who reads or hears with attention and

[2] Both terms have wide currency. See for instance, Gombrich, *Art and Illusion*, 14–16; and Michael Williams, *Groundless Belief*, 102.

understanding, takes little notice of the Characters, or Sounds, but of the *Ideas*, that are excited in him by them. (2.9.9)

The ostensible uniqueness of visual inference is now generalized and finds its corollary in our constructions of verbal meaning. We do not "see" a world of raw optical impressions any more than we hear or see the individual elements (whether character, sound, word, or even phrase) of common discourse. Both the operations of sight and our operations with language involve leaps and substitutions that aim to contract our field of impressions into a coherent and economical set of signs.[3]

But how precisely does verbal meaning confirm and repeat our experiences of visual perception? Locke begins, as we have seen, by insisting on the distinctiveness of visual perception, and then immediately goes on to propose an analogy between visual and verbal operations. In explaining how "judgment" outpaces "sensation" in both processes, however, Locke resorts back to a strong distinction between the visual and the verbal:

§10. Nor need we wonder, that this is done with so little notice, if we consider, how very *quick* the *actions of the Mind* are performed: . . . I speak this in comparison to the Actions of the Body. Any one may easily observe this in his own Thoughts, who will take the pains to reflect on them. How, as it were in an instant, do our Minds, with one glance, see all the parts of a demonstration, which may very well be called a long one, if we consider the time it will require to put it into words, and step by step shew it another?

In this passage the distinction between "actions of the Mind" and "Actions of the Body" is compared to the distinction between a "glance" and a verbal demonstration. The elision of verbal signifiers referred to in the immediately preceding passage ("takes little notice of the Characters, or

---

[3] See Foucault's description in *The Order of Things* of the "classical episteme" and its affinities for a "brief and concentrated kind of knowledge: the contraction of a long sequence of judgments into the rapidly assimilated form of the sign" (60): "Such is the role of feeling in Malebranche or of sensation in Berkeley; in natural judgement, in feeling, in visual impressions, and in the perception of the third dimension, what we are dealing with are hasty and confused, but pressing, inevitable, and obligatory kinds of knowledge serving as signs for discursive kinds of knowledge which we humans, because we are not pure intelligences, no longer have the time or the permission to attain to ourselves and by the unaided strength of our own minds" (59).

Sounds") is explained now by way of visual operations (the "glance" of the mind) rather than the other way round. And yet this is no simple or reciprocal reversal. For the "glance" that converts sensation into judgment when we operate with words is not literally a glance of the eye but a metaphoric glance, the glance of the mind.

Here, and elsewhere throughout Locke's *Essay*, language is at once the most and the least material of phenomena, alternately identified and contrasted with visual perception. Locke's account of "perception" cannot be resolved in the direction of either verbal meaning or visual perception—a line runs constantly back and forth between the two, analogizing visual perception in terms of linguistic signs and verbal meaning in terms of vision, insisting all the while on the categorical distinction between the two. The paired terms of body and mind, sensation and judgment, eyesight and language, will not align themselves symmetrically. Nor is the route back and forth between these two dimensions of experience symmetrical: we move *by analogy* from visual perception to verbal discourse but *by metaphor* back from verbal meaning to visual perception. And all this goes on under the scrutiny of "reflection": "Any one may easily observe this in his own Thoughts, who will take the pains to reflect on them."

We shall return to this passage later—particularly to consider some of the more intricate ways in which it distributes and opposes the ostensibly similar activities of "noticing," "attending," "seeing," "observing," and "reflecting"—but it is sufficient here to outline the stakes of Locke's peculiar oscillation between visual and verbal models of perception. That empiricism may be characterized in part by such an oscillation is not an entirely new observation. John Richetti, for instance, has argued that Locke's literary style in the *Essay* is an attempt to counter both "the merely visible" and "the merely verbal," "negating both the ordinary visual world of common sense and the unexamined verbal world of philosophic formulation."[4] What I would like to suggest here is that the passage we have just considered is paradigmatic in its insistence that verbal meaning and visual perception cannot be separated from each other—not because one is the ground of the other, or even because the inevitable textuality of Locke's philosophical argument reduces all experience to rhetoric, but rather because human experience cannot be separated into

---

[4] Richetti, *Philosophical Writing*, 88–89.

moments of seeing and moments of saying. We *say what we see*, and for empiricism this is one of the most distinctive and constitutive facts about experience, though one that reflection alone can reveal.[5]

To "reflect" is both the most natural and the most contrived of perceptual habits; it is a way of noticing (or a quality of attention) modeled on natural optical phenomena, but it is one that the mind and eye cannot achieve, unaided by special arrangements. The analogy of "reflective" seeing may be unpacked in two ways, and these alternative models additionally complicate the empiricism's oscillation between philosophical and antiphilosophical impulses. Richard Rorty points to a parallel problem in "unpacking" the metaphor of the "eye of the mind." For Rorty, it is the paradoxical status of the mind as both active recorder and passive recording medium that haunts the specular model of experience. Locke, argues Rorty,

> thought the dents in our quasi-tablet to be (as Ryle puts it) self-intimating. . . . It is as if the *tabula rasa* were perpetually under the gaze of the unblinking Eye of the Mind—nothing, as Descartes said, being nearer to the mind than itself. If the metaphor *is* unpacked in this way, however, it becomes obvious that the imprinting is of less interest than the observation of the imprint—all the knowing gets done, so to speak, by the Eye which observes the imprinted tablet, rather than by the tablet itself. Locke's success, accordingly, depended upon *not* unpacking the metaphor.[6]

One of the ways in which Locke attempts to avoid the unpacking of this metaphor is precisely by moving from the general metaphor of the mind's eye to the specific metaphor of "reflection," since the latter suggests equally the processes of passive mimesis and of critical self-scrutiny.[7]

[5] See an apposite remark by Foucault in *The Order of Things*, characterizing the relationship between visual image and verbal commentary in an encounter with a Velasquez painting, which he sees as "the representation, as it were, of Classical representation" (16), a prefiguration of the Enlightenment episteme: "But the relation of language to painting is an infinite relation. It is not that words are imperfect, or that, when confronted by the visible, they prove insuperably inadequate. Neither can be reduced to the other's terms: it is in vain that we say what we see; what we see never resides in what we say. And it is in vain that we attempt to show, by the use of images, metaphors, or similes, what we are saying; the space where they achieve their splendour is not that deployed by our eyes but that defined by the sequential elements of syntax" (9).

[6] Rorty, *Philosophy and the Mirror of Nature*, 143.

[7] Richetti makes a similar point in *Philosophical Writing* when he writes that a "moral-literary tradition helps to sustain" empiricism's paradoxical characterization of the mind "as both spectator and spectacle" (25), though the moral-literary tradition Richetti

What we notice when we reflect is either that which is specularly self-evident (e.g., "clear," "on the surface") or that which is *legible* (that which is imprinted on the mind). The distinction is an important one since these two alternative analogies suggest different difficulties and break down in different ways. The specular model cannot rid itself of the more troublesome connotations of reflected light: that which is revealed as self-evident by way of reflection may always be recognized subsequently as phantasmic, illusory, or unstable. The visual image is clear, but ephemeral. The linguistic model of self-evidence, on the other hand, confronts us with the stubborn materiality and presence of its signifiers. The palpability of the written sign would appear at first to contrast with the phantasms of reflected images, but of course the materiality of language is at least partially a visible one, and thus the verbal model sends us shuttling back to the visual model. Nonetheless, when Locke compares the self-evidence of impressions to a kind of intrinsic legibility, he requires us to consider just what it is we *do* with the signifiers of language when we read or listen; and reflecting in this way we find the category of visual clarity to be of questionable relevance.

According to Locke, both our habitual and our self-conscious uses of language—both our reflective and unreflective discourse—are characterized by a neglect of material signifiers. If we ignore individual characters, words, and even phrases when we attend to discourse without sufficient concentration, so too do we ignore these signifiers when we are straining for meaning. The leap from discourse to ideas, eliding as it does our experience of sounds or written characters as material objects, thus illustrates the fundamental tensions within the empiricist categories of "experience," of "self-evidence," and of "self-observation." In particular, it reveals just how slippery is the concept of "noticing" upon which Locke's argument relies. Noticing is always selective noticing, and the constant empiricist refrain to pay attention to—to reflect on—our own experience reveals itself as a polemical attempt to construct and direct our attention.[8]

---

has in mind here is not so much a particular rhetorical figure ("reflection") as it is the tradition of Socratic satire and irony, in which the philosopher must be prepared to watch himself "fall" (22–23).

[8] See an apposite remark by Williams (*Groundless Belief*) in reference to the tradition of experimental introspection among modern empiricists (H. H. Price and G. E. Moore). Such a process, argues Williams, is not "unbiased," "subjective" introspection but a "sophisticated device" that is "epistemological through and through" (43–44). "The given

"Reflection" is most prominent as a *metaphor* in the *Essay*, and yet the structure of Locke's argument reveals other rhetorical uses of the figure as well: specifically, the *Essay* employs reflection as an extended narrative trope. To reflect is to recognize not only one's own habits of thought and perception but the *adequacy* of those habits, and thus to turn away from speculation. The local figure of reflection is a potential turning point in the philosophical narrative and can trigger the ironic doubling back of an argument.[9] Thus, for instance, Hume's arguments concerning the skeptical effects of "reflection" are retracted or revised at key moments in his *Treatise* where the logic of his philosophical narrative seems to repeat at a different level a logic borrowed from his metaphors:

> Very refin'd reflections have little or no influence upon us; and yet we do not, and cannot establish it for a rule, that they ought not to have any influence; which implies a manifest contradiction.
>
> But what have I here said, that reflections very refin'd and metaphysical have little or no influence upon us? This opinion I can scarce forbear retracting, and condemning from my present feeling and experience. (1.4.7)[10]

---

element is not just found: philosophers are led to it by methods which reflect sophisticated epistemological presuppositions" (45). W.J.T. Mitchell makes a similar point concerning the mechanics of vision that underlie the metaphor of introspection: "'pure' visual perception, freed from concerns with function, use, and labels, is perhaps the most highly sophisticated sort of seeing that we do; it is not the 'natural' thing that the eye does (whatever that would be). The 'innocent eye' is a metaphor for a highly experienced and cultivated sort of vision" (*Iconology*, 118).

[9] Here it should be clear that I am in agreement with Richetti's thesis concerning the generally ironic structure of empiricist writing. See *Philosophical Writing*, 22–23. As the following analysis will show, however, I believe there are advantages to focusing on the figure of "reflection" rather than on the figurative and narrative pattern of a "fall" (Richetti's term) when trying to account for the epistemological complexities of empiricist writing.

[10] A similar turn occurs in the chapter on "scepticism with regard to reason," where Hume writes of his own argument: "I had almost said, that this was certain; but I reflect, that it must reduce *itself*, as well as every other reasoning, and from knowledge degenerate into probability" (*Treatise*, 1.4.1). See also 1.1.1, where Hume retracts his very first use of the term *reflection* (as a characterization of the relationship "betwixt our impressions and ideas"): "Upon a more accurate survey I find I have been carried away too far by the first appearance, and must make use of the distinction of perceptions into *simple and complex*, to limit this general decision, *that all our ideas and impressions are resembling.*"

For a related version of this repetition of local figures at the level of narrative trope, see Anthony Earl of Shaftesbury, "Miscellaneous Reflections," in *Characteristics of Men, Manners, Opinions, Times, etc.*, 2 vols., ed. John M. Robertson (London: Grant Richards, 1900), vol. 2. Shaftesbury's closing argument against ecclesiastical conservatives (who urge a fundamentalist reading of the Scriptures and decry Shaftesbury's speculative moral philos-

The narrative figure of reflection is central to empiricist writing, and Locke's *Essay* in particular makes use of reflection's potential as a trope of irony, reversal, and inversion. What is both attractive and problematic is that Locke uses the trope of reflection precisely to turn away from difficulties established by the conflicting values and implications of "reflection" as the latter functions metaphorically in his text.

A provisional analysis of the slippage in Locke's text between visual and verbal models of reflection would stress Locke's recognition that connotative meaning threatens constantly to undermine the schematic metaphors of philosophic writing. Accordingly we will first read the shifts back and forth between verbal and visual models (and between specular and material metaphors) as symptoms of a counter-rhetorical impulse: Locke is anxious to "negate" the distracting connotations of his various schematic metaphors.[11] Ultimately, however, the undecidability between the verbal and the visual in Locke's *Essay* must be seen as part of a more positive strategy: specifically, the attempt to prevent our confrontation with sensory evidence and our confrontation with language from becoming disengaged from each other. With this larger strategy of Locke's in mind, we may say that our goal in examining the shifts in Locke's metaphoric schemes will not be so much to show how he retreats from the philosophical difficulties engendered by his own rhetoric, or to show how thoroughly rhetorical is the category of common sense with which he works, but rather to highlight the rhetorical strategies that allow Locke—and subsequent empiricists—to sustain a complicated and constantly shifting relationship between verbal and visual meaning. This relationship is sustained, I will argue, primarily by the diverse, but related, uses that Locke makes of the figure of "reflection." One way of putting this is

---

ophy) is turned back precisely at the point where ecclesiastical arguments are characterized as "reflections" (insinuations, aspersions) upon him. It is at this point in his text that Shaftesbury sets ecclesiastical authority against itself, citing the long history of ecclesiastical debate concerning the canonicity of various scriptural texts. Shaftesbury's opponents are thus characterized as throwing up "reflections" at him, even as the course of the argument turns their reflections back on them (2.354–55, 360–64).

11 See Richetti's admirable account of this "negating" strategy, in *Philosophical Writing*, 75–89. As will become evident, I differ from Richetti in seeing Locke's strategy of playing various rhetorical tropes off against one another as part of an attempt to sustain the irreducible connection between the visual and the verbal rather than as an attempt to dissolve rhetoric and "analogy" by means of "the recurrent force of a literal view of things" (75–76). Cf. also Hagstrum's discussion of Locke's emphasis on the literality of "seeing" as a figure for comprehension (*The Sister Arts*, 137–38).

to say that Locke exploits the full "grammar" of reflection—if we understand "grammar" in Wittgenstein's sense of "the analogies between the forms of expression in different regions of language."[12] Reading Locke's figure of reflection in this way—as the figure for a loosely connected set of activities indispensable to "human understanding"—will in turn enable us to characterize the distinctive trait of this most focused essay as its constantly shifting focus of attention.[13]

THE TRADITIONS OF "REFLECTION"

In a gesture practically inaugural for the tradition of empiricism, Locke begins book 2 of his *Essay* by dividing the sources of all human knowledge into "ideas of sensation" and "ideas of reflection" (2.1.1–2); yet the notorious ambiguity in his use of the word "idea" does not constitute his only rhetorical innovation.[14] In employing "reflection" as a speculative metaphor, Locke is also drawing on a variety of discursive traditions, both scientific and literary.[15] One of our interests here will be with

[12] Ludwig Wittgenstein, *Philosophical Investigations*, trans. G.E.M. Anscombe (Oxford: Blackwell, 1968), part 1, §90. Indeed, Locke's use of "reflection" and its correlative terms (attending, noticing, observing, remembering) has strong affinities with Wittgenstein's favorite examples of grammatically related activities: e.g., "pointing" and "attending to" (§§33–35), "being guided" (§172), "grasping a meaning" and "following a rule" (§§138–202, passim).

[13] For an excellent discussion of the influence that Locke's concept of "attention" had on eighteenth-century poetry and literary criticism, see Ralph Cohen, *The Art of Discrimination*, 97–98.

[14] For a summary of late seventeenth- and early eighteenth-century criticisms of Locke's ambiguous definition of "idea," see John Yolton, *John Locke and the Way of Ideas* (Oxford: Clarendon Press, 1968), 86–98. Ian Hacking summarizes a few modern objections in *Why Does Language Matter to Philosophy?*, 26–27; and Jonathan Bennett gives perhaps the fullest modern critique of Locke's ostensible confusion between "mental items" and "sense impressions" in *Locke, Berkeley, Hume: Central Themes* (Oxford: Clarendon Press, 1971), 6–7, 25–30. For a summary of the literature defending the internal consistency of Locke's "idea," see Kroll, *The Material Word*, 64.

[15] Despite Rorty's masterly account in *Philosophy and the Mirror of Nature* of the mirror-trope's centrality to virtually all of Western philosophy, we must recognize the systematic use of "reflection" (as a speculative metaphor for mental processes) as a distinct subtradition. (I would offer the same caveat as well to Gasché's admirable, if briefer, summary of Western philosophies of "reflection" in *The Tain of the Mirror: Derrida and the Philosophy of Reflection* [Cambridge: Harvard University Press, 1986], 13–54). Even Descartes—who preceded Locke in emphasizing the importance of "clear and distinct" objects of introspection, and whose "Optics" anticipate both Locke and Newton—did not

the way Locke negotiates among the various traditions and registers of the figure of "reflection," exploiting both its shifting moral valence and its ostensible explanatory power.

The late seventeenth century witnessed an efflorescence of literary "Reflections"—a subgenre occupied, in Shaftesbury's words, by "the celebrated wits of the miscellenarian race, the essay writers, casual discoursers, reflection coiners, meditation founders, and others of the irregular kind of writers," its rhetorical method characterized by "different glances and broken views."[16] Frequent extended analogies made it clear that the tradition of "reflection" claimed for itself, *in a thematic way*, many of the putative optical qualities of reflected and refracted light, as they were being analyzed and characterized contemporaneously by Newton and the Royal Society.[17] Newton's friend Robert Boyle, in his own *Occasional Reflections* (1665, 1669), describes the "reflecting" disposition as one characterized particularly by indirectness:

employ the metaphor of reflection frequently or systematically, despite the fortuitous proximity of the scientific and moral-literary registers in his own work. As this is in effect a negative observation, I cannot produce positive evidence for it other than an appeal to a close reading of Descartes's writings. Not only does Descartes fail to use "reflection" schematically as a metaphor for introspection; his *Dioptrics* also distinguishes less categorically than does Newton's *Opticks* between "reflected" and "refracted" light, frequently referring to both phenomena jointly under the general term *détourner* (deflection).

[16] These remarks are made, ironically enough, in Shaftesbury's "Miscellaneous Reflections" (*Characteristics*, 2.215, 295).

[17] A note to philosophers may be in order here. The argument that follows assumes the existence of a late seventeenth-century scientific discourse on optics that gave considerable attention to the phenomenon of reflected light. It further assumes that this discourse was familiar to Locke and his readers, and that Locke expected his readers to recognize an optical analogy implicit in the expression "ideas of reflection." This kind of argument clearly does not observe the strict reasoning of "cause" and "influence" upon which large-scale intellectual histories have traditionally been constructed by historians of science or of philosophy. But this is not an argument about the development of optical theory. The literary and rhetorical influence of discursive traditions on one another works in more nuanced and partial ways, as it is my goal to demonstrate in the present chapter. Though Newton's *Opticks* was not published until well after Locke's *Essay*, Newton had read a paper on optics (and perhaps circulated work) before the Royal Society more than a decade before the publication of the *Essay*. The work of Boyle and others on optics was clearly also available to Locke. For a discussion of Locke's knowledge and use of Newton's optical theory, the reader may consult Marjorie Hope Nicolson's *Newton Demands the Muse: Newton's "Opticks" and the Eighteenth-Century Poets* (Princeton: Princeton University Press, 1946), 6–7. For a more general discussion of the rhetorical prestige and authority of seventeenth-century scientific discourse, see Wimsatt, *Philosophic Words*, 12–13.

Oftentimes, the Subject that is consider'd, appears not to be any thing at all of Kin to the Notion it suggests. And there are many of these Reflections, whose Titles, though they name the occasion of them, do so little assist, ev'n an ingenious Reader, to guess what they contain, that if you tell him what is treated of, he will scarce imagine, how such Thoughts can be made to have a Relation to such remote Subjects;[18]

The indirectness of "reflections" or "meditations" (Boyle uses the terms interchangeably) is not only technically accurate, according to Boyle, but morally instructive as well: "thus sometimes a little Flower may point us to the Sun, and by casting our eyes down to our feet, we may in the water see those Stars that shine in the Firmament or highest visible Heaven."[19] Thus the literary tradition of writing about "reflections" contains within it both a moral trope of self-scrutiny—figured as a specular process—and affinities with the claims and methods of natural philosophy.

Nonetheless, the two discursive registers of "reflection"—the moral-literary and the scientific—remain distinct. The goal of the literary reflection is to avoid the dogmatism of schematic investigation; not only indirectness but a certain informality of discursive usage is essential.[20] In the technical literature of optical theory, precision of definition and consistency of usage are ostensibly paramount.[21] The constant shift between "re-

---

[18] Boyle, *Occasional Reflections upon Several Subjects. With a Discourse about Such Kinds of Thoughts* (Oxford, 1848), 15.

[19] Ibid., 15. In an introductory "advertisement," Boyle hints that the indirectness of "reflections" may be politically strategic as well as morally salutary: "A Reader that is not Unattentive, may easily collect from what he will meet with in some of the ensuing Discourses, That they were written several years ago, under an Usurping Government, that then prevail'd. And this may keep it from appearing strange, That in Papers, which contain some things not likely to be Relish'd by those that were then in Power, the Author should take occasion to speak of himself as of Another person" (xxxv).

[20] Characterizations of this informality, nevertheless, may vary. Boyle characterizes the spontaneity, suppleness, and inventiveness of his meditative vocabulary by distinguishing it from "vulgar and receiv'd forms of Speech," and associating it instead with the "Similitudes" of "Oratory" and "Rhetoric" (*Occasional Reflections* 35–38). Shaftesbury, on the other hand, claims a "familiar style" for his "Miscellaneous Reflections" and distinguishes his discourse explicitly from the formal divisions of declamatory rhetoric—though he assumes the familiar style to include a fairly wide range of rhetorical strategies: "repartees, reflections, fabulous narrations, . . . parables, similes, [and] comparisons" (*Characteristics*, 2.216, 231).

[21] But as W. K. Wimsatt points out, the ostensibly superior clarity and referential powers of the new (and primarily Latinate) seventeenth-century scientific terminology was countered, paradoxically, by an emphasis on the easy translatability of scientific insights into colloquial and vernacular expressions. See Wimsatt, *Philosophic Words*, 12–13.

flection" and "meditation" in Boyle's text (not to mention his occasional confusion of reflection and refraction)[22] and the rigid, even crucial, distinction between "reflection" and "refraction" in Newton's *Opticks* indicate an important tension between scientific and literary employment of the term "reflection."[23] Though Locke employs reflection as a figure for thought—and a morally inflected one at that—he differs from writers in the "Reflections" tradition by distinguishing reflected ideas consistently from the directly encountered ideas of sensation. Locke's claims for "reflection" are not so much stylistic or thematic as empirical and categorical.

One way of describing Locke's project in the *Essay* would be as an attempt to combine the technical specificity of investigations into optics with the moral valences of literary commonplaces about "reflection," the latter exemplified particularly in the trope of moral *self-scrutiny*.[24] Clearly, however, Locke cannot have expected the discourse of the natural sciences to unify or systematize the loose set of rhetorical commonplaces that compared reflected light alternately to revelation and seduction, "depth" alternately to divinely revealed and scholastically obscured knowledge, and "surfaces" alternately to trivial and necessary objects of study.[25] As we have begun to see, Locke's strategy for finessing this set of

---

[22] See, e.g., Boyle's use of the *magnifying glass* as an analogy for *reflection* in *Occasional Reflections*, 28.

[23] Shaftesbury attempts to articulate a distinction between specular figures of reflection and penetration, but only in a passage that ironically displays the easy reversibility of specular figures in general: "Every light reflection might run us up to the dangerous state of meditation. And in reality *profound thinking* is many times the cause of *shallow thoughts*. To prevent this contemplative habit and character . . . we have reason perhaps to be fond of the *diverting manner* in writing and discourse, especially if the subject be of a solemn kind. There is more need, in this case, to . . . bring into the mind, by many *different glances and broken view*, what cannot so easily be introduced by *one steady bent or continued stretch of sight*" (*Characteristics*, 2.295, my emphasis).

[24] See Wimsatt's account of the spectrum, in seventeenth- and eighteenth-century literature, ranging from "the scientific style with moral flourishes to the full-blown theological or moral style embellished by scientific arguments or scientific metaphors" (*Philosophic Words*, 17). Wimsatt returns to this point in a later discussion of the combined theological and scientific rhetoric (and goals) of Johnson's *Dictionary*, itself a cipher for late seventeenth- and eighteenth-century philosophic writing in the widest sense. See Wimsatt, "Johnson's *Dictionary*," in *Day of the Leopards: Essays in Defense of Poems* (New Haven: Yale University Press, 1976), 174–75.

[25] One need only read through the works of Joseph Glanvill to see the constantly shifting valences of surface, depth, and reflection, particularly in an explicitly polemical text. In *A Seasonable Recommendation, and Defence of Reason in the Affairs of Religion against Infidelity, Scepticism, and Fanaticisms of all sorts* (London, 1670), Glanvill refers both to

complications is to replace the optical model with a linguistic model. Language becomes the empirical model for the process of reflection. This is not an explicit shift, and Locke does not wish to forsake the rhetorical advantages and moral overtones of specular figures; his strategy, rather, will be to substitute the concept of *legibility* for that of *self-evidence* while distracting as much as possible from the troublesome material signifiers of language.

LOCKE'S AMBIGUOUS DEPTHS

Locke's metaphor of reflection is closely connected to figures of surface and depth, and the three come into play most frequently in those sections of the *Essay* where Locke attempts to explain the nature of "impressions." In Locke's account of sense impressions, depth is in the first instance a measurement of how intensely and durably ideas have been recorded on the tabula rasa of the mind. The deeper the "impression" or "imprint," the more ineradicable the idea. But reflection is not absent from this operation, and the way in which Locke deems reflection necessary reveals two significantly different notions of "depth." For if the initial intensity of an idea is measured by the depth of the impression it leaves, the durability of that idea—and thus its depth in a very different sense—seems to rely on subsequent reflection.[26] Thus ideas *about* the

---

the "great Deeps of Atheism, and Fanaticism" and to the "deeper things of God" that "shallow" thinkers "must not expect throughly to understand" (2, 13). In "The Vanity of Dogmatizing: or Confidence in Opinions," Glanvill makes constant allusion to the "superficial" inquiries of religious and philosophical dogmatists and yet will offer the telescope's revelations about the "surface" of the moon as a refutation of scholastic philosophy's conceptions of the cosmos. See *The Vanity of Dogmatizing: The Three "Versions"* (Sussex: Harvester Press, 1970), 174. The relative values of penetrating sight and reflected light also shift constantly throughout the "Vanity of Dogmatizing," as in the following passages: "And the best of their [the Aristotelean schoolmen's] *curiosities* are but like paint on Glass, which intercepts and dyes the light the more desirable splendor. I cannot look upon their elaborate trifles, but with a sad reflexion on the degenerate state of our lapsed Intellects; and as deep a resentment, of the mischiefs of this *School-Philosophy*" (168); "His [God's] face cannot be beheld by Creature-Opticks, without the allay of a reflexion; and Nature is one of those mirrours, that represents him to us. . . . The *wonders* of the Almighty are not seen, but by those that go *down into the deep*" (245).

[26] A related, though somewhat different, picture of the relationship of reflection to depth and impressions is given by Boyle in *Occasional Reflections*. Boyle argues that the practice of writing down one's reflections aids in the cultivation of "wit," the particular

mind fail to make deep impressions on children (and, unfortunately, some adults), who are not prone to reflection:

> And hence we see the Reason, why 'tis pretty late, before most Children get *Ideas* of the Operations of their own Minds; and some have not any very clear, or perfect *Ideas* of the greatest part of them all their Lives. Because, though they pass there continually; yet like floating Visions, they make not deep Impressions enough, to leave in the Mind clear distinct lasting *Ideas*, till the Understanding turns inwards upon it self, *reflects* on its own *Operations*, and makes them the Object of its own Contemplation. (2.1.8)

Reflection here seems to be necessary for the preservation of an impression's depth and thus for the preservation of ideas, and indeed a few chapters later Locke acknowledges that "there seems to be a constant decay of all our *Ideas*, even of those which are struck deepest . . . so that if they be not sometimes renewed by repeated Exercise of the Senses, or Reflection . . . the Print wears out" (2.10.5).[27]

Paradoxically, however, in many other passages throughout the *Essay* the absence of something like reflection is held responsible for the disproportionate retention of merely contingent or passing impressions. This is particularly the case in Locke's discussion of the "Association of Ideas." In the chapter from book 2 on that subject, Locke cautions that childhood is "the time most susceptible of lasting Impressions" and, further, that the "strength of the first Impression" may often lead us mistakenly to attribute naturalness or innateness to our sentiments when "early Impressions, or wanton Phancies . . . would have been acknowledged the Original of them *if they had been warily observed*" (2.33.7–8, my emphasis). In short, the absence of self-scrutiny may contribute as much to the intensification as to the "decay" of impressions. Lack of reflection may thus be responsible for either the preservation or the disappearance of depth.

This paradox may help us account for Locke's frequent shift from "impression" to "imprint" as his figure for the way in which the mind's surface is altered in the production of ideas. And such a shift raises questions concerning Locke's concept of legibility, and the degree to

---

virtue of which is the noting of similitudes and comparisons: "Lucky Comparisons being indeed those parts of Wit, that as well make the strongest Impressions upon the Mind, as they leave the deepest on the Memory" (37–38).

27 See also 2.10.3,4.

which the noticing of one's own ideas requires a kind of attention that can
be compared to reading. Ultimately, we shall have to consider whether the
phenomenon of "reflection," so central to Locke's account of human
understanding, is a process that looks beyond the material signifiers of
language (its printed characters and vocalized sounds) or focuses our
attention on those signifiers in the most mechanical way. First, however,
we must look at the way in which Locke employs the figure of depth.

If reflection exerts contrary effects on depth, it is important to know
just what depth of mind (or depth of impression) consists in for Locke.
Yet Locke's figure of depth is even more ambiguous than his figure of
reflection. This ambiguity is foregrounded in the very first chapter of the
Essay, where Locke emphasizes the modest goals of his enquiry: his
intention is to investigate the inherent limits to our acquisition of knowledge, dictated by the nature of our own cognitive apparatus and the
mechanics, structure, and process of human experience. In a crucial analogy, which will reappear later in the *Essay*, Locke compares our cognitive
apparatus to a sailor's "line." In his elaboration of this trope, however,
the "depth" of the ocean becomes a figure for both the knowable and the
*un*knowable: " 'Tis of great use to the Sailor to know the length of his
Line, though he cannot with it fathom all the depths of the Ocean. 'Tis
well he knows, that it is long enough to reach the bottom, at such Places,
as are necessary to direct his Voyage, and caution him against running
upon Shoals, that may ruin him" (1.1.6). Though initially the expression
"depths of the Ocean" suggests something like unfathomability or bot-
tomlessness, the passage also refers to depths that can be gauged: there
are practical instances in which the sailor's line does indeed "reach the
bottom" and thus becomes a mark or figure for depth—which in turn
stands for stable knowledge. However, as Locke begins to play with the
analogy in the following paragraph, the ocean's depth becomes exclusively a figure for the unknowable and, more disturbingly, for skepticism
itself. Until "a Survey of our own Understandings" can be undertaken,
argues Locke,

> I suspected we began at the wrong end, and in vain sought for Satisfaction in
> a quiet and secure Possession of Truths, that most concern'd us, whilst we let
> loose our Thoughts into the vast Ocean of *Being*, as if all that boundless
> Extent, were the natural, and undoubted Possession of our Understandings,
> wherein there was nothing exempt from its Decisions, or that escaped its
> Comprehension. Thus Men, extending their Enquiries beyond their Capaci-

ties, and letting their Thoughts wander into those depths, where they can find no sure Footing; 'tis no Wonder, that they raise Questions, and multiply Disputes, which never coming to any clear Resolution, are proper only to continue and increase their Doubts, and to confirm them at last in perfect Scepticism. (1.1.7)

There are actually three separate figures of depth operating in Locke's extended analogy here. In its modest, domesticated aspect, depth is an entirely adequate figure for the limits of our understanding. We *can* know precisely to what depths our knowledge may reach; the sailor may "know the length of his Line." However depth is also a figure for inaccessible or inadequate knowledge (knowledge of the "vast Ocean of *Being*"), and this second sense of the figure both overlaps and conflicts with the first one. Depth becomes a figure for that which exceeds specific depths. Here something actually corresponds to the knowledge we seek—particular attributes of God, for instance—but our minds can comprehend such things only indirectly, perhaps only metaphorically. "Depth" stands for a phenomenon of an entirely different order from itself, and perhaps for something that does not even have a proper name of its own. Finally, as a figure for the unknowable or the ineffable, depth makes itself further available as a figure for *false* knowledge and for the delusions of knowledge that lead to skepticism ("depths, where they can find no sure Footing"). In this case the figure is a synecdoche; scholastic philosophers debate quite literally about spatial categories (e.g., "extension" and "substantiality"), and the spatial figure of depth is thus a local instance of the very kind of category that leads such philosophers astray.

We encounter a more powerful, if more complicated, version of this particular trope when we turn to book 2, chapter 17: "Of Infinity." Infinity, argues Locke, is something of which we can have no clear and positive idea.[28] Furthermore, though we are capable of comprehending relative or "comparative" ideas, infinity is no more a comparative than a positive idea; it is, finally, only a "negative" concept. In the extended analogy that Locke uses to illustrate this set of relationships, we can again

---

[28] Cf. Thomas Hobbes, *Leviathan*: "No man can have in his mind an image of infinite magnitude. . . . When we say any thing is infinite, we signify only, that we are not able to conceive the ends, and bounds of the things named; having no conception of the thing, but of our own inability" (*Leviathan: Or the Matter, Forme, and Power of a Commonwealth Ecclesiastical and Civil*, ed. Michael Oakeshott [Oxford: Basil Blackwell, 1946], chap. 3, 17). Hobbes's explanation, however, is not articulated in metaphoric terms (e.g. "depth"), as is Locke's.

see the figure of depth take on three different senses: it is at once a figure for positive, relative, and negative ideas:

> When we would think of infinite Space or Duration, we at first step usually make some very large *Idea*, as, perhaps, of Millions of Ages, or Miles, which possibly we double and multiply several times. All that we thus amass together in our Thoughts, is positive, and the assemblage of a great number of positive *Ideas* of Space or Duration. But what still remains beyond this, we have no more a positive distinct notion of, than a Mariner has of the depth of the Sea, where having let down a large portion of his Sounding-line, he reaches no bottom: Whereby he knows the depth to be so many fathoms, and more; but how much that more is, he hath no distinct notion at all: And could he always supply new Line, and find the Plummet always sink, without ever stopping, he would be something in the posture of the Mind reaching after a compleat and positive *Idea* of Infinity. In which case, let this Line be 10, or 10000 fathoms long, it equally discovers what is beyond it; and gives only this confused, and comparative *Idea*, That this is not all, but one may yet go farther. (2.17.15)

Depth is first introduced here as a figure for positive ideas ("he knows the depth to be so many fathoms . . .") in comparison with which we judge certain ideas to be greater ("so many fathoms *and more*"). But then depth is also thereby a figure for the comparative idea. And the sailor's line represents both depths—the first literally, the second only by suggestion.

Curiously, Locke seems to suggest that since the line is merely an arbitrary figure for the "comparative" idea, *any* length of line will do; any length of line "equally discovers what is beyond it." This is true insofar as the purpose of the figure is to represent a *comparative* idea. However the larger purpose of the analogy as a whole was to get not at the nature of comparative but at that of negative ideas. And here it is not clear that the sailor's line *does* offer itself as a figure. As an attempt to explain our ideas of infinity, the focus of the extended analogy is not really on the figures of "line," "depth," or "ocean" but on the sailor's "posture of Mind" given the entirely hypothetical scenario of a bottomless ocean *and* an infinitely long plumb line: "could he always supply new Line, and find the Plummet always sink, without ever stopping, he would be something in the posture of the Mind reaching after a compleat and positive *Idea* of Infinity." And yet even this "posture of mind" is a figure for infinite depth only in a qualified sense, since it is expressive precisely of the *failure* to achieve any such clear and positive idea.

Thus in a sense the idea of an infinite depth *fails* of figuration in Locke's analogy. The analogy begins by offering us clearly designated figures (the line, the ocean, the "bottom") but then shifts to suggest instead the *process* involved in trying to grasp these figures—a process that eludes figurative representation, or at least requires a shift to an incommensurate scheme of figures (the mind's "posture").[29] But of course this is precisely the point. The strategy of the analogy is to represent infinity as a negative idea, expressible only by grammatical negations ("we have no more a positive distinct notion of"; "reaches no bottom"; "no distinct notion") and not in the positive manner of figuration. Locke's whole point is that a "negative" idea such as infinite depth is not simply an *extension* of a positive idea (as the comparative idea is) and thus cannot be understood by using the positive idea as a figure.

We should be cautious of even suggesting that a shift from the figure of depth to the figure of the mind's "posture" brings us closer to a representation of the infinite. The portion of the extended analogy that introduces the figure of the "posture" is not only entirely hypothetical but in fact tautological: *if* the sailor could "*always* supply new Line" and *if* the plummet could "*always* sink, without *ever* stopping," then he would experience a "reaching after a compleat and positive *Idea* of Infinity." But in this way of putting it the idea of infinity is presupposed by the adverbs, and there is little work left for the rhetorical figures to perform. The conceptual work to be performed by the figures of "posture" or "depth" has already been done by the abstractions of "always" and "ever." The point is not that Locke argues circularly without realizing it but that he does not think of rhetorical figuration as something that can sensuously represent the idea of infinity (even though he makes his argument by way of another rhetorical device, analogy).[30] The burden of the argument falls quite purposely on grammatical devices (e.g., adverbs and negative con-

[29] Ironically, and perhaps not coincidentally, "posture" is itself a figure for rhetorical figuration in Lamy's *Art of Speaking* (2.3.3 [99]). Lamy compares rhetorical "figures" to the various "postures" of the body, and argues that figuration is a form of spiritual "defense"—analogous to physical self-defense—rather than a mere "ornament of discourse."

[30] Cf. Kant's account of the paradoxical way in which a sublime sense of infinite magnitude or power may be excited by, though not represented in, a sensuous intuition: "For the sublime, in the strict sense of the word, cannot be contained in any sensuous form, but rather concerns ideas of reason, which, although no adequate presentation of them is possible, may be excited and called into the mind by that very inadequacy itself which does admit of sensuous presentation." See Immanuel Kant, *Critique of Aesthetic Judgement*, in *The Critique of Judgement*, trans. James Creed Meredith (Oxford: Clarendon Press, 1952), 92 (§23).

structions) rather than on rhetorical figures (e.g., "depth" or "posture").[31]

The conflicting uses of Locke's analogy should alert us to the fact that the categorization of cognitive processes in terms of linguistic processes always requires a further specification of the various *kinds* of linguistic processes—specifically the various kinds of figuration—at stake in the comparison. If it is true that we confront experience as we confront a language, that still does not limit or determine the possible range of relationships between signifiers and signifieds. For example, Locke compares our various "ideas" of infinity to a number of different signified-signifier relationships—some of which he explicitly designates as "figurative," others of which he *contrasts* with figuration, though the latter are still highly self-conscious "applications" of signs for all that.

If we regard the "sailor's line" analogy anachronistically, not only its figures but its rhetorical and philosophic issues seem rather familiar. The estimation of natural magnitude, the calculation of depths, and the failure of comprehension are all tropes of eighteenth-century literature on the sublime. Yet there is no aesthetics of the sublime here; the sensation of failure (constitutive of the "confused" comparative idea or the attempt to comprehend the negative as a positive idea) does not present itself as a dramatic solution to the tension between the knowable and the unknowable. We might say that the difference between Locke on the one hand and Burke or Kant on the other is that Locke refuses to *thematize* failure. Whereas for Burke and Kant the failure of comprehension or the inadequacy of sensuous intuition to rational idea produces something distinct and interesting, for Locke such a failure is undramatic and simply prompts a return to more limited investigations.

---

[31] Here I would disagree slightly with Richetti's characterization of the textual dynamic that leads to, and then away from, analogy in the *Essay*. Richetti identifies quite incisively the "recurring thematics of loss" in the *Essay*, "provoked by the difficulty of imagining the understanding," but he characterizes the end result of this dynamic as a return to the literal: "Locke approaches the moment when mental experience actually takes place and then finds that this moment escapes literal description and requires analogy. Analogy is proposed and indeed employed, but then it is frequently dissolved or, better, dismantled by the recurrent force of a literal view of things" (*Philosophical Writing*, 75–76). Locke does indeed approach, and then regress from, analogy in his attempt to represent certain experiences. But what his explanations break down into once the analogy can no longer be sustained is not quite "a literal view of things" but rather a mixture of grammatical devices, contradictory figures, and literal expressions. We might describe the result as a more humble, heterogeneous, or prosaic account of experience than his analogies set out to provide, but I do not believe it is technically accurate to describe the result as a return to the literal.

Though Locke does evoke the rather heady prospect of "the Mind los[ing] it self" in an attempt to arrive at a clear and distinct idea of infinity (2.17.9), it seems clear that such a consequence neither intrigues nor significantly worries him. The mind may lose itself as easily on the near as on the far side of comprehension—as easily in the "confused heap" of unindividuated sense impressions prior to their organization by the understanding as in the "confused incomprehensible remainder of endless addible Numbers" that reach beyond the understanding (2.17.9). Confusion is not some exotic extreme beyond the understanding but simply the background against which understanding gains its significance.

It is precisely because there is no thematization of failure in Locke's *Essay*—no attempt to make the limits of knowledge or the failure of comprehension interesting or productive in their own right—that there can be no consistent or wide-ranging thematization of depth.[32] Locke uses the figure of depth literally, metonymically, synecdochically, metaphorically, allegorically, and ironically, and these various uses correspond, in different ways and at different times, to positive, relative, and negative ideas. But the moral and rhetorical thrust of Locke's *Essay* is neither to condemn nor to exalt certain kinds of enquiry but to assume the aspect of a humble and commonsense self-scrutiny. Locke's purpose in introducing, and then complicating, the figure of depth is not simply to ironize the rhetoric and claims of the "school-men"[33] but to prompt "reflection."

VISIBLE, MATERIAL, AND LEGIBLE: LOCKE'S GRAMMAR OF REFLECTIONS

The metaphor of reflection is perhaps the dominant figure in Locke's *Essay*. It is so pervasive that Locke cannot help using it even in explaining

[32] Richetti points out quite rightly that there is a "staged failure of the understanding" in such passages, and further that "this marking of limits is a recurring theme in the *Essay*" (*Philosophical Writing*, 76, 78). However the thematization of reflexiveness—in those scenes where the inquiring mind notes, and turns humbly away from, the limits of comprehension—is quite different from the thematization of failure and depth, the latter illustrated in the tradition of the sublime, where the sensation of failure itself is the subject of examination and the source of aesthetic value.

[33] Locke uses the figure of depth to characterize scholastic philosophy's fascination with "essences." In his critique of essences in book 3, Locke refers pejoratively to "the Language of the Schools" and to "those learned quick-sighted Men, who look so deep into [Things], and talk so confidently of something more hidden and essential" (3.6.24).

the appropriateness of optical metaphors: "The Perception of the Mind, being most aptly explained by Words relating to the Sight, we shall best understand what is meant by *Clear*, and *Obscure* in our *Ideas*, by reflecting on what we call *Clear* and *Obscure* in the Objects of Sight" (2.29.2). Locke's specular figure for self-scrutiny, it seems, lies back of all other specular figures. "Clear" and "obscure" are merely helpful analogies; "reflection" is an essential one. But reflection does not mean the same thing at all times in the *Essay*. As a specular figure it remains closely tied to one of its discursively specific meanings—as an optical process—and stands for a process of self-observation whose object is a visual image. As a more generalized figure for mental attentiveness, however, its sense begins to wander from the strict scheme of optical self-observation and to take on a different set of objects: "impressions" and, in particular, *language*.

As we observed earlier, the figure of reflection seems to answer a call made in the very first paragraph of the *Essay*, where Locke compares the understanding to an eye that must be brought to see itself: "the Eye, whilst it makes us see, and perceive all other Things, takes no notice of it self: And it requires Art and Pains to set it at a distance, and make it its own Object." Though Locke does not use the term "reflection" in this passage, its connection to the "painful" process of self-scrutiny is made explicit in the following chapter: "Those who will take the Pains to *reflect* with a little attention on the Operations of the Understanding, will find . . ." (1.2.11, my emphasis).

Curiously, though, when Locke finally comes to define "reflection" at the beginning of book 2, neither the metaphor of the eye nor the emphasis on "pain" are particularly central to the account. Locke seems more concerned to show how reflection is an internal, mental process analogous to—and thus mirroring—the external phenomenon of "sensation":

> The other Fountain, from which Experience furnisheth the Understanding with *Ideas*, is the *Perception of the Operations of our own Minds* within us, as it is employ'd about the *Ideas* it has got; which Operations, when the Soul comes to reflect on, and consider, do furnish the Understanding with another set of *Ideas*, which could not be had from things without: and such are, *Perception, Thinking, Doubting, Believing, Reasoning, Knowing, Willing,* and all the different actings of our own Minds; which we being conscious of, and observing in our selves, do from these receive into our Understandings, as distinct *Ideas*, as we do from Bodies affecting our Senses. This Source of *Ideas*, every Man has wholly in himself: And though it be not Sense, as

having nothing to do with external Objects; yet it is very like it, and might properly enough be call'd internal Sense. But as I call the other *Sensation*, so I call this REFLECTION, the *Ideas* it affords being such only, as the Mind gets by reflecting on its own Operations within it self. By REFLECTION then, . . . I would be understood to mean, that notice which the Mind takes of its own Operations. (2.1.4)

For Locke, "reflection" is not properly a "sense," since it has "nothing to do with external objects," yet "it is very like it, and might properly enough be call'd internal Sense." "Reflection" thus has a double relation to "sensation": one of similitude ("it is very like it") and one of antithesis or complementarity (internal vs. external).

Locke claims that he chooses the term "reflection" because it conveys the fact that the mind takes "notice" of itself (thus resembling the optical process by which an eye would see itself); but we may also suspect that such an operation deserves the name of "reflection" precisely because as an "internal sense" it mirrors or *reflects* our "external" sense. (Here is where Locke differs at least rhetorically from Hobbes, for whom the relation of ideas to impressions is characterized in terms of attenuation rather than of reflection.)[34] One interpretation of reflection, then, represents the eye of the mind as active and autonomous (here the figure means something like an eye seeking its own image); the other interpretation represents the mind's eye as passive (here the figure is that of a mirror that simply mimics an image). This tension between activity and passivity underlies the entire passage and ultimately haunts Locke's use of the term *reflection* throughout the *Essay*.[35] Sometimes ideas of sensation are char-

[34] Hobbes does not use the metaphor of reflection at all to describe the relationship of "imagination" to "sense." In his famous definition, "IMAGINATION therefore is nothing but decaying sense" (*Leviathan*, 2.9). This is the basis of Hume's subsequent contention that "ideas" differ only in "degree of force and vivacity" from their correspondent impressions (*Treatise*, 1.1.1).

[35] See Rorty's discussion of the tension between activity and passivity implicit in Locke's "eye of the mind" metaphor, a metaphor that, according to Rorty, Locke must not allow to be "unpacked" (*Philosophy and the Mirror of Nature*, 143–46). Hagstrum makes essentially the same point, if conversely, when he argues that Locke must stress the literality of "seeing" and prevent it from becoming too entirely a speculative metaphor (*The Sister Arts*, 137–38). Like Rorty, Ernest Tuveson emphasizes the combination of active and passive qualities implicitly ascribed to the mind in Locke's metaphor of reflection. Tuveson further argues that it is the complex and subtle combination of these two qualities in Locke's account that distinguishes Locke's associational psychology from the ostensibly more mechanistic versions of associationism to be found in Hobbes, Hartley, and Hume (*The Imagination as a Means of Grace*, 18–19, 39–40). Cf. Abrams, who appears to disregard the active

acterized by Locke as being received passively by the mind in contrast to the active production of ideas of reflection. At other times the mind is said to be passive in its reception of both types of ideas. And at yet other times the existence of sensation itself seems dependent on the mind's exercising at least the minimal reflective activity of "noticing." And these shifts in the relation of sensation to reflection are tied throughout to Locke's alternating characterization of "reflection" as a mirroring activity (producing ghostly or shadowy images) and as the activity of paying attention (particularly as exemplified in the act of *reading*).

Let us begin by noting the list of mental activities equated with reflection in the passage just quoted: respectively, to "consider," to be "conscious of," to "observe," and to "notice." We might call these terms the "grammar" of reflection. In its most minimal function (mere noticing, or consciousness), reflection is quite passive; but to "observe" is perhaps more active, and to "consider" (with its implications of estimation and comparison) is certainly a higher-order intellectual activity, one that might well require "pains." This range of possible descriptions for the activity of reflection appears over and over again throughout the *Essay*, and it is clear that Locke considers only the more strenuous and active forms of reflection to be the true embodiment of that faculty. Only a few paragraphs later Locke characterizes the difference between ideas of sensation and reflection as a difference between ideas that "solicit" our notice and those to which we must apply ourselves "with attention":

> *Light*, and *Colours*, are busie at hand every where, when the Eye is but open; *Sounds*, and some *tangible Qualities* fail not to solicite their proper Senses, and force an entrance to the Mind; . . .
> . . . though he that contemplates the Operations of his Mind, cannot but have plain and clear *Ideas* of them; yet unless he turn his Thoughts that way, and considers them *attentively*, he will no more have clear and distinct *Ideas* of all the *Operations of his Mind*, and all that may be observed therein, than he will have all the particular *Ideas* of any Landscape, or of the Parts and Motions of a Clock, who will not turn his Eyes to it, and with attention

---

qualities implicit in Locke's figure of reflection when he identifies Locke rather unproblematically with the Aristotelean tradition of the *tabula rasa* and schematically contrasts metaphors of illumination and emanation with Locke's metaphor of reflection. In Abrams's view, the concept of the reflective mind as an active participant in perception is elicited from Locke's text only retrospectively, by Edward Young and the romantic poets (*The Mirror and the Lamp*, 57, 63).

heed all the Parts of it. The Picture, or Clock may be so placed, that they may come in his way every day; but yet he will have but a confused *Idea* of all the Parts they are made up of, till he *applies himself with attention*, to consider them each in particular.

. . . Children, when they come first into it, are surrounded with a world of new things, which, by a constant solicitation of their senses, draw the mind constantly to them. (2.1.6–8)

Ideas of sensation *solicit* our "notice"; ideas of reflection *require* our "attention." And yet by drawing an analogy between the attention required to notice the operation of our own minds and that required to see a landscape clearly, Locke begins already to blur the distinction between sensation and reflection. For if it is required not only that we "turn our eyes" to a landscape but that we "heed" it and "apply" ourselves to our "idea" of it with "attention," then the "solicitation" of our senses by the external world may not be complete or successful without some degree of reflection entering into the process. If "attention" is part of the grammar of "reflection," it is part of the grammar of "sensations" as well.

There is in fact a third category of ideas lurking in the apparently binary scheme of sensation/reflection. For when we fail to *notice* the operations of our own minds, the ideas of such operations are not entirely nonexistent. Rather, such ideas exist as phantasms, which only reflection can convert into "deep Impressions." In a passage from these paragraphs, which we have discussed earlier, Locke writes:

And hence we see the Reason, why 'tis pretty late, before most Children get *Ideas* of the Operations of their own Minds; and some have not any very clear, or perfect *Ideas* of the greatest part of them all their Lives. Because, though they pass there continually; yet like floating Visions, they make not deep Impressions enough, to leave in the Mind clear distinct lasting *Ideas*, till the Understanding turns inwards upon it self, *reflects* on its own *Operations*, and makes them the Object of its own Contemplation. (2.1.8)

The existence of prereflective "floating Visions" disrupts the neat binary distinction between ideas of sensation and ideas of reflection, and at the same time casts doubt upon the propriety of "reflection" as a figure for that activity that produces "deep impressions." For as we shall see, the specular—and for Locke, threatening—characterization of ideas as phantasmic or shadowy images is related to the equally specular conception of the mind as a reflecting mirror.

Locke concludes this first chapter of book 2 ("Of Ideas in general, and their Original") by characterizing the "Understanding" as "meerly *passive*" in its reception of *both* ideas of sensation and ideas of reflection. Reflection, it turns out, does not entirely depend on our intentional scrutiny, since "the Operations of our minds, *will not let us be without*, at least some obscure Notions of them" (my emphasis). The chapter's presiding distinction between sensory ideas that "solicit" or "force" their way into the mind and reflective ideas that require our voluntary attention disappears in the concluding paragraph, and the mind is characterized as a mirror in relation to both sensation and reflection: "These *simple Ideas* [i.e., of sensation and reflection], when offered to the mind, *the Understanding can* no more refuse to have, nor alter, when they are imprinted, nor blot them out, and make new ones in it self, than a mirror can refuse, alter, or obliterate the Images or *Ideas*, which, the Objects set before it, do therein produce" (2.1.25). Here the mind's ideas are pictured first as imprints but then, in a shift from material to specular figures, are immediately compared to mirror images.[36] The mind understood as a mirror generalizes the figure of reflection—which now characterizes ideas both of sensation and of reflection—and yet at the same time trivializes it in a threatening way.[37] The salient features of the mirror image—by Locke's own account—are its transience and derivativeness. Only pages earlier Locke had employed the picture of the mind as a mirror in order to ridicule the notion of innate ideas. Locke's critique of "innate ideas" assumes that the mind is incapable of possessing ideas without at the same time being aware of those ideas (1.2.5,25; 1.3.1; 2.1.9–20), and in responding to the argument that our "soul" might be capable of thinking during our sleep without our being conscious of the fact, Locke asserts that such a hypothesis implies a vulgar, mechanical conception of the soul, one that he compares to a mirror:

> *To think often, and never to retain it so much as one moment, is a very useless sort of thinking*: and the Soul in such a state of thinking, does very

[36] Cf. Ernst Cassirer, *The Platonic Renaissance in England*, trans. J. P. Pettegrove (Austin: University of Texas Press, 1953). Cassirer considers this picture of the reflective mind as a passive recipient of sensation to be particularly—if not uniquely—characteristic of Locke's model of mind (63). See also Abrams, cited in n. 35.

[37] See Hagstrum's discussion of the tension between two contrasting meanings implicit in the conventional metaphor of *art as a mirror*. The tension—between visual particularity and abstract ideal—is captured, according to Hagstrum, in the two-part definition of *mirror* in Johnson's *Dictionary* (*The Sister Arts*, 135–36).

little, if at all, excel that of a Looking-glass, which constantly receives variety of Images, or *Ideas*, but retains none; they disappear and vanish, and there remain no footsteps of them; the Looking-glass is never the better for such *Ideas*, nor the Soul for such Thoughts. (2.1.14)

The soul as mirror is a soul without activity or will; this cannot be an accurate characterization of the human mind, according to Locke.[38]

The characterization of ideas as immaterial images is almost always in Locke tied to a characterization of them as fleeting, impermanent, not fully perceived. In explaining why God has "join[ed]" to our "several Thoughts, and several Sensations, a *perception* of *Delight*," Locke describes how ideas would float randomly through our minds if there were no pleasure associated with them:

If this [delight] were wholly separated from all our outward Sensations, and inward Thoughts, we should have no reason to preferr one Thought or Action, to another; Negligence, to Attention; or Motion, to Rest. And so we should neither stir our Bodies, nor employ our Minds; but let our Thoughts (if I may so call it) run a drift, without any direction or design; and suffer the *Ideas* of our Minds, like unregarded shadows, to make their appearances there, as it happen'd, without attending to them. (2.7.3)

---

[38] For a related though more morally inflected critique of the mind-as-mirror trope, we might look to Francis Bacon, *The Advancement of Learning and New Atlantis* (London: Oxford University Press, 1969). Bacon writes: "For the mind of man is far from the nature of a clear and equal glass, wherein the beams of things should reflect according to their true incidence; nay, it is rather like an enchanted glass, full of superstition and imposture, if it be not delivered and reduced" (153). Bacon's critique is considerably different from Locke's, however, because the Renaissance tropes of microcosm/macrocosm and of the human mind as an image of God's creation still function as ideals for Bacon, obscured and distorted as they are by ignorance and superstition. Early in *The Advancement of Learning* Bacon paraphrases Solomon, with approval: "God hath framed the mind of man as a mirror or glass, capable of the image of the universal world, and joyful to receive the impression thereof, as the eye joyeth to receive light" (8). It is not knowledge itself, or the mirroring capacity of the mind, that is responsible for man's spiritual degradation, but the lack of a corresponding spiritual humility: "There is no danger at all in the proportion or quantity of knowledge, how large soever, lest it should make it swell or out-compass itself; no, but it is merely the quality of knowledge, which, be it in quantity more or less, if it be taken without the true corrective thereof, hath in it some nature of venom or malignity, and some effects of that venom, which is ventosity or swelling" (8–9).

For a somewhat different interpretation, see chaps. 2 and 3 of Foucault's *The Order of Things*. Foucault sees Bacon as an early critic of the Renaissance episteme's reliance on "similitude"—the latter a principle that relies for its significance upon a universe understood as divided into microcosm and macrocosm.

Locke is generally far more comfortable with a characterization of ideas (whether of sensation or reflection) as impressions or imprints rather than as images. Though admittedly even impressions and imprints may "wear out" or be "effaced by time" (2.10.5) Locke still tends to shift from material to specular figures whenever he wants to emphasize the transience and fragility of ideas, as we can see in each of the following two passages:

> And in some, where they [ideas] are set on with care and repeated impressions, either through the temper of the Body, or some other default, the Memory is very weak: In all these cases, *Ideas* in the Mind quickly fade, and often vanish quite out of the Understanding, leaving no more footsteps or remaining Characters of themselves, than Shadows do flying over Fields of Corn; and the Mind is as void of them, as if they never had been there. (2.10.4)

> Thus the *Ideas*, as well as Children, of our Youth, often die before us: And our Minds represent to us those Tombs, to which we are approaching; where though the Brass and Marble remain, yet the Inscriptions are effaced by time, and the Imagery moulders away. *The Pictures drawn in our Minds, are laid in fading Colours*; and if not sometimes refreshed, vanish and disappear. (2.10.5)

Each of these passages derives a considerable amount of its rhetorical strength from its material figures (footsteps, tombs, etc.), yet in each instance Locke chooses to shift to a specular image (shadow, fading colours) in order to emphasize the fragility of the mind's ideas.

The quality of instability associated with the *eidos*, however, along with Locke's general preference for material over specular figures, conflicts with his pervasive and generalized use of "reflection." Throughout the *Essay* "reflection" is a figure for everything positive and constructive about the mind: not only for those ideas we have *concerning* the operations of our mind but indeed for almost any active, critical, operation of the mind itself, including memory (2.27.10), deduction (1.2.21; 1.4.9; 4.7.11), and analogy (4.3.27). Once again we run up against a paradox in rhetorical usage. Although reflection is essential in order for our ideas to become deeply impressed (2.1.8), those ideas that make the least (or least durable) impression are precisely those that Locke characterizes as mere reflected images.

Although the figure of depth is implicated in this paradox it is nonetheless the figure that allows Locke to sustain his two contrasting attitudes toward "reflection." For it is precisely the description of ideas and impressions as having the quality of depth that allows Locke to treat an abstract temporal distinction between kinds of ideas (fleeting vs. lasting) as if it were a sensory difference (specular vs. material). Thus Locke can distinguish between deeply impressed ideas and mere shadows or images. The rhetorical distinction simply ignores the fact that under Locke's generalized understanding of "reflection," *all* ideas are specular objects. Locke recognizes, implicitly, that to speak of lasting ideas as "deeply impressed" is only metaphorical. After having used another material figure, in describing the memory as a "Store-house," Locke confesses:

> But our Ideas being nothing, but actual Perceptions in the Mind, which cease to be any thing, when there is no perception of them, this laying up of our Ideas in the Repository of the Memory, signifies no more but this, that the Mind has a Power, in many cases, to revive Perceptions. . . . And in this Sense it is, that our Ideas are said to be in our Memories, when indeed, they are actually no where, but only there is an ability in the Mind, when it will, to revive them again; and *as it were* paint them anew on it self, though some with more, some with less difficulty; some more lively, and others more obscurely. (2.10.2, emphasis altered)

The ideas recorded in our memories "are actually no where," and thus are not etched—deeply or otherwise—on brain tissue or nerve endings. Though he clearly inclines toward something like a physiological account of mental processes, Locke nonetheless emphasizes the figurativeness of the expression "*in* the memory" and claims that memories "are actually no where." He even declines to state definitively whether or not the retention of ideas is in any way a physiological process: "How much the Constitution of our Bodies, and the make of our animal Spirits, are concerned in this; and whether the Temper of the Brain make this difference, that in some it retains the Characters drawn on it like Marble, in others like Free-stone, and in others little better than Sand, I shall not here enquire, though it may seem probable, that the Constitution of the Body does sometimes influence the Memory; since we oftentimes find a Disease quite strip the Mind of all its *Ideas*" (2.10.5). But then by this logic, ideas are no more images than they are deep impressions; both descriptions are figurative. (The mind *as it were* paints images on it self, says Locke). Ideas are no more properly specular than they are material, and the distinction between the two remains a thoroughly rhetorical strategy throughout the *Essay*. This explanation may help us negotiate the paradox involved in Locke's antithetical characterizations of "reflection" as a process on the one hand connected to "deep impressions" but on the other hand hostile to specular images. But it leaves unexplained the question of how "reflection" in its most restricted sense (as the passive observation of our mind's operations) is related to reflection in its most general sense (as any attentive operation of the mind).

In order to make sense of this problem we need to consider some of the other ways in which Locke understands the process of "reflection," apart from its role as that faculty which observes and reproduces ideas of sensation. We may recall that the very existence of mere specular, shadowy, phantasmic, or otherwise ephemeral ideas was first introduced in the passage from book 2, chapter 1, where Locke hinted at a category of ideas (those concerning our own minds) that fell somewhere between being noticed and going unnoticed ("they pass there continually . . . like floating Visions" [§8]). This category, however, turned out to share its quality of transience with *all* ideas, there being "a constant decay of all our *Ideas*, even of those which are struck deepest, and in Minds the most retentive" (2.10.5). Thus an initial discrepancy in Locke's account of "reflection" (disrupting the binary alternatives of being noticed and not being noticed) led us to consider recurrent tensions of a similar kind contained in the figure of reflection itself when treated as an optical or specular process. We may now turn to yet another tension implicit in the figure of reflection, one that leads us to consider its material and linguistic aspect rather than its phantasmically specular one.

Leaving aside the ambiguity introduced by the fact that in Locke's account not only ideas of reflection but those of sensation as well seem to require at least some "attention," we may conclude that some sort of attention or "noticing" is a minimal criterion for the production of an idea of reflection. Though we must be cautious about mistaking necessary for sufficient causes, it is important to note that Locke's privileged example of something that cannot exist in the mind without being noticed is *language*.[39] This point is made indirectly, but repeatedly, in book 1 of the *Essay* where Locke is concerned to refute the notion of "innate ideas."

[39] Cf. Hobbes's introduction to *Leviathan*, in which he counsels the reader to "read thyself" (6). Despite his emphasis on this phrase in the introduction, however, Hobbes does not generalize or dramatize the metaphor of self-reading throughout *Leviathan*, any more than he does the metaphor of self-seeing.

There could be no innate ideas in our minds, so the argument goes, because if there were we could not help but notice them immediately. And the putative incoherence of not recognizing ideas within one's own mind is figured consistently as the incoherence of the concept of an *illegible language*:

> It seem[s] to me near a Contradiction, to say, that there are Truths imprinted on the Soul, which it perceives or understands not; imprinting, if it signify any thing, being nothing else, but the making certain Truths to be perceived. For to imprint any thing on the Mind without the Mind's perceiving it, seems to me hardly intelligible. (1.2.5)

> Can it be imagin'd, with any appearance of Reason, That they perceive the Impressions from things without; and be at the same time ignorant of those Characters, which Nature it self has taken care to stamp within? Can they receive and assent to adventitious Notions, and be ignorant of those, which are supposed woven into the very Principles of their Being, and imprinted there in indelible Characters? (1.2.25)

> . . . moral Principles require Reasoning and Discourse, and some Exercise of the Mind, to discover the certainty of their Truth. They lie not open as natural Characters ingraven on the Mind; which if any such were, they must needs be visible by themselves, and by their own light be certain and known to every Body. (1.3.1)

Printed characters are a figure for that which the mind cannot help but perceive, for that which is "indelible," "open," "visible by [itself]" and most importantly "by [its] own light . . . certain and known."[40] Locke denies that we are born with such characters imprinted on our minds, but he sets down clearly and consistently the conditions that would define mental "imprints." Thus, though "impulses" and "impressions" may fail to pass from our "organs" to our "mind," if they do "reach . . . the

[40] Locke does on occasion resort to other metaphors or analogies to illustrate the concept of an idea that *could not fail of recognition*, as when he suggests that if there were innate ideas we would have to know how *many* we possessed, as clearly as we know "the number of our Fingers" (1.3.14). In general, however, throughout book 1 of the *Essay*, it is language rather than the body that stands as his figure for that which cannot fail to be recognized and comprehended.

Ironically, the idea of something that could not go *unrecognized* in our minds is precisely the basis for Berkeley's later rejection of Locke's argument concerning the role of "judgment" in optical impressions (*Essay*, 2.9.8). See Berkeley, *Essay towards a New Theory of Vision*, in *Works*, vol. 1 (§§88–97).

observation of the Mind" they attain the status of "imprints" for the very fact of being noticed:

> How often may a Man observe in himself, that whilst his Mind is intently employ'd in the contemplation of some Objects; and curiously surveying some *Ideas* that are there, it takes no notice of impressions of sounding Bodies, made upon the Organ of Hearing . . . ? A sufficient impulse there may be on the Organ; but it not reaching the observation of the Mind, there follows no perception: . . . that which uses to produce the *Idea*, though conveyed in by the usual Organ, not being taken notice of in the Understanding, and so imprinting no *Idea* on the Mind, there follows no Sensation.[41]
> (2.9.4)

Though there is no systematic distinction in the *Essay* between "impressions" and "imprints," when Locke describes ideas as "imprints" or compares them to some form of language, he clearly means to emphasize the intelligibility and self-evidence of the ideas under consideration. He may refer on occasion to unclear impressions or confused ideas, but never to illegible (or even obscure) imprints. If to "reflect" is to notice, and "imprinting" implies the solicitation of attention, we may posit at least tentatively some point of contact between language—particularly, though not exclusively, in the form of printing—and reflection in Locke's scheme. Let us look briefly, then, at a few of the crucial passages where ideas are described as a kind of alphabet or language and examine the relation of reflection to the material traces of experience in the mind.

If an impression is noticed by the mind, an idea is imprinted; but is it clear that this imprint is a word? Locke's favorite synonym for "imprint" is "character," suggesting at least an elementary unit of a written language. Given Locke's repeated insistence throughout the *Essay* that the relationship of ideas to the external world is arbitrary and conventional rather than pictorial or mimetic (with the exception of our simple ideas of primary qualities) we would appear to be justified in regarding his reference to "imprints" as a reference to linguistic or protolinguistic units.

---

[41] Just as he will not commit himself on the question of whether ideas are physiologically recorded and retained, Locke will not commit himself on the question of what ideas might consist of when they are not "earnestly" attended to. On one occasion, at least, he sidesteps the issue simply by noting that the English language has no word for such a phenomenon: "When *Ideas* float in our mind, without any reflection or regard of the Understanding, it is that, which the *French* call *Reverie*; our Language has scarce a name for it" (2.19.1).

Even in the case of our ideas of "primary qualities" (e.g., bulk, figure, texture, motion), which according to Locke have an immediate, mimetic relation to the actual qualities of external objects (2.8.9–10), the relationship of idea to object is still linguistic rather than pictorial. As we saw at the beginning of this chapter, Locke's account of visual perception suggests that we read our simple sensations of the external world in much the same way that we read language (this passage is followed directly by the Molyneux Question and the shift to issues of linguistic comprehension [2.9.8–9]).[42] Both in visual perception and in our operations with words we pass almost imperceptibly from the actual elementary units or "characters" of experience to the "ideas" with which we customarily find them connected. Yet this account is in turn complicated when we reflect on the attention we pay to *words* and *names* as opposed merely to characters and sounds. In book 4, Locke suggests that when it comes to the names of complex ideas we tend to reflect on the words themselves and to suspend any consideration of the ideas they stand for:

> When we would consider, or make Propositions about the more complex *Ideas*, as of a *Man*, *Vitriol*, *Fortitude*, *Glory*, we usually put the Name for the *Idea*: Because the *Ideas* these Names stand for, being for the most part imperfect, confused, and undetermined, we reflect on the *Names* themselves, because they are more clear, certain, and distinct . . . so we make use of these Words instead of the *Ideas* themselves, even when we would meditate and reason within our selves. (4.5.4)

This new, middle focus—on words as opposed to characters, sounds, or ideas—illustrates the problem we have been outlining here concerning the diverse senses of "noticing" or "attention" assimilated in Locke's figure of "reflection." In 2.9, Locke had stated that we fail to "notice" "characters and sounds" precisely when we are *attending to and understanding* language; but also that we do not "notice" our own words when "by custom" we "have got the use of a By-word" (§10). Yet these by rights should be almost antithetical situations: one in which we are concentrating as we listen or hear, the other in which we might legitimately speak of a lack of concentration—of the habitual rather than the intentional. Ob-

---

[42] See Land, *From Signs to Propositions*: "Locke appears to consider sensations themselves as signs interpreted by the mind in perception. The suggestion is that even the mental image has meaning not by resemblance to its object but by convention and habitual association" (25).

viously these distinctions define rather than resolve a problem. Locke's argument constantly assumes what it is *natural* or *obvious* for us to "notice" in any given situation, but the situation is defined in part by what he asks us to "reflect" on. My point is not that the argument is circular but that it demonstrates the slipperiness—and inevitably polemical use—of the concepts "attention," "noticing," and ultimately "reflection." The positive assertion lying behind the polemic is that experience in a broad sense—including at least the processes of perception and judgment—is composed of an intricate and constantly shifting structure of attention and inattention, these two dispositions of mind being synchronous rather than mutually exclusive and intermittent.

The imprinting of ideas on our understanding is clearly a process with some affinities to language, but whether the connection is by way of physiological processes, logical processes, analogy, or even metaphor remains to be determined. In a passage that accords impressions a more elementary semantic status than language and suggests a relationship of analogy rather than of formal or physiological identity between impressions and words, Locke defends his contention that all ideas—no matter how complex or abstract—must have their origin in simple ideas of sensation and reflection. He compares the relationship between simple and complex ideas to the relationship between alphabetic letters and words: "Nor will it be so strange, to think these few simple *Ideas* sufficient to employ the quickest Thought, or largest Capacity; and to furnish the Materials of all that various Knowledge, and more various Fancies and Opinions of all Mankind, if we consider how many Words may be made out of the various composition of 24 Letters" (2.8.10). This analogy receives confirmation in book 3 when Locke argues that simple ideas cannot be explained by words, while the names for complex ideas— standing in the first instance only for a collection of other words— virtually "imprint" an "understanding" on our mind:

> *Simple Ideas*, as has been shewn, *are only* to be *got by* those *impressions* Objects themselves make on our Minds, by the proper Inlets appointed to each sort. If they are not received this way, all the *Words* in the World, *made use of to explain, or define any of their Names, will never be able to produce in us the* Idea *it stands for.* . . .
> The case is quite otherwise *in complex Ideas*; which consisting of several simple ones, it is in the power of Words, standing for the several *Ideas*, that

make that Composition, to imprint complex *Ideas* in the Mind, which were never there before, and so make their Names be understood. (3.4.11,12)

According to this scheme, our impressions of simple ideas are not unlike letters of the alphabet; they are the elementary units out of which complex ideas—which we receive literally as words—are constructed.

Yet there is something wrong about this description of simple ideas as protolinguistic. For in another sense they could not be further or more categorically removed from language. *No* word—not "all the words in the world"—can explain or define a simple idea, according to Locke. This point is emphasized earlier in his discussion of "perception," itself a "simple idea" of reflection: "*What Perception is*, every one will know better by reflecting on what he does himself, when he sees, hears, feels, *etc.* or thinks, than by any discourse of mine. Whoever reflects on what passes in his own Mind, cannot miss it: And if he does not reflect, all the Words in the World, cannot make him have any notion of it" (2.9.2). This passage returns us to the issue of the relationship between reflection and language. Earlier we had proposed that reflection was the act of noticing, and that *being noticed*—legibility—was a constitutive feature of language. Inasmuch as all impressions were forms of imprinting and thus forms of language, nothing could be impressed on our minds without our noticing it; and all impressions would then involve at least some reflection. But now a gap on the order of a category distinction seems to open up between simple ideas and language. While complex ideas are in a sense *already language*, simple ideas are not translatable into words. All our impressions are either literally linguistic or quite incommensurable with language. But in the former case, as we have seen, the recognition of an impression as a linguistic sign is an invitation for us to replace it automatically with the idea it is customarily associated with—just as when we read *attentively* (according to Locke) we ignore the words and notice only the ideas (2.9.9).

Instead of a figure for our attention to the material signifiers of language, then, reflection becomes a figure for the various ways in which understanding *bypasses* language. On the one hand, through reflection we observe or experience those simple ideas that language itself cannot communicate to us. On the other hand, by reflecting we may notice how little notice we often take of language: "Any one may easily observe this in his own Thoughts, who will take the pains to reflect on them. . . . Men, that by custom have got the use of a By-word, do almost in every sentence, pronounce sounds, which, though taken notice of by others, they themselves neither hear, nor observe" (2.9.10). Reflection alternately foregrounds and dissolves the mediating function of language.

Locke's emphasis in book 2 is on the way language's signifiers fall out of focus when we reflect on what is being said (not when we reflect on what happens when we reflect, which is a different case). Locke takes this process to be a salutary one. It is part of the generally *economical* process of human understanding, which includes the habits of generalization, abstraction, judgment, and other forms of leaping over, bundling, collecting, or otherwise condensing the raw data of experience.[43] Book 4 affirms this relation between reflection and writing but reverses the poles of valorization associated with it in book 2. In book 4, Locke's figure for the superiority of nonreflective experience is the *tabula rasa* or blank sheet of paper, but now literalized with a vengeance and relocated outside the mind.

Nothing could be more intuitively and immediately certain to us, argues Locke, than that the paper before our eyes is of a different color than the marks recorded on it:

> *Another difference between intuitive and demonstrative Knowledge*, is, that though in the latter all doubt be removed, when by the Intervention of the intermediate *Ideas*, the Agreement or Disagreement is perceived; yet before the Demonstration there was a doubt, which in intuitive Knowledge cannot happen to the Mind that has its Faculty of Perception left to a degree capable of distinct *Ideas*, no more than it can be a doubt to the Eye, (that can distinctly see White and Black,) Whether this Ink, and this Paper be all of a Colour. If there be Sight in the Eyes, it will at first glimpse, without Hesitation, perceive the Words printed on this Paper, different from the Colour of the Paper. (4.2.5)

Here our attention to the actual material figures of ink on paper is exemplary of an intuitive knowledge that contrasts strongly with the distortions of reflection. (Locke opposes intuition to "demonstrative Knowledge," which he characterizes in the following paragraph as "a Face reflected by several Mirrors one to another" and which "in every successive reflection" loses its "Clearness and Distinctness" [4.2.6].)[44] The term

[43] See Foucault's remarks, cited in n. 3.
[44] Though Locke's emphasis on the material signifiers of language in book 4 recapitulates the *Essay*'s pervasive tension between the specular and material aspects of "reflection" and is thus part of a tension within Locke's own philosophic scheme, that emphasis might

"attention" is perhaps not quite appropriate here, for Locke is attempting to articulate a mode of certainty that anticipates even the reflective activities of attending and noticing. Nonetheless, our attention to the material signifiers here has dramatically different value than in 2.9. This new value is reaffirmed in a similar passage a few chapters later, when Locke turns to our next most certain kind of knowledge, our *"Knowledge of the Existence* of any other thing" (i.e., other than God and self)—a knowledge that "we can have only by *Sensation"* (4.11.1). Our certainty of the existence of external things, which we derive from our senses, is illustrated, not coincidentally, by the acts of writing and reading:

> Whilst I write this, I have, by the Paper affecting my Eyes, that *Idea* produced in my Mind, which whatever Object causes, I call *White;* by which I know, that that Quality or Accident (*i.e.* whose appearance before my Eyes, always causes that *Idea*) doth really exist, and hath a Being without me. And of this, the greatest assurance I can possibly have, and to which my Faculties can attain, is the Testimony of my Eyes, which are the proper and sole Judges of this thing, whose Testimony I have reason to rely on, as so certain, that I can no more doubt, whilst I write this, that I see White and Black, and that something really exists, that causes that Sensation in me, than that I write or move my Hand. (4.11.2)

Nothing in the phenomenal world could be more certain than the material signifiers of language, writes Locke. And yet we recall from book 2 that such faculties as judgment and reflection involve precisely the bypassing of sensation's immediate signifiers, a process of figurative, substitutive reading in which "by an habitual custom" we "[alter] . . . Appearances

---

also be given an intellectual-historical explanation. Murray Cohen points out that an interest in the immanent structural qualities and cognitive value of material signifiers was characteristic of the seventeenth-century English grammarians, who believed that "the relationship between language and reality . . . must be sought in the physical parts of writing and speech-letters and sounds" (*Sensible Words*, 1). Cohen adds: "Whether seventeenth-century English grammars are explicitly organized according to the materials of language—letters, syllables, words, and sentences—or according to its processes—orthography, pronunciation, etymology, syntax, and prosody—virtually all of them give initial and extensive attention to the materials, specifically to the shapes and sounds of letters and to the images of words" (8). According to Cohen, the grammarians' emphasis on the language-nature analogy is superseded somewhat during the last quarter of the century by the Port Royalist emphasis on the language-mind analogy (26–27). However, Locke clearly retains the grammarian emphasis, even while using the figure of reflection to complicate the notion of *paying attention* to the signifier.

into their Causes" and "collecting the Figure, . . . [make] it pass for a mark of Figure" (2.9.8).

What does reflection teach us? That when we reflect on what is being said or written, we do not reflect on the words, characters, or sounds themselves but on our *ideas* (which are figured, paradoxically, precisely in terms of material signifiers: imprints, alphabetic characters, etc.). We pass from "figure" to "a mark for figure." If this paraphrase sounds circular, that is no coincidence. A continual doubling or multiplying of the figure of reflection (and its various equivalents or functions) takes place throughout the *Essay*. "Noticing," "attending," "observing," "considering," and "contemplating" are articulated from the start as part of the grammar of "reflection." Yet often these terms will appear in a single passage playing different, even opposing, roles in a complex dynamic of perception. Different kinds of attention may be mutually reinforcing, mutually exclusive, or simply categorically distinct and incommensurable. Consider a passage we have already cited:

> A Man who hears with *attention* and understanding, takes little *notice* of the Characters, or Sounds, but of the Ideas, that are excited in him by them.
>
> Nor need we wonder, that this is done with so little *notice*, if we *consider*, how very quick the actions of the Mind are performed. . . . Any one may easily *observe* this in his own Thoughts, who will take the pains to reflect on them. (2.9.9–10, emphasis altered)

Each of the italicized words in this passage has been offered elsewhere by Locke as a synonym for "reflection," and the passage could quite reasonably be restated in the following way: "a Man who hears with reflection . . . reflects little on the Characters, or Sounds . . . Nor need we wonder, that this is done with so little reflection, if we reflect." Can we say that it is on purely stylistic grounds that Locke avoids such a formulation?[45] Or should we conclude instead that the rhetorical variegation of apparently equivalent terms in this passage signals the fact that *reflection* is not a

---

[45] There are, as Richetti points out, passages in which Locke's deliberate avoidance of anaphora seems intended to make a polemical statement about the relationship of genuine "experiential relationships" to the inauthentic, "exact repetitions of rhetorical patterns" (*Philosophical Writing*, 63). However even in such situations one can hardly consider Locke's strategy to be merely stylistic, since the relationship of "experience" to "rhetoric" is itself a philosophic issue.

consistent quality, direction, or configuration of psychic energy but rather a set of (necessarily) loosely related dispositions, states and behaviors?

Throughout the *Essay* Locke figures both our attention to signifiers and our attention to signifieds in terms of the immediacy and self-evidence of written characters. Reflection thus short-circuits language, but not by having the reader focus beyond actual words and attend instead to "meanings" or "intentions." Rather, Locke wants us to notice what is going on in our *own* minds when we use words; his assumption is that we will see how often it is we skip words and proceed directly to ideas. But of course this is based on the further assumption that what we *see* when we look past language are ideas that have all the characteristics of *legibility*.

This connection of "reflection" to reading is not entirely novel, since it is a commonplace of literary-moral "Reflections" that the world is a hieroglyph awaiting the patient meditator's observation.[46] But Locke does not want to emphasize the half-mysterious, half-wonderful hiero-glyphic nature of the objects of human knowledge. He wants to portray the sources of knowledge as immediately legible, as self-evident in a way that requires only "reflection"—to see reflection, as he uses the term, being as simple and clear as light, as morally essential as self-scrutiny, and as concrete as the printed page. What Locke wants, then, is neither a literal reading of his text nor a reading by way of a particular rhetorical trope. "Reflection" is the dominant figure of the *Essay*, but it is a con-stantly varying figure, in accordance with constantly varying rules of transformation. It is a figure for whatever Locke happens to think we should be focusing on at the moment—but that focus constantly changes, and it is only by "reflecting" that we can notice how frequently our attention shifts direction and how unreflectingly we proceed in the nor-mal course of things.

[46] See, for instance, Boyle, *Occasional Reflections*: "The World is the great Book, not so much of Nature, as of the God of Nature, which we should find ev'n crowded with instructive Lessons, if we had but the Skill, and would take the Pains, to extract and pick them out: The Creatures are the true Ægyptian Hieroglyphicks, that under the rude forms of Birds, and Beasts, &c. conceal the mysterious secrets of Knowledge, and of Piety" (44). "The Beams of Knowledge, acquired by . . . Reflections, [have] in them, like those of the Sun, not onely Light but Heat. And indeed it were somewhat strange, as well as sad, if a person disposed and accustomed to observe and consider, conversing with such instructive Books as those of God's Creatures and his Providence, with an intention to take out practical Lessons, should not find them" (47).

We have seen that Locke's oscillation between visual and verbal models of experience is accounted for at least in part by two distinctive rhetorical features in the *Essay*. The first is the diverse range of linguistic elements and phenomena that Locke refers to when he reflects on language. Locke compares sense-perception variously to reading, writing, listening, and speaking, and the objects of sense-perception variously to words, characters, sounds, signs, figures, and marks. This comparison is additionally complicated by the fact that Locke characterizes the relationship between the two orders of visual perception and verbal behavior in a variety of different linguistic terms: sometimes the two orders are offered as *analogies* for one another, sometimes they are described metaphorically in terms of one another, and at other times they are described as two components within a linguistic system. This alone should make us cautious in suggesting that Locke's accounts of perception and of language can be explained systematically in terms of one another. Locke is rarely referring to the same aspect of language or of language use from one passage to the next, despite the frequency with which language appears as a model or analogy within the *Essay*.

The second rhetorical feature of the *Essay* that contributes to the mutual implication of language and sense-perception is Locke's diverse grammar of reflection, that is, the fact that his various synonyms for reflection (noticing, attending, observing) are played off against one another in a way that prevents reflection from being reduced to a single or unitary phenomenon. We are always attending to something at the expense of something else. This structure of attention and inattention—of reflection and nonreflection—is exhibited in both our verbal behavior and our sense-experience, and is reenacted by the constant motions of Locke's text, which direct our attention variously to the functions of language, the functions of sense, and the functions of judgment and reflection that divide and join them.

Locke's commentators have tended to locate his most distinctive reflections on language in the latter half of the *Essay*—in his discussion of abstract ideas (2.32.6–8), his account of the "Beginn[ings] of Language" (3.1.5), his famous "confession" of language's "connexion" to knowledge (3.9.21), and in the infamous attack on rhetoric (3.10.34).[47] As we

---

[47] Notable exceptions to this include de Man ("The Epistemology of Metaphor") and Aarsleff (*From Locke to Saussure*, esp. 44, 107).

have seen, however, accounts and discussions of language are integral to Locke's investigation of "human understanding" even in the *Essay*'s early sections on sense perception. Locke simply cannot consider impressions and sensations without recourse to metaphors and analogies that introduce some aspect of language use. And that use of language is, in turn, explained in terms of analogies and metaphors of sense perception. Thus it is not only in terms of the *Essay*'s overall narrative structure that Locke's account of human understanding moves from an account of sensation to an account of language; the *Essay* slides constantly back and forth between the two even at the level of local arguments concerning the most minute aspects of sense experience. If Locke's ostensible, and most famous, contribution to the empiricist tradition is his theory of sensations and impressions, his subtler legacy lies in the interweaving of sense perception with a large and loosely defined entity called language—and with the articulation of that relationship in terms of the equally large and loosely defined figure of reflection.

It is perhaps not surprising, then, that Berkeley's critique of the *Essay Concerning Human Understanding* begins with the charge that Locke had insufficiently "reflected" on the role of language.[48] But paradoxically Berkeley's strategy for correcting Locke's ostensible misprision is to conflate as far as possible the relationships among world, mind, and mediating language. Locke's mistake, according to Berkeley, was not so much in taking words for things (e.g., the word *substance* for some general property of bodies) as in failing to reflect that they were never separate categories in the first place.

Despite this charge of inadequate reflection, reflection can never be the dominant figure for Berkeley that it is for Locke because for Berkeley there is no sustained distinction between mind and body, or between self and world, for "reflection" to explain or negotiate. There is no real problem for Berkeley about how the world gets "into" our minds, or how we communicate our ideas that are "invisible" to other people. Relationships among world, medium, and mind must be explained, in Berkeley's philosophy, in terms of linguistic relationships such as "analogy," "metaphor," "transference," and "literal and accepted significations." This

---

[48] Berkeley, introduction (§§18–25) to *The Treatise Concerning the Principles of Human Knowledge*, in *Works*, vol. 1.

compels him, as we shall see, to give a more systematic account than does Locke of the various relationships constituting the elements and operations of language.

For Berkeley our ideas and our faculties are *essentially* linguistic; ideas of sensation (particularly optical ones) are only a special case of language. It seems, then, that Berkeley should be able to dispense with figures of reflection, surface, and depth altogether, since no mechanical model of mind—whether specular or material—is necessary to explain the congruency of mind and world that constitutes human knowledge. But those figures persist: and if Locke finds it difficult to explain the process of reflection without recourse to the model of language, Berkeley finds it equally difficult to explain the process of language without the figures of reflection, surface, and depth.

3

Toward the Surface and Back Again: Berkeley's Reflections on Language

Nothing, in a certain sense, more flippant has ever been invented than the gimcrack world of façades of Berkeley—that of tables and chairs that come and go, of hollow and one-sided mountains, like theatrical structures of stucco. . . . It is an extremist philosophy for *surface-creatures*: and it is as that, essentially, as I have remarked in an earlier part of this book, that we should, I believe, regard ourselves.

—WYNDHAM LEWIS, *Time and Western Man*

THE PHILOSOPHER OF SURFACES

BERKELEY IS THE quintessential philosopher of surfaces. To modernist literary writers in particular he is a virtual philosophical hero, author of an "extremist philosophy for *surface creatures*," of a "gimcrack world of facades . . . of tables and chairs that come and go, of hollow and one-sided mountains, like theatrical structures of stucco."[1] According to scientists and philosophers as well, Berkeley presents us with a world in which "everything is surface";[2] he is even held uniquely responsible for the constructivism of eighteenth- and nineteenth-century optics, according to which "we 'see' a flat field but 'construct' a tactile space."[3]

The great irony of these characterizations is that they fly in the face of both the rhetoric and the empirical concerns of Berkeley's writings. Berkeley is far more interested in verbal "signs" than he is in physical "surfaces"; more concerned with "analogies" than with "impressions." More than any other writer in the empiricist tradition, Berkeley articulates his theory of perception in terms of linguistic categories. While

[1] In addition to Lewis, other modernist writers such as Yeats, Joyce, and Beckett were particularly fascinated with Berkeley.

[2] Popper, *Conjectures and Refutations*, 168.

[3] Gombrich, *Art and Illusion*, 330–31.

Locke's *Essay* restricts itself generally to the literal/figurative and signifier/signified distinctions, Berkeley's work is populated by a host of heterogeneous linguistic oppositions: characters and sounds, sounds and ideas, ideas and things, signifiers and signifieds, the literal and the metaphoric, true and false analogies, numerals and numbers, and so on. Berkeley's linguistic categories and terms multiply to such an extent, in fact, that the sensory world often seems to drop out of his account altogether. Far from making language into a transparent window onto the empirical world, Berkeley's philosophy seems almost to render the sensory world transparent before language. This may help explain why he is so often thought of as an idealist rather than an empiricist, and it helps account as well for our frequent impression that the "surfaces" with which he is concerned are such hypothetical films as to be nonexistent—a mere "gimcrack world of facades."

The central paradox of Berkeley's philosophical career lies in the fact that everything he could say or do to make the world appear more real, more accessible, more certain, served only to make it appear more chimerical, fantastical, and theatrical. No philosopher has ever produced more counterintuitive-sounding claims from more thoroughly empirical observations or from more commonsense axioms. Berkeley somehow manages to take the most traditional and familiar set of empiricist figures—surfaces, impressions, imprints—and to render them suspect by insisting on the literalness of the analogy between sense-experience and verbal signification. He thus epitomizes the constantly shifting relationship between language and perception that so often makes empiricism seem to tilt over from the most dogmatically positivistic to the most unwittingly skeptical of philosophies.

As we shall see, however, such a tilt in Berkeley's work is neither the result of logical inconsistency nor the product of metaphorical drift. It is the result, rather, of a constant analogizing process that links language and perception by means of a common set of rhetorical figures. According to Berkeley, language reflects meaning much in the same way as visual perception reflects the tangible world; and the virtual mirror-relationship between these two processes is something that mental reflection both exposes and preserves. But this apparent circularity is necessary and constructive so far as Berkeley is concerned. We would be just as much mistaken in assuming that the world is all language as we would be in assuming that it is all sensation. And Berkeley's figures of reflection, surface, and depth help sustain the constant oscillation between sensory and linguistic criteria that is the hallmark of his work and of empiricist philosophy in general.

It is a philosophical commonplace to point out that Berkeley pushed Locke's empiricism to its logical conclusions, extending Locke's critique of secondary qualities to a critique of primary qualities as well. Berkeley thus appears more rigorously empiricist than Locke, more scrupulously phenomenalist in his insistence that we can know only our impressions of things.[4] Like a later empiricist, Hazlitt, Berkeley pushes the common-sense claims of empiricism to their counterintuitive extremes. Unlike Hazlitt, however, Berkeley is not interested in the ironic potential of this tension but wishes to resolve it through a constant appeal to the opposition between proper and improper uses of language—the single distinction toward which his entire miscellany of linguistic categories and terms are channeled. One of the central dramas of Berkeley's philosophy—as it unfolds over the course of his three major essays—is his development of a rhetoric that can accommodate both the technical claims of his immaterialism and his commonsense opposition to philosophical abstractions.

Berkeley's principal task is to dramatize his doctrine of "immaterialism" (the belief that there is no material reality independent of the mind) in such a way as to make it appear congenial to common sense; this ultimately comes down to showing that immaterialism does not require any reformation of our common figures of speech. Despite his virtually commonplace protests against rhetorical language, Berkeley does not object to rhetoric so much as to the habit of inferring philosophical categories and distinctions common figures of speech. What is implied by our trust in a substantial, external, material world (a trust presupposed by our actions as well as by the very terms of our ordinary discourse) is simply not what philosophers understand by the terms *external, material,* or *substance*—or so Berkeley's argument goes. But this is a difficult position to maintain without contradiction since it requires Berkeley to acknowledge the close affiliation of the most philosophical and the most commonsensical attitudes and at the same time to argue for philosophy's profound misreading of common discourse. For instance, while material substance *as it is conceived by the philosophers* may indeed seem an

---

[4] I am using "phenomenalist" in the general sense of a philosophical position that interprets knowledge as the knowledge of our experiences (and not of things-in-themselves); not in the more modern and restricted sense of a philosophy that interprets knowledge as a *logical construction* out of sense impressions. See the Appendix.

absurd abstraction, any attack on "material substance" is bound to appear equally suspicious from the perspective of "common sense."

Berkeley's philosophy, then, struggles with the question of how to make an account of the world (which is ultimately an account of our *perception* of the world) compatible with our habits of describing the world, even while discriminating consistently and dogmatically between proper and misleading habits of description. At the heart of this dilemma lies the rhetorical constellation of surfaces, depths, and reflections with its multiple registers. These figures are central to scientific descriptions of the empirical world (e.g., the surfaces of a cube or a globe, the depth of an ocean or an eyeball, the iridescent reflections of a water fountain or prism), to descriptions of the intellectual mechanism (e.g., the impressible or imprintable surfaces of the mind, and the reflective capacity of judgment), and additionally to descriptions of the qualities of mental life (e.g., deep or superficial problems).

According to Berkeley we will not be tempted to infer conflicting meanings from this overdetermined rhetorical structure if we acknowledge that the inference of *any* philosophical meaning from a figure of speech is specious. The overdetermination of philosophical figures simply exemplifies the general analogy between sensory and linguistic signification. But contrary to Lockean epistemology, this is not an analogy between inner and outer worlds; rather it is an analogy between different systems for predicting future experiences in the light of past ones. Over the course of his three major works Berkeley moves toward, and then turns away from, a rhetoric of surfaces, even as he moves progressively closer to a rhetoric of depth. But this pattern is countered at a different level by a changing attitude toward rhetoric that discounts the philosophical significance of the surface/depth scheme altogether and points the way to a quite different metaphor, one for the very trajectory of thought that first entertains and then finally rejects the philosophical implications of figurative language altogether: the metaphor of reflection.

Berkeley's first major work—a technical essay on optics—would appear to be his most empirical, and yet in that essay Berkeley goes to great lengths to avoid any systematic reference to the "surfaces" of the phenomenal world, and indeed to avoid any rhetorical evocation of surfaces via the empiricist metaphor of "impressions." The world, according to *An Essay towards a New Theory of Vision*, is *spoken* to us by God.[5] It is

[5] George Berkeley, *An Essay towards a New Theory of Vision*, in *Works*, vol. 1. All subsequent references will cite paragraph numbers from this edition.

in his second work, the *Treatise Concerning the Principles of Human Knowledge*, that Berkeley begins to sound like the "surface" philosopher with whom we are familiar, as he describes a world "imprinted" on our senses and rails against "deep" philosophical speculation.[6] Yet by the end of the *Treatise* Berkeley finds himself backed into a counterintuitive description of the phenomenal world, and in the more popularly oriented *Dialogues* he attempts to reclaim a discourse of common sense.[7] At one level he does this by toning down his rhetoric of "imprinting" and acknowledging the "depth" of our phenomenal experiences; but, even more important, he does this by articulating a pragmatic attitude toward rhetoric, which distinguishes between the ordinary and the philosophical employment of figures rather than between literal accuracy and rhetorical distortion. Though in the *Dialogues* Berkeley retreats again from the empiricist rhetoric of impressions and imprints, he nonetheless remains firmly within an even more important empiricist rhetorical tradition: that of describing the *criticism* of knowledge claims as a kind of "reflection."

"REFLECTION" AND THE EXPANSION
OF THE LANGUAGE ANALOGY

Despite their differences, it is possible to give the same general description to both Berkeley's and Locke's most basic philosophical project and most basic figurative habits: both complain that we habitually mistake contingent associations for natural and necessary connections, and both propose to address this error by exposing the contingent connections forged in our minds through the critical process of "reflection." Where the two differ is in their characterization of illusory associations (Locke figures them as "deep"; Berkeley depicts them as "false analogies"), in their understanding of the precise nature—and perils—of "reflection," and in their understanding of the analogy between physiological and linguistic processes.

For Locke, reflection is the act of "reading" our own mental contents but also the act of watching what happens when we engage in reading and

[6] George Berkeley, *A Treatise Concerning the Principles of Human Knowledge*, in *Works*, vol. 1. All subsequent references will cite paragraph numbers from either the introduction or the body of the *Treatise*; the two are numbered separately.

[7] George Berkeley, *Three Dialogues between Hylas and Philonous*, in *Works*, vol. 1. All subsequent references will cite page numbers from this edition.

other linguistic activities. For Berkeley, the double sense of "reflection" is somewhat different. Reflection is both the process of analogizing and the process of discerning false analogies. Since the analogies Berkeley is most concerned with are those that define the status, nature, and contents of language, we might say that Berkeley's "reflections" both make and unmake language. Ultimately two contradictory claims distinguish Berkeley's discussion of language: one, his insistence that experience in the most general sense of the word be reducible, or at least analogous, to language; and two, his insistence that linguistic relationships and their analogies be distinguished sharply, even categorically, from other kinds of relationships.

For Berkeley, reflection is primarily the process of recognizing linguistic phenomena as such and not mistaking them for natural or necessary phenomena. Ironically (but not, for all that, contradictorily), this includes not mistaking optical impressions for anything more natural or immediate than a language. This analogy is so consistent, so thoroughly insisted upon, in Berkeley's work that it makes optical models of cognition almost useless. Anything optical immediately becomes dissolved, in Berkeley's scheme, into a question of language. We can see aspects of Locke's argument being developed here (e.g., *Essay*, 2.9.8–10), but Berkeley's concern with language is ultimately so dominant that it makes the optical model somewhat beside the point. But if Berkeley is thus in a sense even more suspicious than Locke of reflection, he also presents a more complicated account of what we "see" when we reflect on language. All this turns, of course, on Berkeley's understanding of "language."

Berkeley's best interpreters agree that the analogy or model of language is central to Berkeley's philosophy.[8] Colin Murray Turbayne has written extensively on Berkeley's use of language (or a "theory of language") as his privileged "model" for visual, natural, physiological, and metaphysical relationships.[9] And John Richetti, while sensing a greater

---

[8] See general remarks by Foucault in *The Order of Things*, 58–61.

[9] Turbayne's definition of "model" corresponds, in traditional rhetorical terms, to what we would call an extended analogy or allegory: "I define 'model' in terms of 'metaphor.' . . . If a metaphor is extended and its features spelled out and applied, we have what I shall call a 'model.' " See Colin M. Turbayne, "The Origin of Berkeley's Paradoxes," in *New Studies in Berkeley's Philosophy*, ed. Warren E. Steinkraus (New York: Holt, Rinehart, and Winston, 1966), 33. Turbayne extends this discussion of Berkeley's theory of language in "Berkeley's Metaphysical Grammar" and to a lesser extent in "Berkeley's Two Concepts of Mind," both in Turbayne's edition of Berkeley's *A Treatise Concerning the Principles of*

instability in Berkeley's conception of language than does Turbayne, concludes that "at the center of Berkeley's thought . . . lies the analogy of language."[10]

Language is certainly the great, the abiding, analogy throughout Berkeley's work. But if Berkeley's interest in language, like Locke's, is based on the exemplariness of language as a system of arbitrary signs and conventional relationships, he nonetheless describes a more complicated range of linguistic activities than does Locke. There are in Berkeley's view a number of different relationships that may be described, roughly, as "linguistic." When Berkeley compares visual impressions to language, he has in mind a general picture of the arbitrary, even intermittent, relationship of "words" to "ideas" (e.g., *Essay*, §32), but as soon as one turns to his specific examples, this reduces, variously, into relationships between characters and sounds, between "sounds" and "things," between written signs and ideas, between "names" and "definitions," between literal expressions and "extended" figurative senses, between numerals and numbers, and between the "countenance" and the "passions." And these relationships in turn are glossed, variously, as relationships of "analogy," of "suggestion," of "mediation," of "close and customary connexion," and of "signifying indifferently," to list but a few.

The language model, then, is not a single structural relationship,

---

Human Knowledge (Indianapolis: Bobbs-Merrill, 1970), 3–36, 145–60. Berkeley's theory of language is also a passing subject in chaps. 4, 5, and 8 of Turbayne's *The Myth of Metaphor*, rev. ed. (Columbia: University of South Carolina Press, 1970).

Turbayne's view is implicitly challenged in more recent work by Michael Williams and Ian Hacking, both of whom stress the great divide between Enlightenment and modernist "theories" of language. Williams and Hacking argue that a philosophical theory of language in the modern sense is a highly technical theory of "meaning" and "significance" and is neither a theory about the discursive character of the mental operations nor simply the "assumptions about language" coded into a philosopher's own discursive practice. However, Hacking also goes on to claim that a theory of "ideas" as "mental discourse" played the same philosophical role for the early British empiricists that theories of language play for modern philosophers; in short, we can make a translation from what seventeenth-century philosophers say about "ideas" to what we would be inclined to say about language. See Williams, *Groundless Belief*, 172; and "Hume's Criterion of Significance," 302–3. See also Hacking, *Why Does Language Matter to Philosophy?*, chaps. 1–3 and 13.

10 In *Philosophical Writing*, Richetti writes: "The verbal language Turbayne identifies as the stable vehicle of Berkeley's master metaphor has a turbulent uncertainty of its own, and Berkeley's literary facility collides with his own deep sense of the unreliability of language" (137). Richetti's remarks concerning Berkeley's "analogy of language" appear in *Philosophic Writing*, 165.

infinitely extended or reproduced, but a collection of relationships.[11] When Berkeley says at one point that our optical impressions are related to our sensations of touch in the same way that words are to ideas (e.g., ibid., §32), and then at another point that our words for tangible and optical impressions are related in the same way as literal to "transferred" expressions (ibid., §98), do we have two aspects of the same model, or two different models? And when that same relationship is further compared to the relationship between a man's "countenance" and the "passions" it "signif[ies]" (ibid., §65), have we passed beyond the language analogy entirely, or has the verbal model of language simply been replaced by a more general conception of language as a semiotic system? The arbitrary/nonarbitrary distinction essential to Locke, Berkeley, and their empiricist heirs, *appears* to have a simple analogy in the working of language, and yet there are innumerable diverse verbal, grammatical, semiotic, and rhetorical relationships that fall under this general description. There are, in short, numerous pictures of language, some of which simply reproduce rather than clarify those relationships that the language model is introduced to explain.

We may sharpen our understanding of this dynamic by focusing on the role of "analogy" in Berkeley's articulation of the relationship among objects of sight, objects of touch, and language.[12] "Analogy," as Berkeley uses the word in the *Essay*, entails a natural and necessary connection, a relationship of "resemblance" or "similitude" as opposed to one of mere "arbitrary" suggestion or signification (§§140–47). We are so "dispose[d]," writes Berkeley, as to "imagine a likeness or analogy between the immediate objects of sight and touch," but in this we are mistaken (§145). There is, Berkeley admits, a "habitual connexion," indeed a "strict and close connexion," between these two orders of objects, but this does not constitute any "likeness or identity of nature" or

---

[11] Turbayne's essay "The Origin of Berkeley's Paradoxes" provides an excellent analysis of the various ways in which the analogy of language is invoked throughout Berkeley's work (i.e., directly, indirectly, by simile, through metaphor, etc.). But Turbayne tends to assume a certain uniformity within the analogy itself; that is, he assumes that "language" is a uniform concept, despite the variety of modes in which it is invoked or alluded to. Turbayne acknowledges, importantly, that the language analogy leads Berkeley into paradoxes or apparent absurdities when linguistic *laws* are projected back into physical laws, but Turbayne sees such paradoxes as symptoms of the instability of *analogy* rather than as something about the complexity and instability of Berkeley's conception of language itself.

[12] Foucault emphasizes that *analogy* in classical rhetoric is a relation between relations rather than a relation between objects. See *The Order of Things*, 21.

"same[ness]" of "species" (§§143, 145, 147). By contrast, the relationship between visual ideas and verbal language (which Berkeley introduces precisely to illustrate the arbitrariness of the sight:touch relationship) *is* one of similarity: "visible figures represent tangible figures *much after the same manner* that written words do sounds" (§143); "the manner wherein they [visible figures] signify and mark out unto us the objects which are at a distance *is the same* with that of languages and signs of human appointment" (§145).[13] The relationship between visible figures and tangible figures is arbitrary; the relationship between verbal language and its objects is arbitrary; but the relationship between these two orders of facts is *not* arbitrary. The irony of the "language analogy" is that nonanalogical relationships (i.e., sight and touch) are illustrated precisely through their analogical similarity with the nonanalogically based system called language. And what further complicates the irony is that genuine relations of natural resemblance (i.e., sight:language) are less readily apparent to view than the "strict and close connexions" of arbitrary relationships. Opposed categories run very close here: though there is a *more natural* connection (i.e., a relationship of genuine similitude) between the operations of sight and the operations of language than between words and ideas or between visible and tangible figures, there is nonetheless a *stricter*, a *closer*, a more *habitual* connection at work in the latter two cases.[14] Though "nature" and "habit" should be logically distinct, the confusion of them is hardly surprising. Thus, according to Berkeley, we are constantly imposed on by false analogies and fail to see true analogies.

---

[13] Berkeley complicates this description somewhat at §159.

[14] This imminent confusion of categories leads to problems only a few sections later, at §152, where Berkeley denies that God's language of visible signs possesses an "arbitrary" relation to its tangible signifieds: "There is, indeed, this difference betwixt the signification of tangible figures by visible figures, and of ideas by words—that whereas the latter is variable and uncertain, depending altogether on the arbitrary appointment of men, the former is fixed, and, immutably the same in all times and places. . . . Hence it is, that the voice of the Author of nature, which speaks to our eyes, is not liable to that misinterpretation and ambiguity that languages of human contrivance are unavoidably subject to." Berkeley wishes to insist on the invariability of God's sign-language and yet to dissociate himself from any suggestion that God is necessarily bound to consistency (see the *Treatise*, §106, where Berkeley writes, concerning the analogous and harmonious relationships of the physical universe, that "there is nothing necessary or essential in the case, but it depends entirely on the will of the Governing Spirit"). The result is that the principle of arbitrariness is inconsistently applied; sometimes suggesting lack of *resemblance*, sometimes suggesting *nonnecessity*.

In *Alciphron, or the Minute Philosopher* (1732), Berkeley undertakes to distinguish between two traditional conceptions of "analogy."[15] One of them, he suggests, will help us understand just how it is that we can "know" God; the other would mislead us into thinking that our knowledge of God can never be "direct or proper." Yet Berkeley will not go so far as to suggest that one of these conceptions of "analogy" is true and the other false. Rather, "analogy" divides into a literal and a metaphorical component. Will this allow us to reinterpret the false-analogy/true-analogy distinction of the *Essay* as a distinction between metaphoric analogy and literal analogy? Analogy, writes Berkeley, has both an original, "strict" signification and a "looser and translated sense":

> Every one knows that *analogy* is a Greek word used by mathematicians to signify a similitude of proportions. . . . And, although proportion strictly signifies the habitude or relation of one quantity to another, yet, in a looser and translated sense, it hath been applied to signify every other similitude of relations or habitudes whatsoever. Hence the Schoolmen tell us there is analogy between intellect and sight. (§21)[16]

Berkeley might well have added that Locke, as well as "the Schoolmen," had relied heavily on the "analogy between intellect and sight." Berkeley's privileged analogy is of a different order. As he proceeds to elaborate on his distinction between "proper" and derivative senses of "analogy," the latter type becomes more explicitly a "metaphorical" sense:

> For the further clearing of this point, it is to be observed that a twofold analogy is distinguished by the schoolmen—metaphorical and proper. Of the first kind there are frequent instances in Holy Scripture, attributing human parts and passions to God. When he is represented as having a finger, an eye, or an ear; when He is said to repent, to be angry, or grieved; every one sees that analogy is metaphorical. Because those parts and passions, taken in the proper signification, must in every degree necessarily, and from the formal nature of the thing, include imperfection. . . . But the case is different when wisdom and knowledge are attributed to God. . . . Knowledge . . . in the

---

[15] George Berkeley, *Alciphron: Or, the Minute Philosopher*, in *Works*, vol. 2, §21. All subsequent citations will be to paragraph numbers from this edition.

[16] Cf. Quintilian, *Institutio Oratoria*, 4 vols., trans. H. E. Butler (London: William Heinemann, 1920–22), vol. 1, chap. 6, 3: "But in all these cases we have need of a critical judgment, especially as regards *analogy* (a Greek term for which a Latin equivalent has been found in *proportion*)."

proper formal meaning of the word may be attributed to God proportionably, that is, preserving a proportion to the infinite nature of God. We may say, therefore, that as God is infinitely above man, so is the knowledge of God infinitely above the knowledge of man.

Berkeley does not deny the value of metaphor. His point, rather, is that metaphor confesses a radical nontranslatability between two orders of facts (there are certain aspects of God's being to which we give representation only at the expense of logical incoherence or self-contradiction), whereas "proper" analogy relates two orders of facts that differ in degree but not in formal structure. Analogy is usually thought of as a relation between relations; but Berkeley's "metaphorical analogy" involves orders or categories so incommensurable that any postulated relationship among them is a heuristic fiction rather than an objective representation of similar functions or structures. Accordingly, the Scholastic and Lockean representation of "intellect" in terms of "sight" is, in Berkeley's estimation, metaphorical, whereas Berkeley's own consistent representation of "sight" in terms of "language" is quite explicitly *not* metaphorical. (Berkeley, as we shall see, reserves the term "metaphorical" to describe the application of sensory figures—for example, "upper" and "lower"—to "things that are intangible, and of a spiritual nature— . . . thoughts and desires, [the] passions, and in general all the modifications of [the] soul" [ibid., §94]).

But this now leaves us with three different linguistic models. There is the system of "strict" but arbitrary signification that characterizes a "language," whether a verbal language or the language of visual ideas. Aside from this there are relationships by some species of "analogy"; but this further breaks down into analogy "proper" (or "strict")—exemplified by mathematical or quantitative relations—and analogy in the "loose," "translated," or "metaphoric" sense, exemplified, paradoxically, by rhetorical language. To understand "analogy" in the metaphorical sense, is, ironically, to understand analogy *as* metaphor, that is, as generic "similitude." "Language" is something that at once contains and is defined both by and in contrast with "analogy."[17]

[17] For a similar classical caution concerning the perils of systematic analogizing in linguistics and grammar, see ibid.: "Language is based on reason, antiquity, authority and usage. Reason finds its chief support in analogy and sometimes in etymolygy. . . . The essence of *analogy* is the testing of all subjects of doubt by the application of some standard of comparison about which there is no question, the proof that is to say of the uncertain by

According to Berkeley, our most useful modes of knowledge and signification are quite expressly *not* analogical. Both the language of sense experience—which God "speaks" to us (ibid., §§32, 152; *Alciphron*, §14)—and the human institutions of verbal language are distinguished by the arbitrary imposition of signs. And yet Berkeley acknowledges that analogy is an important critical and investigative tool. First, we would not recognize the arbitrariness of the relationship between our visual and tangible experiences if it were not for our recognition of the analogy between optical and verbal language. Second, Berkeley acknowledges that "analogy" is essential if we are to *extend* our knowledge through the admittedly useful inductive procedures of scientific investigation.

For Berkeley, "reflection" results in the recognition of an analogy (between sight and language) that itself reveals to us the nonanalogical relationship of signifiers to signifieds. This reduction of all cognitive processes into questions of language in turn neutralizes the specular implications of the figure *reflection*. Neither "seeing" ourselves nor "seeing" what happens when we "see" can be models of any critical significance. Any specular model that fails of translation into the language model is an illusion, and once we understand the language model properly, the ostensible critical edge or exemplary nature of the specular model seems beside the point.

Why *reflection*, then? Why does Berkeley retain the term as his figure for our most important activities of self-scrutiny? Though Berkeley's *Treatise* opens with a proto-Humean attack on the skeptical and incapacitating consequences of reflection,[18] he uses the term with approval throughout his work, and by the end of the *Dialogues*—the culmination

---

reference to the certain" (1.6.1). "But we must remember that *analogy* cannot be universally applied, as it is often inconsistent with itself" (1.6.12). "Analogy was not sent down from heaven at the creation of mankind to frame the rules of language, but it was discovered after they began to speak and to note the terminations of words used in speech. It is therefore based not on reason but on example, nor is it a law of language, but rather a practice which is observed, being in fact the offspring of usage" (1.6.16).

[18] As soon as we depart from "plain common sense" and "instinct," and begin "to reason, to meditate, and reflect on the nature of things," we become "forlorn" skeptics, according to Berkeley (introduction, §1). For Hume's famous opposition of "reflection" to our instinctive thoughts, perceptions, emotions, and activity, see *A Treatise of Human Nature*, 1.4.1–2. Hume concludes: "As the sceptical doubt arises naturally from a profound and intense reflection on those subjects [the "understanding" and the "senses"], it always encreases, the farther we carry our reflections, whether in opposition or conformity to it. Carelessness and in-attention alone can afford us any remedy" (1.4.2).

of his philosophical development—reflection is responsible for nothing less than our knowledge of God.[19] What accounts for his simultaneous defense and critique of the figure? In order to answer this we must look at Berkeley's changing conception of rhetorical language—of similitude, transference, metaphor, borrowing, and figuration—over the course of his three major philosophical treatises. And in order to do that we shall have to make a detour through two other figures connected to Berkeley's use of reflection: surface and depth.

BERKELEY'S ILLUSORY "SURFACES": FROM "VOICE" TO "IMPRINT" AND BEYOND

The counterintuitive implication of Berkeley's *Essay* on vision, in the words of William James, is the "notion that depth cannot possibly be perceived in terms of purely visual feeling," a notion that in James's estimate had dominated British psychology and philosophy well into the nineteenth century.[20] A further implication is that all objects of visual perception must then be *surfaces* inasmuch as they possess extension but lack depth.[21] Strictly speaking, our visual experience lacks depth because three-dimensionality is simply not a property of optical impressions. "Distance, of itself and immediately," writes Berkeley, "cannot be seen" (§2). Solidity and three-dimensionality are only *tactile* qualities and, though coordinated with, are not derived from our visual impressions: "All that is properly perceived by the visive faculty amounts to no more than colours with their variations, and different proportions of light and shade" (§156). Since our sight cannot of itself yield "an idea of distance," neither can it yield an "idea of a solid or quantity of three dimensions"

---

[19] Berkeley writes: "But that—setting aside all help of astronomy and natural philosophy, all contemplation of the contrivance, order, and adjustment of things—an infinite mind should be necessarily inferred from the bare *existence* of the sensible world, is an advantage to them only who have made this easy reflection: that the sensible world is that which we perceive by our several senses; and that nothing is perceived by the senses beside ideas; and that no idea or archetype of an idea can exist otherwise than in a mind" (*Dialogues*, 305). "All the notion I have of God is obtained by reflecting on my own soul, heightening its powers, and removing its imperfections" (326).

[20] James, *Principles of Psychology*, 2.212.

[21] This is clearly the implication of Berkeley's discussion, though no explicit definition of surfaces as such actually appears in the *Essay*. For an explicit definition of "surface" as extension without "depth," see Hume's *Treatise*, 1.2.4: "A surface is *defin'd* to be length and breadth without depth."

(§154), and these ideas must thus be "*suggested* to the mind" through the constant association of visual with tactile impressions (§§16–17).

It is this rejection of depth—the denial of a visually *immediate* three-dimensional world—that gives Berkeley's philosophy the air of a "gim-crack world of facades." Yet in fact Berkeley's essay on vision neither champions "surfaces" nor depreciates "depths." As we shall see, it is even unclear precisely what a *visual surface* could *be* in Berkeley's scheme. What Berkeley's immaterialist doctrine denies is that matter has an existence independent of the sensations God imparts to our minds; "immaterialism" does not deny our experience of solidity or three-dimensionality (we "experience" these sensations tactilely), *nor does it assert that the visible world is only two-dimensional.* This latter fact is emphasized at the conclusion of the *Essay*, where Berkeley asserts that "planes are no more the immediate object of sight than solids":

> All that is properly perceived by the visive faculty amounts to no more than colours with their variations, and different proportions of light and shade—but the perpetual mutability and fleetingness of those immediate objects of sight render them incapable of being managed after the manner of geometrical figures; . . .
>
> I must confess, it seems to be the opinion of some very ingenious men that flat or plane figures are immediate objects of sight, though they acknowl-edge solids are not. And this opinion of theirs is grounded on what is ob-served in painting, wherein (say they) the ideas immediately imprinted on the mind are only of planes variously coloured, which, by a sudden act of the judgment, are changed into solids: but with a little attention, we shall find the planes here mentioned as the immediate objects of sight are not visible but tangible planes. For, when we say that pictures are planes, we mean thereby that they appear to the touch smooth and uniform. But then this smoothness and uniformity, or, in other words, this planeness of the picture is not perceived immediately by vision; for it appeareth to the eye various and multiform.
>
> From all which we may conclude that planes are no more the immediate object of sight than solids. What we strictly see are not solids, nor yet planes variously coloured—they are only diversity of colours. And some of these suggest to the mind solids, and others plane figures. (§§156–58)

Here Berkeley mocks precisely the distorted version of his philosophy that has had taken on such a fascinating appeal for literary modernism: the idea, parodied by James Joyce in *Ulysses*, that the world jumps sud-

denly into three-dimensional relief once prereflective judgment is added
to our pure optical sensations, which are "really" flat: "The good bishop
of Cloyne took the veil of the temple out of his shovel hat: veil of space
with coloured emblems hatched on its field. Hold hard. Coloured on a
flat: yes, that's right. Flat I see, then think distance, near, far, flat I see,
east, back. Ah, see now. Falls back suddenly, frozen in stereoscope."
Berkeley would in fact reject Stephen Dedalus's description of pure optical
sensation ("veil of space . . . coloured on a flat"), just as he rejects the
"flat or plane figures" offered by "very ingenious men." Our immediate
ideas of optical sensation are neither flat nor planar, because such adjec-
tives refer to tactile rather than to visual qualities.

We can see that Berkeley effectively denies any purely optical distinction between planes and solids. What happens, then, to the category of
"surface" if the distinction between planes and solids, between extension
and distance, is dismantled? Is "surface" ultimately discarded as a mere
rhetorical device devoid of any real visual referent, a strategy for "manag-
ing" the "mutability and fleetingness" of optical sensations? What is the
force of Berkeley's term *visible surface* (e.g., *Essay*, §131) when no *visual*
distinction between planes and solids is allowed? Throughout the *Essay*
and the *Treatise*, "surfaces" are both ubiquitous and chimerical. In his
attempt to deny the existence both of abstract ideas (e.g., a color without
extension or shape) and of a material substratum to experience (e.g., a
"material" cube to which both our visual and tangible impressions refer,
and in which they both inhere), Berkeley is led, respectively, both to
affirming the ubiquity of surfaces in our visual impressions and yet to
denying any "strict" existence of a visible surface.[22] What, then, could
constitute a visual surface?

If there is a source for the powerful figure of surface within Berkeley's
work, it is not to be found in his technical speculations on visual and
tangible surface, or, in fact, in the essay on vision at all, since the analytical method of the *Essay* dispenses with surfaces as rigorously as it does
with visual "depths." Yet within the *Essay* are to be found the origins of
Berkeley's trope of surface: his account of language. According to Colin
Murray Turbayne, Berkeley conceives of "the language of nature . . . as a
written language," and Turbayne calls particular attention to the Lockean metaphor of impression and imprinting in the *Treatise* and the *Es-*

---

[22] Both Berkeley's attack on abstraction and his denial of a material substratum are
aimed, of course, at Locke. For Locke's discussion of the distinction between primary and
secondary qualities, and his definition of abstract ideas, see his *Essay*, 2.8 and 2.11.

say.[23] John Richetti also emphasizes Berkeley's fascination (in the *Essay*) with the physical surface of written language. Berkeley, writes Richetti, believed that "we decipher . . . visual signs in an incomplete fashion, bowled over by the surface complexity of it all, marvelling at the closely printed pages."[24]

It is surely a fascinating testimony to the power of the surface/writing motif that both Turbayne and Richetti claim to recognize its presence within the *Essay*, a text whose principal analogy for perception is phono-centric (i.e., "voice") and in which Berkeley is largely unconcerned with the activities of reading and writing. Throughout the later *Treatise*, it is true, Berkeley consistently describes God as "imprinting" sensations on our minds, but in the earlier *Essay* the controlling analogy is that of *voice* rather than of print. That Berkeley is self-conscious about this choice of analogies is indicated by his parenthetically calling attention to its awk-wardness when he first employs it. Describing the way in which visible objects suggest familiar tangible sensations to us, Berkeley writes: "The object speaks (if I may say so) with words that the eye is well acquainted with" (§32). Written language would be a less powerful analogy for Berkeley here because his intention is to show how two categories that are in reality distinct (visible and tangible sensations) come to be identified and conflated through habitual association. Though on the one hand Berkeley recognizes that graphic signs are as arbitrarily related to mean-ing as are phonic ones (and thus provide as suitable an analogy for a relationship whose conventional nature has become invisible to us), on the other hand he believes that the mediating function of written symbols is too conspicuous. Writing does not mystify or obscure its own conven-tionality the way speech does. (In his only discussion of writing in the *Essay*, Berkeley describes "written words" as having a relationship to "things" as well as to "sounds" [§§140, 143], thus skirting the question of whether writing is at a further remove from its object than is voice).[25] Accordingly, in the *Essay*, Berkeley chooses *hearing* rather than *reading* (or, indeed, "imprinting") as the paradigm for a habitual principle of association that has become mistaken for a natural and immediate act of

[23] See Turbayne, "Berkeley's Metaphysical Grammar," 14–15. The locus classicus can be found in Locke, *Essay*, 1.3 and 2.1.

[24] See Richetti, *Philosophical Writing*, 134.

[25] Locke skirts—or resolves—the issue in another way by referring to words as "sensi-ble Marks of *Ideas*," thus granting material status to the very concept of language. See Locke, *Essay*, 2.2.1.

comprehension. The reason we have difficulty in separating the "second-ary" objects of sight (figure and extension) from the "proper" objects (light and color), he argues, is that the two are as habitually and closely connected as are the meanings of words with their *sounds*:

> No sooner do we *hear* the words of a familiar language pronounced in our *ears* but the ideas corresponding thereto present themselves to our minds: in the very same instant the *sound* and the meaning enter the under-standing: so closely are they united that it is not in our power to keep out the one except we exclude the other also. We even act in all respects as if we *heard* the very thoughts themselves. So likewise the secondary objects, or those which are only suggested by sight, do often more strongly affect us, and are more regarded, than the proper objects of that sense; along with which they enter into the mind, and with which they have a far more strict connex-ion than ideas have with words. (§51, my emphasis)

The comparison of sense perception in general to the "hearing" of a language is not arbitrary, because for Berkeley it is axiomatic that our sense perceptions are nothing more or less than God *speaking* to us:

> It is therefore plain that visible figures are of the same use in geometry that words are. And the one may as well be accounted the object of that science as the other; neither of them being any otherwise concerned therein than as they represent or suggest to the mind the particular tangible figures connected with them. There is, indeed, this difference betwixt the significa-tion of tangible figures by visible figures, and of ideas by words—that where-as the latter is variable and uncertain, depending altogether on the arbitrary appointment of men, the former is fixed, and, immutably the same in all times and places. . . . Hence it is, that the *voice of the Author of nature, which speaks to our eyes*, is not liable to that misinterpretation and ambi-guity that languages of human contrivance are unavoidably subject to. (§152, my emphasis)

We noted previously (p. 103) that this passage is somewhat at odds with Berkeley's earlier contention that God's optical language and the human institutions of verbal language operate analogously, that is, each in accor-dance with principles of "habitual connexion" rather than of "likeness or identity of nature" (§147). The catachresis of God "speak[ing] to our eyes" (which Berkeley will later ridicule [*Treatise*, §142]) foregrounds the difficulties in this "metaphoric" (as opposed to "proportional") analogy likening God's actions to a language. The apparent contradiction and the catachresis have two causes. First, Berkeley is quite self-consciously maintaining a counterintuitive position here, and the catachresis challenges us to see this; second, Berkeley needs to avoid the figure of "surface," and thus the figure of "imprinted" language, in his description of God's actions. For Berkeley, God's "voice" is not a mere figure for divine authority, as Berkeley feared the more graphic figure of written language might seem to imply; God's voice constitutes the world itself at every moment.[26]

Yet before we can comprehend the world as voice, Berkeley argues, we must first comprehend it as an *alien voice*. Accordingly, Berkeley concludes the *Essay* by asking his reader to "consider how hard it is for any one to hear the words of his native language pronounced in his ears without understanding them" and suggests that the (philosophically necessary) attempt to "disentangle in our thoughts the proper objects of sight from those of touch" requires that we put ourselves "in the posture of a foreigner that never learnt the language, so as to be affected barely with the sounds themselves, and not perceive the signification annexed to them" (§159). The final "posture" of the *Essay* is to reinforce the analogy of voice, and thus to set aside troubling questions about the function of surfaces, since the figure of *surface* is drawn primarily from the visual world.

If the *Essay* raises a question that it cannot answer (i.e., What is a "visual surface"?) and avoids it by imagining the world in terms of a nonspatial figure ("the voice of the Author of Nature"), then the *Treatise* would seem to subvert this solution. Almost from the beginning, the physical world is described in terms of "lines," "surfaces," and "solids,"[27] and from the very first sentence the world is figured as "ideas . . . imprinted upon the senses" by God. As Turbayne and Richetti have noted, the dominant figure of the *Treatise* is the Lockean–Cartesian *imprint*. Not only is the world imprinted upon our minds by God; our own capacity for "reflection" also produces "imprint[s]" of "ideas, sensations, [and] notions" (§74; though later in the *Treatise* Berkeley distinguishes between the ideas "*generated* from within" and those "*imprinted* by a Spirit" [§90, my

---

[26] Cf. a similar passage in *Alciphron*, where Crito describes our visual sensations as God's "optic language," "equivalent to a constant creation, betokening an immediate act of power and providence" (§14).

[27] Berkeley, *Treatise*, §§8, 11, 18. Cf. Berkeley's *Essay*, where the first reference to "surface" occurs two-thirds of the way through the text.

emphasis]). This scheme not only borrows Locke's favorite analogy but also more or less duplicates the Lockean distinction between ideas of sensation and those of reflection.[28] Yet the *Treatise* is as hostile to Lockean notions of abstraction and primary qualities as was Berkeley's earlier *Essay*. What, then, explains this crucial shift in Berkeley's description of God's linguistic mode, from voice to print?

Berkeley's ambivalence about the nature and existence of surfaces in the *Essay* arose from the fact that he allowed the tangible world to exist outside the mind but the visible world to exist only in it: "[All] visible things are equally in the mind, and take up no part of the external space; and consequently are equidistant from any tangible thing which exists without the mind" (*Essay*, §111). By assigning the objects of visible and tangible sensation respectively to two distinct and incommensurable spaces—"within" and "without" the mind—Berkeley made it impossible to assimilate the concepts of visible and tangible "surface" in a single graphic figure—thus his recourse to the trope of "voice." In the *Treatise*, however, Berkeley takes the bolder step of denying the externality of "tangible things."[29] This places all modes of sense perception on a level, as it were, and allows them to be collected in a single figure—ironically, if not contradictorily, in the planar and graphic figure of the world as "imprint."

The connection between "imprinting" and the newly equivalent relationship between visible and tangible impressions is demonstrated in the passage from the *Treatise* where Berkeley addresses the apparent inconsistency of the *Essay*. Here, Berkeley argues that our coordinated optical and tangible impressions of a particular object may occur at *temporal* distances from one another but cannot occupy distinct *spaces* (i.e., "within" and "without" the mind). The apparent failure of the earlier *Essay* to dispense entirely with the interior/exterior distinction is now retrospectively excused as a mere tactical oversight:

> That the proper objects of sight neither exist without the mind, nor are the images of external things, was shown even in that treatise [the *Essay*]. Though throughout the same the contrary be supposed true of tangible objects—not that to suppose that vulgar error was necessary for establishing the notion therein laid down, but because it was beside my purpose to examine and refute it in a discourse concerning *Vision*. So that in strict truth

[28] See Locke, *Essay*, 2.1.4.
[29] Externality always meaning, for Berkeley, exteriority to *mind*. See *Treatise*, §90.

the ideas of sight, when we apprehend by them distance and things placed at a distance, do not suggest or mark out to us things actually existing at a distance, but only admonish us what ideas of touch will be imprinted in our minds at such or such distances of time, and in consequence of such or such actions. It is, I say, evident from what has been said in the foregoing parts of this Treatise, and in sect. 147 and elsewhere of the Essay concerning Vision, that visible ideas are the Language whereby the Governing Spirit on whom we depend informs us what tangible ideas he is about to imprint upon us, in case we excite this or that motion in our own bodies. (§44)

Berkeley describes the interior/exterior distinction of the *Essay* as a heuristic rather than a logical or necessary one.[30] More significantly, however, he now summarizes a passage from the *Essay* (§147) that had referred indifferently to the "language of the Author of Nature" (without any distinction between speech and writing) as a passage specifically about ideas "imprint[ed] upon us." Despite this retrospective redescription, the rhetorical differences between the *Essay* and the *Treatise* (and between their respective models of cognition) remain clear. Where the *Essay* had ended with a reference to the "voice of the Author of nature," and had challenged us to try to "hear" our actual sense perceptions as a "foreign language" (§§152, 159), the *Treatise* ends by asserting that God's presence is "plainly *legible*," despite (and, in fact, *because* of) the artificiality of "this mighty machine of nature" whose "motions and various phenomena strike on our senses" (§151, my emphasis).

Clearly it is the rhetorical figures of the *Treatise*, and not those of the *Essay*, which are the source for the traditional characterization of Berkeley as a philosopher of "surfaces." In the *Essay*, Berkeley's purpose was to distinguish the objects of visible sense perception from the objects of tangible sense perception. Given this project of *differentiation*, the interior/exterior distinction is helpful, and the figurative expressions

---

[30] J. D. Mabbott defends Berkeley's contention that an external tangible world was not presupposed in the *Essay*. See Mabbott, "The Place of God in Berkeley's Philosophy," in *A Treatise Concerning the Principles of Human Knowledge*, ed. Colin M. Turbayne (Indianapolis: Bobbs-Merrill, 1970). Mabbott points out that Berkeley had already refuted such an idea in his commonplace book a few years earlier and that the apparent shift between *Essay* and *Treatise* was part of an "intentional policy of gradualness" (213–14). However, it is one of the axioms of this study that a major shift in the figurative scheme whereby a philosophical theory is presented cannot be devoid of consequences for the theory itself. Whether or not Berkeley had wrestled already in the commonplace book with the issue of an external tangible world, the rhetorical figures of the *Essay* clearly reintroduce the possibility of such a world.

"within" and "without" the mind are assigned strategically to the faculties of sight and touch, respectively. In turn, the only figure that can account for God's production of both sense experience ("without the mind") and ideas of reflection "within the mind," is "voice."

In the *Treatise*, however, Berkeley's primary object is not to distinguish the various faculties of sense perception but to challenge the putatively Lockean distinction between sensation and substratum (or between idea and matter). Given the project of *denying* this central distinction, the interior/exterior distinction becomes a rhetorical liability. Once the three-dimensional distinction between the inside and the outside of the mind is dissolved (i.e., once Berkeley denies the possibility of physical objects existing exterior to all minds), the entire world, including individual minds, can be described in terms of a two-dimensional image—and everything becomes an "imprint."

In trying to escape the implications of the *Essay's* interior/exterior model, Berkeley finds himself in the *Treatise* relying on a figure of surface; but the "gross" implications of such graphic figures are in turn denounced in the subsequent *Dialogues* (1713). In the *Dialogues*, Berkeley recognizes that in order to deny the idea/matter distinction it is not necessary to deny the interior/exterior distinction and to reduce everything to a printed plane.[31] Instead, the implicitly spatial distinction between the inside and outside of the mind is transformed into an abstract, logical distinction. Instead of being "outside" of the mind, ideas are to be conceived as existing *independently* of the mind:

> *Phil.* . . . It is evident that the things I perceive are my own ideas, and that no idea can exist unless it be in a mind: nor is it less plain that these ideas or things by me perceived, either themselves or their archetypes, exist *independently* of *my* mind, since I know myself not to be their author, it being out of my power to determine at pleasure what particular ideas I shall be affected with upon opening my eyes or ears: they must therefore exist *in some other Mind*, whose Will it is they should be *exhibited* to me. (307, my emphasis)

> *Phil.* . . . When I deny sensible things an existence *out of the mind*, I do not mean my mind in particular, but all minds. Now, it is plain they have an

---

[31] Richetti writes, "Berkeley is protesting that outer is 'inner,' that an invidious opposition of outer and inner is nonsense" (*Philosophic Writing*, 176). What Richetti takes to be a general Berkeleyan project of dismantling conventional metaphors, however, I take to be a more local and strategic project concerning the interior/exterior scheme, a project begun only within the *Dialogues* and in response to specific problems of philosophical rhetoric raised by the *Treatise*.

existence *exterior* to my mind; since I find them by experience to be *independent* of it. There is therefore some other mind *wherein they exist*, during the intervals between the times of my perceiving them: as likewise they did before my birth, and would do after my supposed annihilation. And, as the same is true with regard to all other finite created spirits, it necessarily follows there is an *omnipresent eternal Mind*, which knows and comprehends all things, and *exhibits* them to our view. (325, emphasis altered)

As the empirical and spatial category of "exteriority" is transformed into the logical category of "independence," so God's graphic "imprinting" is reconceived as the more abstract action of "exhibiting" (and also, later, of "producing" and "affecting" [e.g., §§307, 308]).[32] There are only two references in the *Dialogues* to the activity of "imprinting," and since the analogy is no longer crucial for Berkeley's theory he even takes the opportunity of warning against its misleading connotations:

> *Phil.* Look you, *Hylas*, when I speak of objects as existing in the mind, or imprinted on the senses, I would not be understood in the gross literal sense—as when bodies are said to exist in a place, or a seal to make an impression upon wax. My meaning is only that the mind comprehends or perceives them; and that it is affected from without, or by some being distinct from itself. (346)

Berkeley's ability to retain (or at least acknowledge) some form of the interior/exterior distinction by recasting it as a logical one obviates any need for the rigidly two-dimensional figure of "imprinting"; Berkeley now allows himself to criticize the empiricist rhetoric of "impressions" and "imprints." This critique, in turn, is extended to cover all putatively analogical descriptions of the mind's operations. It is in accordance with the "general analogy of language," argues Philonous, that "mental operations" are "signified by words borrowed from sensible things; as is plain in the terms *comprehend, reflect, discourse, &c.*, which, being applied to the mind, must not be taken in their gross original sense" (347). For Berkeley, this "general analogy" operates purely metaphorically, since it has "nothing to do with external Objects" and is not a metonymy or proportional analogy grounded in congruency, contiguity, or some logically articulated relationship. There is a significant departure from Locke

[32] It should be noted, however, that even the term "independence" has a figurative component (cf. Milton's "pendant world" in book 2 of *Paradise Lost*), one allied, ironically, with the figure of depth.

here in that Berkeley denies we can *learn* anything by paying attention to the sensory figures that constitute language's "general analogy." Etymology reveals nothing to us about the origins or sources of knowledge, since for Berkeley all knowledge simply comes to us immediately from God.

DEPTH AND IMMATERIALISM

The drama of Berkeley's argument, as it unfolds over the course of the *Essay*, the *Treatise*, and the *Dialogues*, is generated by an almost obsessive need to anticipate ostensibly commonsense objections to his philosophy. While the *Essay* is concerned chiefly with refuting scholastic and philosophical theories, almost half of the *Treatise* (§§ 34–84) is devoted to a rhetorical confrontation with an imaginary lay interlocutor (addressed generally in the second person, e.g., "You will say perhaps . . ."), and the *Dialogues* are given over entirely in form to a dramatized debate between two young men, both claiming to argue against metaphysical discourse and on behalf of common sense (Philonous contests the existence of "what *Philosophers* call *material substance*," and Hylas objects that immaterialism is "repugnant to Common Sense" [*Dialogues* 262–63]). Berkeley conceives the *Dialogues* as a popularization of the ideas expounded in the *Treatise*, and his tendency toward the dramatization of immaterialism is intimately connected with the figure of depth.[33] Hylas, who embodies a popular understanding of, and resistance to, immaterialism, also represents a set of rhetorical habits that Berkeley recognizes must be satisfied if immaterialism is to claim the allegiance of common sense. This set of habits includes certain conventional ways of talking about aesthetic and spiritual experience, in which the figure of depth plays a prominent role—conventions that can be seen at a glance in the moral and literary essays of the day.

It is significant that the name "Hylas" (etymologically an allusion to the Greek *hyle*, "matter") is associated with beauty, nature, and, allusively, with the trope of *depth* (Hylas, the armor-bearer of Hercules, leans

---

[33] Both Richetti (*Philosophical Writing*, 122) and David Marshall (writing on Shaftesbury in *The Figure of Theater*) point to the significance of a shift toward the *dialogue* form over the course of a writer's career. Richetti sees Berkeley's choice as dictated by the need to combat the *recurrent* tendency toward philosophical error on the part of his readers; Marshall sees Shaftesbury's choice as part of a complex strategy for avoiding the ostensible artificiality of "theatricality" in writing, while leaving for the reader the fiction of being an objective witness rather than a partisan participant (29, 30–32, 45, 65–66).

over a forest pool and is drawn down into it by a love-struck water nymph). Hylas thus represents a vast range of sensual experiences and poetic sentiments that would seem to have no place in the austere Berkeleyan surface-world of "imprints" and geometric figures. The task of the *Dialogues* is precisely to demonstrate that the Hylean motifs of sensuality, aesthetics, and depth are not challenged—either as common-sense experiences or as rhetorical traditions—by Philonous's claims. It is thus Philonous (the lover of mind and reason) who employs the figure of depth most conspicuously, and who articulates the aesthetic, sensual, and spiritual values that Berkeley intends his philosophy to confirm rather than deny:

> *Phil.* Look! are not the fields covered with a delightful verdure? Is there not something in the woods and groves, in the rivers and clear springs, that soothes, that delights, that transports the soul? At the prospect of the *wide and deep ocean*, or some huge mountain whose top is lost in the clouds, or of an old gloomy forest, are not our minds filled with a pleasing horror? . . . How vivid and radiant is the lustre of the fixed stars! How magnificent and rich that negligent profusion with which they appear to be scattered throughout the whole *azure vault*! Yet, if you take the telescope, it brings into your sight a new host of stars that escape the naked eye. Here they seem contiguous and minute, but to a nearer view immense orbs of light are various distances, *far sunk in the abyss of space*. (302–3, my emphasis)

It was never Berkeley's intention to deny the legitimacy of such sentiments or expressions, and one of Philonous's consistent claims in the *Dialogues* is that the doctrine of immaterialism challenges only the description of the world offered by philosophers, not the descriptions conventionally offered by either lay persons or poets. The same position is developed by Shaftesbury in *The Moralists*, where a similar tension develops between the theist Theocles's "deep . . . romantic way" (and "sublime" rhetoric of depth) and the ironic rhetoric of surface employed by his "moralist" antagonist Philocles.[34] Theocles laments that he has been unable in his "poetic ecstasies" to "have led you [Philocles] into some deep view of Nature" and later claims that Philocles must become more "deeply engaged" in these issues (128, 141). Philocles, in turn, protests ironically that "I am now obliged to go far in the pursuit of beauty, which lies very absconded and deep; and if so, I am well assured that my enjoyments

---

[34] Shaftesbury, *Characteristics*, 2.124–25.

hitherto have been very shallow. I have dwelt, it seems, all this while upon the surface, and enjoyed only a kind of slight superficial beauties, having never gone in search of beauty itself, but of what I fancied such" (130). Yet Philocles never denies the poetic significance and appeal of Theocles's apostrophes to Nature's "deep horrors," "deep precipices," and "deep shades"; he criticizes only Theocles's insistence on drawing theological inferences from them.[35]

The distinction between the unobjectionable practical use of figures of speech in "common" discourse and the objectionable philosophical conclusions drawn from such figures by philosophers is a virtual commonplace of late seventeenth-century and early eighteenth-century philosophy.[36] Nevertheless, if a rhetoric so interfused with figures of depth is to be allowed, and even celebrated, within Berkeley's system, then the Lockean rhetoric of surface "imprints" will appear increasingly awkward and problematic. If figures of surface begin to lose their importance in the *Dialogues* (as we shall see they do), it is not only because of the shift from a three-dimensional interior/exterior distinction toward a more abstract dependent/independent distinction but also because of pressure from the figure of depth as it is asserted for rhetorical and dramatic purposes.

One further aspect of Philonous's apostrophe to nature deserves some consideration. After his reference to the "abyss of space," Philonous continues:

> Now you must call imagination to your aid. The feeble narrow sense cannot descry innumerable worlds revolving round the central fires; and in those worlds the energy of an all-perfect Mind displayed in endless forms. But, neither sense nor imagination are big enough to comprehend the boundless extent, with all its glittering furniture. Though the labouring mind exert and strain each power to its utmost reach, there still stands out ungrasped a surplusage immeasurable. (303)

Unlike the famous passages in Locke that figure philosophical inquiry (and particularly the philosophical conception of infinity) in terms of the ocean's depth, there is no final adjuration to "reflect" or "return" to a

[35] See Ernst Cassirer, "Fundamental Problems of Aesthetics," in *The Philosophy of the Enlightenment*: "Although in the apostrophes to nature in the *Moralists* Shaftesbury shows a profound sensitivity to all the charms of the sublime, yet he always treats the idea of form as the fundamental principle of aesthetics" (329).

[36] See, e.g., Locke, *Essay*, 2.21.20, 3.9.3–8, and 3.11.2–3; and Berkeley, *Treatise*, §§51–52, and *Dialogues*, 358.

more humble inquiry in this passage. Berkeley is entirely content, as is Shaftesbury, to accept the aesthetic thematization of "depth" as something sublime and inspirational, so long as epistemological consequences are not deduced from such descriptions. The rhetoric of depth indeed speaks to our sense of awe at the prospect of God's creation; and furthermore, we can interpret our perception of the natural world as "a direct and immediate demonstration . . . of the *being of God*" (304); but this is done *immediately* and without the aid of theology, "science," "reason," or "philosophy":

> Divines and philosophers had proved beyond all controversy, from the beauty and usefulness of the several parts of the creation, that it was the workmanship of God. But that—setting aside all help of astronomy and natural philosophy, all contemplation of the contrivance, order, and adjustment of things—an infinite mind should be necessarily inferred from the bare *existence* of the sensible world, is an advantage to them only who have made this easy reflection: that the sensible world is that which we perceive by our several senses; and that nothing is perceived by the senses beside ideas; and that no idea or archetype of an idea can exist otherwise than in a mind. You may now, without any laborious search into the sciences, without any subtlety of reason, or tedious length of discourse, oppose and baffle the most strenuous advocate for Atheism. (305)

In the rather exceptional passage that begins this sequence ("Look! are not the fields covered . . ."), Berkeley lets his philosophical protagonist speak for a moment in the moral-literary rhetoric of the day. Despite the consistent denial of visual "depth" throughout Berkeley's work, we are momentarily treated to a description of "deep oceans," "azure vaults," and "abyss[es] of space." And Berkeley's claim for such poetic sensations is that they lead us by "immediate" and "easy reflection" to an acknowledgment of God's existence.

At first glance we would appear to be closer here to Kant's third Critique than to Locke's reflections on infinity. In a famous passage from the *Critique of Aesthetic Judgement*, Kant too suggests that our sense of nature's sublime "finality" and "totality" cannot be grounded in rational or scientific estimations:

> So, if we call the sight of the starry heaven *sublime*, we must not found our estimate of it upon any concepts of worlds inhabited by rational beings, with the bright spots, which we see filling the space above us, as their suns moving

in orbits prescribed for them with the wisest regard to ends. But we must take it, just as it strikes the eye, as a broad and all-embracing canopy: . . . Similarly, as to the prospect of the ocean, we are not to regard it as we, with our minds stored with knowledge on a variety of matters, (which, however, is not contained in the immediate intuition,) are wont to represent it in *thought*, as, let us say, a spacious realm of aquatic creatures, or as the mighty reservoirs from which are drawn the vapours that fill the air with clouds of moisture for the good of the land, or yet as an element which no doubt divides continent from continent, but at the same time affords the means of the greatest commercial intercourse between them—for in this way we get nothing beyond teleological judgements. Instead of this we must be able to see sublimity in the ocean, regarding it, as the poets do, according to what the impression upon the eye reveals, as, let us say, in its calm, a clear mirror of water bounded only by the heavens.[37]

Like Berkeley, Kant insists that there is something about nature that is best comprehended *rhetorically* ("as the poets do"). The crucial difference, however, is that Kant is only trying to account for our aesthetic appreciation of nature, while for Berkeley the very existence of God is at stake in such appreciation. Kant excludes not only empirical calculations but *teleological* judgments as well from our estimation of natural sublimity, whereas for Berkeley it is precisely our immediate intuition of God's hand in the natural world that constitutes our sense of the sublime.

Philonous's paean to nature ultimately remains closer to Locke than to Kant in its refusal to link cognitive failure with a rhetoric of depth. The rhetoric of depth, Berkeley implicitly admits, is finally indissociable from the celebration of God's handiwork. But the *recognition* of that fact is not represented as a deepening of experience or as a plumbing of depths. It is, rather, a *reflection* we make upon the "language" of God and upon the language of the poets concerning the language of God. As the line between rhetorical language and the putatively nonrhetorical analogies out of which experience is structured begins to disintegrate in the *Dialogues*, "reflection" begins to emerge as that activity that both sustains common discourse and yet guards against the philosophical errors latent in common figures of speech. This double function of reflection will allow Berkeley, finally, to represent his entire philosophical undertaking as yet a third kind of reflection—that is, as a "revolt" in the sense of a "return."

[37] Kant, *Critique of Aesthetic Judgement*, 1.2.29.

"EXCEPT ONLY IN A METAPHORICAL SENSE":
REFLECTION AND THE RETREAT TO COMMON SENSE

Figures of surface and depth take on different overtones and degrees of prominence at different points in these three Berkeleyan texts. In part this is because they are in service to a shifting philosophical project (or at least to a philosophical project whose emphasis undergoes shifts). There is another factor, however, affecting the dynamic of the surface/depth relationship, and that is the shift in Berkeley's attitude toward rhetorical figuration itself as it develops over the course of his three major works.

In a passage from the *Essay* that we have already touched on, Berkeley discusses the conventional explanation of the inverted relationship between retinal images and supposedly "external" objects, and in outlining the explanation he employs the phrase "the bottom of the eye" (§88).[38] It is the first use of the word "bottom" in the *Essay*, and only a few paragraphs later he concludes his critique by writing that "it remains, therefore, that we look for some other explication of this difficulty. And I believe it not impossible to find one, provided we *examine it to the bottom*, and carefully distinguish between the ideas of sight and touch" (§91, my emphasis). This is the first occurence in the *Essay* of the expression *examining something to the bottom*, and it is striking that the first figurative use of the word *bottom* should follow so closely upon its first discursive usage. Until this point, Berkeley has made frequent use of such figures of speech as examining something *further*, or looking into something more *closely*, but not of examining an idea or a problem *to the bottom*. The coincidence appears even more striking when in the following paragraphs, concerning the Molyneux Question, Berkeley explicitly raises the issue of the relationship between physical sensations and their figurative application to mental phenomena:

> It is certain that a man actually blind . . . would, by the sense of feeling, attain to have ideas of upper and lower. By the motion of his hand, he might discern the situation of any tangible object placed within his reach. That part on which he felt himself supported, or towards which he perceived his body to gravitate, he would term "lower," and the contrary to this "upper;" and accordingly denominate whatsoever objects he touched.
> But then, whatever judgments he makes concerning the situation of

[38] The phrase is common in period optics. See, e.g., Newton's *Opticks* (New York: Dover, 1952), 15.

objects are confined to those only that are perceivable by touch. All those that are intangible, and of a spiritual nature—his thoughts and desires, his passions, and in general all the modifications of his soul—to these he would never apply the terms upper and lower, except only in a metaphorical sense. (§§93–94)

Berkeley's purpose in this passage and in the immediately following paragraphs is to explain how "terms relating to the position of tangible objects" are "transferred" to our "ideas of sight" by association, so that we come to designate visual sensations with terms that properly designate only tangible sensations (e.g., *down*ward):

> To the immediate objects of sight, considered in themselves, [we should] not attribute the terms high and low. It must therefore be on account of some circumstances which attend them. And these, it is plain, are the actions of turning the eye up and down, which suggest a very obvious reason why the mind should denominate the objects of sight accordingly high or low. And, without this motion of the eye—this turning it up and down in order to discern different objects—doubtless "erect," "inverse," and other the like terms relating to the position of tangible objects, would never have been transferred, or in any degree apprehended to belong to the ideas of sight, the mere act of seeing including nothing in it to that purpose. (§98)

It turns out that the explanation for the "transference" of terms is a physiological one: the tangible sensation of the eye moving up and down instructs us to coordinate the accompanying visible sensations with a tangible world that we have already mapped out by touch.[39] In rhetorical terms we can designate this associational contiguity as a relationship of

[39] Richetti, in explaining Berkeley's theory of analogy, also avoids the specifically linguistic aspect of analogy. Berkeley's theory, Richetti argues, involves a general transformation of external into internal relationships. However, Richetti mentions only the transformation of physiological analogies into *thought*, not their transformation into language, and he describes the process simply as one of *imitation*: "Berkeley begins with an elaboration of the mind's connections with the world in which visual and physical contiguity and adjacency are affirmed and then gradually transformed into deeper and more difficult relationships, first epistemological then metaphysical and theological. . . . In Berkeley's elaboration of its progress, mind changes its relationship to the world from extrinsic to intrinsic, learning in effect to imitate the divine mind, which maintains the forms of nature intimately and continuously" (*Philosophical Writing*, 143). What Berkeley describes as the "exceptional" nature of linguistic analogy is not acknowledged here by Richetti, and similarly Berkeley himself found the issue impossible to pursue or explain, opting instead for a more general theory about *all* analogy in the *Dialogues*.

metonymy. But the physiological explanation then renders even more problematic the phenomenon to which Berkeley had only a few paragraphs earlier alluded, that is, the "metaphorical" transference of terms of tangible relation to functions of the mind. Though the metonymic theory of "transference" gives a historical or etiological explanation to the ultimately false analogy that relates tangible signs to optical signs, it does not explain our *metaphorical* application of a rhetoric of sensation to ideas and feelings.[40] Berkeley identifies this latter phenomenon as an exceptional case, and one not requiring explanation ("things that are intangible, and of a spiritual nature . . . to these [one] would never apply the terms upper and lower, *except only in a metaphorical sense*"), yet his unwillingness to explain the transference seems to constitute an almost necessary blind spot, considering he has only a few paragraphs earlier made his first significant derivation of a rhetorical term from a discursive, empirical designation (the "bottom" of a "difficulty" from the "bottom of the eye"). What is unclear here is what distinguishes the "false analogy" from the "metaphorical." And the point is not that Berkeley contradicts his own principles but that he is working with several different paradigms for nonliteral signification. (His solution in the *Dialogues*, as we shall see, is to retreat into a generalized conception of "analogy" that simply avoids the question of how metonymy and metaphor, false and necessary analogy, are related.)

Having raised as an issue the legitimacy of transferring descriptive terms from one discursive scheme to another, Berkeley finds himself unable to explain one of the key kinds of transference upon which his discourse depends. Though Berkeley's subject is the analogies we habitually and unconsciously make among our various sensory schema, analogy is the single phenomenon for which he cannot establish a consistent definition. This perhaps explains why the *Essay*'s presiding figure for all perception and experience is "voice," a metaphor that by its very intangibility attempts to evade questions about how the sensory can represent the spiritual. Though the *Essay* provides various tangible and visual figures for abstract mental operations (e.g., "ill-grounded" analogies, the "bottoms" of difficulties, "deeply struck" habits of association), the au-

---

[40] In these passages Berkeley distinguishes implicitly between metonymy and pure metaphor. The application of tangible ideas to related visible sensations is essentially metonymic, while the application of either to the operations of the mind can only be metaphorical. As I have argued above, Berkeley's eventual critique of figurative language in the *Dialogues* focuses implicitly on metaphor alone.

thority for such figures is never articulated, and as a result they never attain the consistency or prominence that would allow them to govern the discourse.

In the *Essay*, the rhetorical figure of "metaphor" seems to constitute a minor and inexplicable subset of that more general principle of "analogy" according to which we coordinate all our ideas of sensation. Berkeley is constrained in his representation of mental operations by sensory figures, precisely because figures that *negotiate between the sensory and the spiritual* are conceived of as exceptions to the more general rules of analogy and relation in the Berkeleyan system. They are conceived, as I have argued above, as pure metaphor—the necessary borrowing of an identity from a logically incommensurable realm—rather than as metonymic figures drawn from a contiguous realm (e.g., the "outside" representing or being reflected in the "inside," as in Locke's ideas of sensation and reflection; or tangible ideas representing the visible ideas with which they are temporally connected, as in Berkeley's *Essay*). In the *Treatise*, however, Berkeley's thoughts about figuration change in a way that allows him systematically to employ concrete figures for abstract and mental phenomena. The motive for such a change is his anticipation of a quite particular objection to his immaterialism—that it requires us to change our way of talking about the world: "It will . . . be demanded whether it does not seem absurd to take away natural causes and ascribe everything to the immediate operation of Spirits? We must no longer say upon these principles that fire heats, or water cools, but that a Spirit heats, and so forth. Would not a man be deservedly laughed at, who should talk after this manner?" (§51). Berkeley answers this objection by pointing to a set of figurative expressions that his post-Copernican readers presumably understand to be false in a literal sense but that they also understand the expediency of retaining for pragmatic discursive purposes:

> They who by demonstration are convinced of the truth of the Copernican system do nevertheless say "the sun rises," "the sun sets," or "comes to the meridian"; and if they affected a contrary style in common talk it would without doubt appear very ridiculous. . . .
>
> In the ordinary affairs of life, any phrases may be retained, so long as they excite in us proper sentiments or dispositions to act in such a manner as is necessary for our well-being, how false soever they may be if taken in a strict and speculative sense. Nay, this is unavoidable, since, *propriety being*

regulated by custom, language is suited to the received opinions, which are not always the truest. Hence it is impossible—even in the most rigid, philosophic reasonings—so far to alter the *bent and genius of the tongue* we speak, as never to give a handle for cavillers to pretend difficulties and inconsistencies. (§§51–52, my emphasis)

Here, figuration is no longer explained in terms of either an inexplicable transference or a standing "analogy" but rather in terms of convention— something "regulated by custom," a "bent and genius of the tongue we speak." This still, of course, evades the question of how, or by whose authority, metaphor specifically makes its mark on the language, but it relieves individual speakers of the responsibility for explaining and justifiying their figurative expressions.[41] Berkeley may now exploit the familiarity of sensory figures (e.g., surface and depth) without having to worry about the "inconsistencies" they might produce within his own philosophic scheme.

In a passage I have already cited, Philonous warns that when—in conformity with the "general analogy of language"—"mental operations" are "signified by words borrowed from sensible things" they "must not be taken in their gross original sense" (347). In the *Essay,* the habit of attributing "words borrowed from sensible things" to our "mental operations" is seen as an exceptional species of "metaphorical" analogy; here in the *Dialogues* it is seen as part of the *general* analogical process of language. And as opposed to the *Treatise,* which uneasily suppresses questions about the authority of analogy precisely by using a few key figures so consistently and boldly, the *Dialogues* implicitly renounce the project of organizing philosophical discourse around a unified figurative scheme. The strategy of the *Dialogues* is thus to substitute general figurativeness for a specific figurative scheme, to exploit the general associative and evocative force of rhetorical language while trying to appear independent of a governing metaphor.[42] This explains perhaps why the

----

[41] See Locke on the roles of "common Use" and social "Propriety" in the regulation of linguistic signification (*Essay,* 3.ix–xi).

[42] Here again I would disagree somewhat with Richetti, who argues that in general "Berkeley's self-imposed task is the invention of a new set of precise terms (or a radical revision of the old ones) for dramatizing the conditions of knowing" (*Philosophical Writing,* 120). Berkeley's project in the *Dialogues,* I argue, is finally to dispense (or at least to *appear* to dispense) with any precise rhetorical scheme for describing knowledge and perception, in acknowledgment of the fact that ordinary discourse is too resistant to such schemes, and professional philosophers too opportunistic and sophistical in their critiques of philosophical vocabularies.

privileged figures of the *Essay* ("voice") and the *Treatise* ("imprint") give way to the *Dialogues*' rhetorical play of "mazes," "labyrinths," "vaults," "abysses," "grounds," "extensions," "imprints," and "superficialities." Berkeley recognizes that the force of rhetoric is more cumulative and impressionistic than systematic, that philosophical persuasion is an effect of presenting ideas in "different lights" (an activity figured in the *Dialogues* as one of "reflection"), and that philosophical *error* lies precisely in attributing philosophical consistency and explanatory power to common figures of speech.

For a philosophical demonstration to be convincing, it must avoid the appearance of *reliance* on a single figurative scheme, since rhetorical rigor only turns "custom" into "method" and is certain to aggravate a reader's prejudices.[43] To Hylas, who halfway through the *Dialogues* finds himself still unable to give up "matter," Philonous responds:

> Though a demonstration be never so well grounded and fairly proposed, yet, if there is withal a stain of prejudice, or a wrong bias on the understanding, can it be expected on a sudden to perceive clearly and adhere firmly to the truth? No, *there is need of time and pains*: the attention must be awakened and detained by a frequent *repetition of the same thing placed oft in the same, oft in different lights.* (317, my emphasis)

Repetition, time, and pain replace logical rigor and rhetorical consistency as the necessary conditions for persuasion. The literal implications of figurative language no longer seem to pose a risk to Philonous, because he appears not to rest his philosophy on any particular figure. Thus by the end of the *Dialogues*, when Hylas declares himself persuaded and no longer "in pain" (360), Philonous even allows him to retain a vocabulary whose figures implicitly contradict the principle of immaterialism:

> *Hyl.* . . . In denying Matter, at first glimpse I am tempted to imagine you deny the things we see and feel: but, upon reflection, find there is no ground for it. What think you, therefore, of retaining the name *Matter*, and applying it to *sensible things*? This may be done without any change in your sentiments: and, believe me, it would be a means of reconciling them to some

---

[43] The rhetorical need to cloak one's rhetoricity is a classical trope, and the best discussion of it is in Neil Hertz, "A Reading of Longinus," in *The End of the Line: Essays on Psychoanalysis and the Sublime* (New York: Columbia University Press, 1985), 1–20 (especially 15–18).

persons who may be more shocked at an innovation in words than in opinion.

Phil. With all my heart: retain the word *Matter*, and apply it to the objects of sense, if you please; provided you do not attribute to them any subsistence distinct from their being perceived. I shall never quarrel with you for an expression. (358)

At stake in Hylas's passage from a condition of shock and pain to one of tranquil acceptance is a "quarrel for an expression." To be released from pain is to be freed from the imperative of confronting the misleading figurativeness of language. Instead of having to renounce false concepts ("*in* the mind" or "*outside* the mind") or develop rigorous new ones, Hylas is allowed simply to speak as he always has. In a sense this represents a passage out of pain for Berkeley as well, since the possibility of his reader's being "shocked" poses a risk not only for the reader but for the author whose intentions are at once conciliatory and suasive.

It is worth noting that Hylas describes his final conversion to immaterialism in terms of reflection: "At first glance I am tempted to imagine . . . but upon reflection, find there is no ground for it." Ironically, "reflection" is precisely the activity that had led to Hylas's "pain" in the first place. The first dialogue begins with Hylas confessing his disturbed state of mind to Philonous and requesting "that you would suffer me to impart my reflections to you" (261). Reflection here is used in its more general moral-literary sense as meditation rather than in the strict Lockean sense of passive awareness of mental operations or in the more generalized Lockean sense of self-scrutiny and self-criticism. The figure of reflection seems to frame the *Dialogues*, both initiating and resolving its problems, yet it is still less prominent here than in Berkeley's more Lockean *Treatise*, where ideas of reflection are subordinated to ideas of sensation (ideas are created, according to the *Treatise*, primarily by being imprinted upon us by God and secondarily by our own process of reflection upon such imprints).

Berkeley's figure of reflection, like Locke's, provides a model of self-scrutiny and self-criticism that appears to be objectively articulated; and yet both Locke and Berkeley quite purposely abstain from any systematic extension of their central analogy. Despite the repeated claim of both philosophers to gauge the limits and conditions of the knowing self, both are ultimately more interested in correcting views of the world than in correcting views of the self. In reflecting we pay careful attention to our impressions and then either *correct* them (as, according to Lockean "judgment," we "read" a three-dimensional world into two-dimensional optical impressions) or correct our understanding of their *relationship* (as in Berkeley's argument concerning true and false analogies among our sense impressions). What we do not achieve, by reflecting, is some more detailed knowledge of the kind of machine the human mind is. We do not elucidate transcendental categories, or articulate the formal conditions or criteria implicit in the activities of perceiving and knowing.

There is no particular reason to assume that the eschewal of such transcendental explanations should constitute the more humble or practical philosophic route, but of course that is precisely how British empiricism has tended to characterize its own course. We have seen how the figure of reflection operates in Locke's *Essay* not only as a local figure for the activity of concentrating one's attention but also as a more extended narrative figure for the circular or reflexive route taken by a philosopher who properly observes the limits of human inquiry. Such a representation of philosophical inquiry is shared by Berkeley, whose *Dialogues* stress the theme of "return"—figured alternately as "reflection" and "revolt." In his preface to the *Dialogues*, Berkeley argues that philosophical reflection will reveal to us the perhaps unflattering fact that true wisdom lies in "think[ing] like other men"; though once we have acknowledged this, reflection may in fact become a quite pleasant activity:

> And, although it may, perhaps, seem an *uneasy reflection* to some that, when they have taken a *circuit through so many refined and unvulgar notions, they should at last come to think like other men*; yet, methinks, this *return* to the simple dictates of nature, after having wandered through the wild mazes of philosophy, is not unpleasant. It is like *coming home* from a long voyage: a man *reflects with pleasure* on the many difficulties and perplexities he has passed through, sets his heart at ease, and enjoys himself with more satisfaction for the future. (259)

Though the theme of a return "home" is not particularly Lockean, the representation of philosophy as a humble retreat from speculative inquiry certainly fits the Lockean paradigm. Just a few pages into the *Dialogues*, however, Berkeley strikes a less humble and domestic chord and describes the philosophical return that he hopes to initiate as a "revolt." Philonous assures Hylas that "since this revolt from metaphysical notions, to the plain dictates of nature and common sense, I find my understanding strangely enlightened" (262). And the twin tropes of reflection and revolt converge in the Second Dialogue, when Berkeley argues that the the "whole system of Atheism, is . . . *entirely overthrown by this single reflection* on the repugnancy included in supposing . . . the visible world, to exist without a mind" (305, my emphasis). Finally, Berkeley ends the dialogues with a comparison of his "principles" to the self-reflexive course of water in a fountain:

> *Phil.* You see, Hylas, the water of yonder fountain, how it is forced upwards, in a round column, to a certain height; at which it breaks, and falls back into the basin from whence it rose: its ascent as well as descent proceeding from the same uniform law or principle of *gravitation.* Just so, the same principles which, at first view, lead to Scepticism, pursued to a certain point, bring men back to Common Sense. (360)

Berkeley represents "reflection" as something easy, natural, almost inconsequential (since it leaves us back where we began), and yet at the same time as something difficult, unsettling, even revolutionary. This double sense of "reflection," which amplifies the latent tension between the active and passive roles assigned to reflection in Locke, is an essential element in empiricism's self-characterization and perseveres even in contemporary work in the Anglo-American tradition, labeled as pragmatist, antitranscendentalist or antifoundationalist.[44]

The double sense of reflection is paralleled by—though not reducible to—another paradox. The activity of reflection as Berkeley and Locke conceive it is modeled alternately on the mechanics of sensation (particularly on those of optics, with its epistemological implications) and on the mechanics of language. Both these models contain problems that empiricism would prefer to ignore. Optics provides empiricism with an objectively articulated analogy for *self-seeing* but also with a host of technical anomalies and pejorative traditional associations (e.g., Platonic and neo-Platonic distrust of the image or *eidos*) that undermine the ostensible objectivity, self-evidence, and stability of the specular image. The language model (which presents philosophical reflection as a kind of correct reading) has the advantage of acknowledging custom's share in the formation of our perceptions (thus preempting the charge of solipsistic or subjective delusion) but fails to provide a self-consistent account of

[44] See my "Uncertain Grounds: Wittgenstein's *On Certainty* and the New Literary Pragmatism," in *New Literary History* 19 (Winter 1988): 319–20, 325–28.

the way words are related to one another and to ideas. The constant shift back and forth between these two models for the activity of self-criticism is both the strength and the weakness of empiricist "reflection." It manages to keep both *language* and *sensation* constantly in view, but only at the cost of a somewhat tautological argument that explains the mechanics of sensation in terms of the operations of language *and vice versa*, and that furthermore assumes language to work in a far more homogeneous and self-consistent fashion than Locke's and Berkeley's various examples actually demonstrate.

For all their interest in the historical development and logic of sense-relations, Berkeley and Locke seem little concerned with the physical details and physiological complexities of sensation. They have, ironically, little interest in the characteristics and consequences of the entire phenomenon of reflected light, though they have much to say about mental reflection. Technical issues in optics are the anecdotal and analogical cornerstones upon which Locke and Berkeley's philosophical arguments are based, but both philosophers tend to describe the objects of perception as those objects are received by common experience and as they are described in common language. It is of interest to Berkeley, for instance, that we see "one part of the sky red, and another blue" (*Dialogues*, 265), but it is not his concern to explain this fact in terms of light rays, incidences of reflection and refraction, or the corpuscular composition of matter. Locke and Berkeley both see their ultimate philosophical task as the sharpening of our capacity for self-scrutiny and self-criticism. But paradoxically the continual process of correcting and revising initial impressions, a process that they would have us internalize, is to their minds already entailed in the ordinary course of perception. There is no need to revert to technical explanations of sensation in order to correct our perceptions; what is important is simply that we recognize our impressions of sensation to require just as much—*and just as little*—interpretive supplementation as our attention to "common" language requires when we are engaged in ordinary conversation or reading.

When we turn to Burke's *Philosophical Enquiry into the Origin of Our Ideas of the Sublime and Beautiful*, we encounter a very different relationship between accounts of the mechanics of sensation and those of our common perceptions. In Burke, quasi-technical descriptions of the mechanics and physiology of perception abound. Although he follows Locke and Berkeley in claiming to be concerned only with the "efficient causes" and not the "ultimate causes" of our perceptions, his account of

efficient causes takes us wholly into the realm of physiology and mechanics. The irony is that Burke describes this realm at least as much in
literary, figurative terms as in the period jargon of optics, corpuscular
mechanics, or physiology. The figures of reflection, surface, and depth are
central to Burke's descriptions of physiology and sensation, but they are
not necessarily the same "reflections," "surfaces," and "depths" as might
be encountered in the technical literature on optics and other sciences.
Nonetheless, in Burke's *Enquiry* we encounter not only a philosophical
method figured as "reflection" but an *object of study* figured in terms of
surfaces, depths, and reflections as well. The increasingly schematic way
in which the object of interpretation is figured in terms of surfaces and
depths may fit nicely with the characterization of interpretation itself as a
process of reflection. But the double role of reflection as both the object
and the act of interpretation creates ironies and paradoxes in Burke's
discourse far exceeding anything we have seen in Locke and Berkeley. In
turn, the adjuration to the reader to reflect on his or her own experiences
in order to test the writer's claims becomes more problematic than ever.

4

Empiricist Aesthetics: Burke's "Analogy" of the Senses

All the senses bear an analogy to, and illustrate one another.

—BURKE, *A Philosophical Enquiry into the Origin of Our Ideas of the Sublime and the Beautiful*

FROM REFLECTION TO PERPLEXION

IF THE CENTRAL dramatic scene of empiricist philosophy depicts the recovery of sight by one born blind—and thus an ostensibly unmediated moment of sensory experience by someone already in possession of both language and judgment—then Burke's *Philosophical Enquiry into the Origin of Our Ideas of the Sublime and Beautiful*[1] would appear to offer a significant voice of dissent. For as we saw in Chapter 1, Burke argues that the born blind may construct perfectly accurate, striking, and recognizable verbal accounts of visual objects. Burke's insistence on the rhetorical propriety of the blind poet Blacklock's visual descriptions challenges Locke's and Berkeley's contention that direct, firsthand experience must stand somewhere back of all significant verbal expression. Yet Burke's implicit purpose in celebrating Blacklock's descriptive accuracy is not to refute empiricist epistemology or the constructivist optics central to it but rather to emphasize the rhetorical nature of perception. This may seem an odd characterization of the *Enquiry*, which, after all, gives systematic treatment to questions concerning the psychology, the objects, and the physiology of the sublime and the beautiful long before it turns to questions of language in part 5. Yet as we shall see, Burke's belief in the

---

[1] Edmund Burke, *A Philosophical Enquiry into the Origin of Our Ideas of the Sublime and Beautiful*, ed. James T. Boulton (Notre Dame, Ind.: Notre Dame University Press, 1968), part 4, chap. 11, 139. All subsequent references to Burke refer to part, chapter, and page numbers from this edition.

essential "analogy" of the senses renders sensory perception rhetorical from the very start; for Burke, impressions received through the various sense faculties are always already "illustrating" one another.

Oddly enough, neither Locke nor Berkeley are interested enough in the physiology of perception or the sensory qualities of the material world to develop a systematic set of rhetorical terms for describing differentiations within sensory experience. Just enough of the sensory world gets into Locke's and Berkeley's philosophy to illustrate their principles of cognition; unlike Burke they have little interest in developing a systematic vocabulary to describe and relate the vast range of experiences offered by the sense faculties. Indeed, Locke's distinction between primary and secondary qualities (*Essay* 2.8) and Berkeley's immaterialism virtually preclude the possibility of an analogy among the senses in the strong sense intended by Burke.[2]

The vast analogy that gives unity to Burke's highly synesthetic and rhetorical vision of the world is not simply an underlying logic of signification that governs all impressions (as in Berkeley) but rather a fundamental set of properties shared by objects, sensations, and descriptions alike. For Locke and Berkeley, by contrast, sights and sounds could hardly possess empirical properties in common, nor could the sensory qualities of phenomenal objects share some fundamental structure with the physiology of our sense faculties; perception is not to be accounted for by literal congruence of that sort.

Nonetheless, empiricist philosophy provides the crucial set of tropes by which Burke links physiology with rhetoric and transforms perceptual psychology into aesthetic psychology. Both Locke and Berkeley, we recall, emphasize the constructedness of our three-dimensional visual impressions and offer that construction as an exemplary instance of the relationship between sensation and reflection. Their account of this perceptual process is implicitly, and sometimes quite explicitly, linked to figures of surface and depth. Burke extends and systematizes this figurative scheme with a vengeance, structuring virtually every object of sensation as well as every aspect of human physiology in terms of surfaces and depths. Burke's categorical distinction between the "beautiful" and the "sublime," in fact, reduces to a distinction between impressions of surface and those of depth, respectively. Yet when we inspect Burke's descriptions of these

---

[2] According to Berkeley the visual and tactile sensations of an object can have nothing in common, though there is a common logic or principle to the *manner in which these sensations signify.*

impressions closely, we discover that the qualities of surface and depth are less categorically distinct than they first appear. An element of perceptual confusion enters into almost every aesthetic impression, whether of beauty or sublimity or of surface or depth. This perceptual confusion—figured as "reflection"—may take the form of optical illusion, of vertigo, of synesthesia, or even of rhetorical deception, but in virtually every case it tends to blur the distinction between surfaces and depths.

The trajectory of empiricist philosophy from Locke to Hume involves a progressive acknowledgment of reflection's double role: reflection both constructs and undermines our "commonsense" view of the world, synthesizing discrete sensory impressions but also exposing their synthetic nature. Burke's work preserves the double valence of empiricist "reflection" but reworks it as a tension between the production and destruction of *aesthetic* effects. For instance, those impressions that—when "modified"—are constitutive of the sublime may nonetheless destroy sublimity if "reflected" on. Yet such a formulation marks a distinction between "modification" and "reflection" that Burke's *Enquiry* does not sustain. The line that runs from the most direct and spontaneous sensations to the most deliberately cultivated and conventional aesthetic responses blurs the subtle distinctions between "modified" and "reflective" feelings. Reflection provides the distance or mediation necessary for a truly aesthetic effect and at the same time threatens to overwhelm aesthetic response by turning it into a rational idea.

Burke's empiricist aesthetic grounds the psychology of aesthetic response in physiology: in vibrating surfaces, vertiginous depths, reflected and refracted light, and the tension and recoil of nervous tissue. But this physiological drama is itself rhetorically conditioned. The principle of analogy that informs Burke's *Enquiry* is not merely the analogy of one sense faculty to another but the analogy of mind, body, and world. The phenomenal world, the physiology of nervous response, and the mind all share the same rhetorical configuration; all are structured in terms of surfaces, depths, and reflections. The sight of deep chasms or deep colors and the sound of deep notes strike our nervous tissues deeply and affect us deeply. The sight or touch of a smooth surface and the taste of a viscous fluid impinge lightly on our nervous tissue and give us superficial pleasures. And reflection allows us to perceive these connections even as it perplexes us with their mutual determinations.

In this chapter we shall see how Burke's "sublime" depths are consistently complicated by a physiology of surfaces, how his "beautiful" surfaces are consistently problematized by a psychology of depth, and how the manifold reflections that confuse surface and depth should somehow work to the figurative advantage of *depths*. At stake is the relationship of figurative language to Burke's physiological aesthetics and that of his conceptual and critical terminology (e.g., the rhetoric of "reflection") to the descriptive language seemingly intrinsic to his subject matter (e.g. heights, depths, surfaces, reflections).

THE ANALOGY OF THE SENSES

As tradition has it, Berkeley's common sense told him that all perception was mediated by—and most accurately described in terms of—simple surfaces. But like Locke, he also recognized a resistance to such a description, given the organization of such discourse around various traditional rhetorics of depth (e.g., the metaphysical, ethical, and aesthetic vocabularies of "foundations," "grounds," "bottoms," and "depths"). Burke, by contrast, is comfortable with conventional idioms of depth (e.g., "deep impressions," "deep affection," "profundity") but cannot fully account for their *relationship* to our impressions of surface qualities, impressions that are essential to his aesthetic theory. Burke's essentially binary aesthetic scheme (i.e., beauty vs. sublimity) requires that impressions of depth be contrasted with something, but as soon as he moves beyond the traditional metaphors structured implicitly in terms of surfaces and depths (e.g., bodies of water or solids) and comes to consider the more abstract and generalized phenomenon of surfaces in general, he finds it difficult to determine their relationship to deep impressions. "Water" may be "plumbed," "solids" may be "penetrated," but it is unclear whether "surfaces" (which Burke comes to acknowledge as virtually ubiquitous) are to be "troubled," "cleared," "broken," or "mimicked" in order to discover their depths. The problem of getting *beyond* surfaces is itself symptomatic for a writer who wants to employ surfaces as mere contrastive figures for depth and yet to derive an entire aesthetic (or set of complimentary aesthetics) from that contrast.

Burke in fact begins with a quite different problem from Berkeley's or Locke's: perception is by no means simple, unproblematic, or internally consistent, and it is by no means clear that perception can be accounted for in terms of our ability to learn, recognize, and coordinate sense impressions. Many of the phenomena that affect us seem inscrutable or obscure, and in fact this may be the very condition of their affective power. Yet if it is not necessary to explain how the inscrutable is made *clear*, it is still necessary to explain how something inscrutable, hidden, or absent can *affect* us. Burke's foregrounding of the depth/surface distinction obliges him to explain how depths might be communicated. However, the figure of surface is little help in this, as Burke is both unable and unwilling to describe depths as *functions* of surfaces or as surfaces modified by an act of judgment or reflection.

Burke begins his book with a rather traditional depreciation of surfaces. "On a superficial view," he writes at the beginning of his introduction to the *Enquiry*, "we may seem to differ very widely from each other in our reasonings, and no less in our pleasures" ("Introduction on Taste," 11). These "superficial" differences, however, are immediately designated as "rather apparent than real," and a few pages later the "superficial view" is contrasted with "principles" that are "*grounded* and certain" (13, my emphasis). The designation of surfaces as mere appearance—figured here as a distinction between the "superficial" and the "grounded"—is asserted again on the first page of the *Enquiry* proper, where Burke refers disparagingly to "curiosity" as "the most superficial of all the affections" (1.1.31). More important, the figures of surface and depth are implicit in Burke's critical distinction between positive "pleasure" and the "delight which arises from the modifications of pain": "When we recover our health, when we escape an imminent danger, is it with joy that we are affected? The sense on these occasions is far from that *smooth* and voluptuous satisfaction which the assured prospect of pleasure bestows. The delight which arises from the modifications of pain, confesses the stock from whence it *sprung*, in its *solid*, strong, and severe nature" (1.5.38, my emphasis). Here a quality of surfaces (smoothness) is contrasted with the tactile qualities of three-dimensional objects ("sprung," "solid") in order to dramatize the distinctions among various levels of complexity and intensity in our emotions. Yet the "voluptuous" nature of "satisfaction" hints at more dangerous waters ahead in Burke's text and suggests something of the disruptive power of surfaces. Burke concludes part 1 of the *Enquiry* in fact by describing his project in terms of an aquatic metaphor, in which the distinction is clearly one between surface and *depth*: "These waters must be troubled before they can exert their virtues. A man who works beyond the surface of things, though he may be wrong himself, yet he clears the way for others, and may chance to make even his errors subservient to the cause of truth" (1.19.54).

Though elsewhere Burke echoes the traditional empiricist caution against "deep" speculation, he nonetheless proceeds to depict his philosophical inquiry as a kind of penetration. This tension leads Burke to mix his metaphor here, or at least to leave his analogy incomplete. The troubled surface of "these waters" becomes the "surface of things," and the project of penetrating "beyond" the surface is figured as an act of "clearing the way"; the obvious complementary metaphor of "depth" is never invoked. We shall return later in this section to Burke's apparent anxiety about depths. For the moment it is sufficient to note that the preface, the introduction, and part 1 of the *Enquiry* all continually set figures of surface against figures loosely aligned with the concept of spatial depth (e.g., "springs," "grounds," and "foundations") and that in general surfaces are depreciated while depths are admired.

As we make our way into the *Enquiry* it starts to become clear that the beautiful is most effectively described in terms of surfaces, while the sublime demands recourse to metaphors of depth. Such a scheme is evident, for instance, in the contrasted metaphors of the "graft" and the "foundation" in the following passage: "I have before observed, that whatever is qualified to cause terror, is a foundation capable of the sublime; . . . I observed too, that whatever produces pleasure, positive and original pleasure, is fit to have beauty engrafted on it" (4.3.131). Though Burke never explicitly describes sublime effects as "deep" or beautiful effects as "superficial," the qualities by which the sublime is known seem always to involve reference to a vertiginous verticality or three-dimensionality, while the characteristics by which the beautiful is known almost always require reference to the qualities of physical surfaces.

The two most important factors contributing to beauty in all things, according to Burke, are *smoothness* and *gradual variation*, and both are described explicitly as qualities of surface:

> In trees and flowers, smooth leaves are beautiful; smooth slopes of earth in gardens; . . . in fine women, smooth skins; and in several sorts of ornamental furniture, smooth and polished *surfaces*. A very considerable part of the effect of beauty is owing to this quality; indeed the most considerable. For take any beautiful object, and *give it a broken and rugged surface*, and however well formed it may be in other respects, it pleases no longer. (3.14.114, my emphasis)

If a body presented to [the eye] has such a *waving surface* that the rays of light reflected from it are in a continual insensible deviation from the strongest to the weakest, (which is always the case in a *surface* gradually unequal,) it must be exactly similar in its effect on the eye and touch; upon the one of which it operates directly, on the other indirectly. And this body will be beautiful if the lines which compose its *surface* are not continued, even so varied, in a manner that may weary or dissipate the attention. (4.23.155–56, my emphasis)

Though the mutually constitutive relationship between surface and depth ensures that the opening up of depth remains a constant possibility in these passages (whether in the successful effect of a "waving surface" or in the ostensible failure of a "broken and rugged surface"), qualities of surface are clearly the starting point for definitions of "smoothness" and "gradual variation."[3]

By contrast, the "passion caused by the Sublime" is clearly dependent on qualities of depth. Burke asserts that "greatness of dimension" alone is not enough to make something sublime unless we "annex" to it "an adventitious idea of terror," and he illustrates this by referring to the difference between a landscape and an oceanscape: "A level plain of a vast extent on land, is certainly no mean idea; the prospect of such a plain may be as extensive as a prospect of the ocean; but can it ever fill the mind with any thing so great as the ocean itself? This is owing to several causes, but it is owing to none more than this, that the ocean is an object of no small terror" (2.2.57–58). Though the ocean's depth is not explicitly mentioned here, it is at least metonymically present. The ocean's depth is the source of its danger and terror, and depth is precisely the dimension that distinguishes an ocean's surface from the surface of a "level plain."[4] This

---

[3] "Smoothness" and "gradual variation" are not only two of the first three "causes" of beauty enumerated by Burke; they appear also as significant contributing factors in virtually every other "cause" he discusses: smoothness is a part of "delicacy" (3.16.116), of "elegance and speciousness" (3.23.120), of "feeling" (3.24.120), of "sweetness" (4.22.153) and of "colour" (4.25.159), while gradual variation is a key factor in the beauty of "colour" (3.17.117), of "grace" (3.22.119), of "feeling" (3.24.120), and of "sound" (3.25.122). The only cause of beauty that does not seem dependent in some way on smoothness or gradual variation—and thus on surface—is "smallness" (3.13.113–14; 4.24.156–59).

[4] Boulton (editor's introduction to Burke, *Enquiry*, xlvii) refers Burke's discussion of the oceanic sublime to an eighteenth-century commonplace derived originally from Longinus. Interestingly enough, Hume gives the "idea of sinking"—stimulated instinctively by the sight of a body of water—as an example of an idea that need not be "noticed" for it to "operate on our mind" (*Treatise*, 1.3).

is implicitly confirmed a few sections later, when Burke singles out verticality, and perhaps especially depth, as the most affecting factor in the
sublime of "vastness":

> Greatness of dimension, is a powerful cause of the sublime. . . . Exten-
> sion is either in length, height, or depth. Of these the length strikes least; an
> hundred yards of even ground will never work such an effect as a tower an
> hundred yards high, or a rock or mountain of that altitude. I am apt to
> imagine likewise, that height is less grand than depth; and that we are more
> struck at looking down from a precipice, than at looking up at an object of
> equal height, but of that I am not very positive. (2.7.72)

Burke's hedging uncertainty about the precise relationship between the
sublimes of depth and height is an issue we shall take up shortly. However, the provisional emphasis on literal depths in this particular passage
is confirmed by its continuation into the discussion of the miniature
sublime, further on in the same paragraph:

> It may not be amiss to add to these remarks upon magnitude; that, as the
> great extreme of dimension is sublime, so the last extreme of littleness is in
> some measure sublime likewise; when we attend to the infinite divisibility of
> matter, when we pursue animal life into these excessively small, and yet
> organized beings, that escape the nicest inquisition of the sense, when we
> *push our discoveries yet downward*, and consider those creatures so many
> degrees yet smaller, and the still diminishing scale of existence, in tracing
> which the imagination is lost as well as the sense, we become amazed and
> confounded at the wonders of minuteness; nor can we distinguish in its effect
> this extreme of littleness from the vast itself. (2.7.72, my emphasis)

Here, the vertiginous physical sensation of "looking down from a precipice" is transferred to the experience of "descending" into—and being
overwhelmed by—"infinite divisibility."[5] Literal and figurative depths
turn out to be closely allied, and the rhetorical tradition in which "descent" describes a particularly intense kind of discovery or experience is
authorized by the special aesthetic intensity of physical depths.[6]

[5] Cf. similar passages in Locke, *Essay*, 2.17.15; and in Addison's tenth essay on the
pleasures of the imagination, *Spectator*, no. 420 (in Joseph Addison and Richard Steele,
Selections from the "Tatler" and the "Spectator," ed. Angus Ross [Harmondsworth: Penguin, 1982]).

[6] See Northrop Frye, *The Secular Scripture: A Study of the Structure of Romance*
(Cambridge: Harvard University Press, 1976), 121–26, on the ambiguities in traditional
narrative correlations between "descent" and "self-knowledge."

The linking of literal with figurative depths (or literal with figurative surfaces) raises the whole question of the relationship between the *sensations* and the *language* of the sublime and beautiful.[7] Though the relation between sensation and language is not addressed in detail by Burke until part 5, it is implicit throughout the *Enquiry*, particularly in the frequently invoked connection between physiological causation and figurative language. Throughout his discussion of the beautiful in part 3, Burke is fond of referring to "smoothness" as a quality of nontactile sensations such as sound and color, yet he concludes with a recognition that some principle must be articulated to justify his synesthetic language.[8] In this particular passage it is the application of "sweetness" to sounds and sights that Burke calls into question, but his metaphoric use of the term "smoothness" is clearly also at issue:

> We metaphorically apply the idea of sweetness to sights, and sounds; but as the qualities of bodies by which they are fitted to excite either pleasure or pain in these senses, are not so obvious as they are in the others, we shall refer an explanation of their analogy, which is a very close one, to that part, wherein we come to consider the common efficient cause of beauty as it regards all the senses. (3.26.123)

The justification for describing sights and sounds as "sweet" (or "smooth") is "referred" to a subsequent discussion, where Burke attempts to prove that there are physiological grounds for synesthetic descriptions, and concurs with Hartley that "all the senses bear an analogy to, and illustrate one another" (4.11.139).[9] As in Hartley's work, the demonstration of an analogy among the five senses does not address the question of the relationship between physical sensations ("looking down from a precipice") and the rhetorical description of mental operations ("push[ing] our

---

[7] I prefer the terms *sensation* and *language* to the traditional terms *natural* and *rhetorical* here, since Burke's discussion of "sensations" or "efficient causes" relies so heavily on the trope of synesthesia that it is unclear whether *nature* stimulates any effects that are not conceptually mediated through rhetorical categories.

[8] According to Boulton (editor's introduction), though the phenomenon of synesthesia had attracted considerable interest among eighteenth-century writers, Burke was the first to develop an actual theory of synesthesia (lxxiii).

[9] See David Hartley, *Observations on Man, His Frame, His Duty, and His Expectations*, rev. ed. (London, 1834). Hartley writes: "The sensations must be supposed to bear such an analogy to each other, and so to depend on the brain, that all evidences for the continuance of the sensations in any one sense, will extend themselves to the rest" (7).

discoveries yet downward").[10] However, as we shall see, Burke's conception of "efficient cause" does manage to suggest a causal relationship between the physiology and the language of the sublime, though possibly only at the risk of blurring the boundary *between* the sublime and the beautiful.[11]

According to Burke, all the senses are capable of receiving both sharp and smooth stimuli, and as a general rule, "bodies which are rough and angular, rouse and vellicate the organs of feeling, causing a sense of pain, which consists in the violent tension or contraction of the muscular fibres. On the contrary, the application of smooth bodies relax" (4.20.151). Burke conceives of his major task at this point to be the demonstration of an empirical connection between "sweet" tastes and the tactile sensations of smoothness and gradual variation, and he proceeds to give a thoroughly physiological explanation of their relationship in sweet liquids. Fluids, in and of themselves, depend on "roundness, smoothness, and weak cohesion," writes Burke, and the uniformity of their smoothness renders them "insipid, inodorous, colourless . . . to the touch and taste." The introduction of sugar particles into the liquid, however, adds a "soft variety" that "prevents . . . weariness." Thus,

> In sweet liquors, the parts of the fluid vehicle . . . being so excessively minute
> . . . have a sort of flat simplicity to the taste, resembling the effects of plain
> smooth bodies to the touch; for if a body be composed of round parts
> excessively small, and packed pretty closely together, the surface will be both
> to the sight and touch as if it were nearly plain and smooth. It is clear
> . . . that the particles of sugar are considerably larger than those of water or
> oil, and consequently that their effects from their roundness . . . will induce
> that sense called sweetness. (4.23.153)

It appears that "sweetness"—the beauty of taste—is quite literally an effect of smooth and gradually varied corpuscular surfaces and that analogies among the senses are not merely functions of language (metaphori-

---

[10] Hartley observes, ironically perhaps, that he is unable to give "a full or satisfactory account of the ideas which adhere to words by association," since "it is difficult to explain words to the bottom by words." Ibid., 174.

[11] Samuel H. Monk suggests that the introduction of physiological explanations into discussion of aesthetic response constituted Burke's distinctive contribution to eighteenth-century theories of the sublime. See Monk, *The Sublime: A Study of Critical Theories in Eighteenth-Century England* (New York: Modern Language Association, 1935), 91–93.

cal applications) but rather physiological congruencies. The sensations that constitute beauty are physiologically smooth, and thus quite literally a function of superficial qualities.[12]

Burke provides a similar physiology of the sublime. On introducing part 4 of the *Enquiry*, his investigation into the "efficient cause" of the sublime and beautiful, Burke immediately disclaims any ability to give ultimate explanations for the effect of physiology on the mind,[13] settling instead for a detailed description of precisely those anatomical and mental states that as a rule occur concomitantly:

> I do not pretend that I shall ever be able to explain, *why* certain affections of the body produce such a distinct emotion of mind, and no other; or why the body is at all affected by the mind, or the mind by the body. A little thought will shew this to be impossible. But I conceive, if we can discover what affections of the mind produce certain emotions of the body; and what distinct feelings and qualities of body shall produce certain determinate passions in the mind, and no others, I fancy a great deal will be done. . . . This is all, I believe, we can do. (4.1.129)

Faithful to the minimum empiricist tenets common to Locke, Berkeley, and Hume, Burke modestly claims to resolve philosophical questions of "cause" into determinations of correlative phenomena. Nevertheless, the very impossibility of ever explaining why physical sensations produce emotional states leads Burke to his own sublime.[14] Immediately after the

[12] Boulton points to Burke's sensationist theory of the cause of beauty as the most obvious (and most frequently cited) absurdity in the *Enquiry* (editor's introduction, *Enquiry*, lxvi).

[13] Both Monk (*The Sublime*, 93) and Boulton (editor's introduction, xxxiv–xxxv) point out that Burke strongly resisted the deterministic extremes of associationism.

[14] The most extensive and incisive discussion of the relationship between the natural and rhetorical sublimes is Thomas Weiskel's *The Romantic Sublime: Studies in the Structure and Psychology of Transcendence* (Baltimore: Johns Hopkins University Press, 1976). Weiskel posits a congruency between the natural sublime (the experience of a "discontinuity between sensation and idea") and the rhetorical sublime (the recognition of a discontinuity "between idea and word" [16–17]). Weiskel too makes the argument that *depth* plays a role in the economies of both the natural and rhetorical sublimes. However, he presents depth only as a figurative analogue to the sublime sensation of astonishment: "The sublime moment establishes depth because the presentation of unattainability is phenomenologically a negation, a falling away from what might be seized, perceived, known. As an image, it is the abyss" (24–25). Burke, I will argue, associates the twin sublimes of incomprehension and inarticulateness with the figure of depth not merely because they are "negations," but

last sentence cited, Burke writes: "If we could advance a *step farther*, difficulties would still remain" (my emphasis). Burke's "step" leads him immediately to the example of Newton and the discovery of the laws governing the "motion of a body falling to the ground" (130). Newton should have been content to "consider attraction but as an effect," argues Burke, without attempting to "trace" its "cause"; searching for ultimate causes is the extra step that leads us *out of our depths*. Newton's and Burke's texts thus join for a sublime moment in which Burke's figure of depth reveals the aporia in Newton's argument: "That great chain of causes, which linking one to another even to the throne of God himself, can never be unravelled by any industry of ours. When we go but one step beyond the immediately sensible qualities of things, we go out of our depth. All we do after, is but a faint struggle, that shews we are in an element which does not belong to us" (129–30). Burke here depicts the theory of falling bodies as an intellectual structure that cannot adequately account for the concept or sensation of falling. Paradoxically, however, philosophical inquiry ultimately leads us to an intellectual vertigo, "an element which does not belong to us." It is not at all arbitrary that Burke chooses the case of gravitational theory to illustrate the limitations that his own philosophizing must eventually confront. The sensation of *falling*—with its strange mixture of tension and relaxation, and the attendant "faint struggle" against a foreign "element"—will play a crucial role in the discussion that follows on the sublime's physiological causes. Depth will turn out to be something more than a common metaphorical name for the various particular intensities produced by the sublime; something of the physiological sensation of drowning or falling turns out to be a part of every sublime feeling. In *naming* the limitations of his own inquiry ("we go out of our depth"), Burke is in the same gesture applying his physiological principles to something beyond, to those sensations attendant upon mental operations. In the very gesture of limiting his inquiry, he marks its critical extension.

The "source" of the sublime, according to Burke, is in the "produc[tion]" of "an unnatural tension and certain violent emotions of the nerves," "terror" being the strongest such stimulus (4.5.134). Implicit in

---

because they are *empirically* related to the physiological sensations of falling, drowning, or vertigo. See also Longinus's distinction between—and then subsequent association of— figuration and "natural" sublimity. See Longinus, *On the Sublime*, ed. A. O. Prickard (Oxford: Clarendon Press, 1906), chaps. 8, 17.

this definition of the sublime is the notion of *suddenness*, since the "vio-lence" of the nervous reaction must be sufficient to preempt or "antici-pate" our reasoning powers and "hurr[y] us on by an irresistable force" (2.1.57).[15] Our nervous response is more immediate than our reflection, and the latter is forced to catch up with sensation too quickly, with an effect of irreparable disproportion. If sublime "tension" is sudden, how-ever, it must be experienced in strong contrast with its opposite, relax-ation, and Burke hints at several points that tension, relaxation, and the sensation of *falling* are all integrally associated. Sublime tension is not unlike a "struggle" in an "alien element," the alternating relaxation and contraction of our muscular nervous system against a medium whose resistance is either unfamiliar or completely absent:

> Hence I conclude that . . . pain and fear consist in an unnatural tension of the nerves; that this is sometimes accompanied with an unnatural strength, which sometimes suddenly changes into an extraordinary weakness; that these effects often come on alternately, and are sometimes mixed with each other. This is the nature of all convulsive agitations. (4.3.131–32)

> An association of a . . . general nature . . . may make darkness terrible; for in utter darkness, it is impossible to know in what degree of safety we stand; we are ignorant of the objects that surround us; we may every moment strike against some dangerous obstruction; we may fall down a precipice the first step we take; and if an enemy approach, we know not in what quarter to defend ourselves. (4.14.143)

The proleptic political implications of a commonsense "struggle" against an abstract "element which does not belong to us" are here echoed in the association of depth and darkness with "an enemy." The result of such a sudden and disorienting exposure to depth is our equally violent recoil from it:

> When the eye lights upon one of these vacuities [a black body], after having been kept in some degree of *tension* by the play of the adjacent colours upon it, it suddenly *falls into a relaxation*; out of which it as *suddenly recovers by a convulsive spring*. To illustrate this; let us consider, that when we intend to

---

[15] Burke's remarks here follow closely Longinus's remarks on the rhetorical device of "asyndeton." Longinus offers as his example a passage from Homer in which "the phrases being disconnected and yet none the less rapid give the idea of an agitation which both checks the utterance and at the same time hounds it on." See Longinus, *On the Sublime*, chap. 19.

sit on a chair, and find it much lower than was expected, the shock is very violent; much more violent than could be thought from so slight a *fall* as the difference between one chair and another can possibly make. If, after *descending a flight of stairs*, we attempt inadvertently to take another step in the manner of the former ones, the shock is extremely rude and disagreeable; and by no art, can we cause such a shock by the same means, when we expect and prepare for it. (4.17.147, my emphasis)

The "shock" that forces itself upon Burke seems also to shock him out of his empiricist caution. For he immediately goes on to make an uncharacteristically hyperbolic observation:

I have often experienced, and so have a thousand others; that on the first inclining towards sleep, we have been suddenly awakened with a most violent start; and that this start was generally preceded by a sort of dream of our falling down a precipice: whence does this strange motion arise; but from the too sudden relaxation of the body, which by some mechanism in nature restores itself by as quick and vigorous an exertion of the contracting power of the muscles? the dream itself is caused by this relaxation; . . . The parts relax too suddenly, which is in the nature of falling; and this accident of the body induces this image in the mind. (4.17.148)

The sensation of falling or sinking seems to be characteristic of most varieties of the sublime (cf. Burke's remarks on the sublimity of the ocean [2.2.57]); our senses are submitted to an "alien element," producing drastic and sudden alternations of convulsion and release. The protogothic sublimities of "darkness," "depth," the "ocean," "vastness," and "infinitude" all threaten us with the prospect, if not the actual sensation, of a vertiginous descent or fall. Nevertheless, though the fear of "depth" is in a quite literal sense what the sublime confronts us with, the investigation of that phenomenon constitutes a potential sublimity in itself, one that Burke is not entirely prepared to experience. Thus he describes his own project as a "troubling" of the "surface" of "these waters" (1.14.54) yet cannot bring himself to complete the metaphor by referring to that water's "depth" and in fact later warns against pursuing inquiry "out of our depth."

Burke's investigation of the sublime points increasingly to the function played by physical depths, yet he shies away from naming depth definitively either as the goal of his investigation or as a principal source of the sublime. Much of this has to do with the divided role played by figures of surface throughout the *Enquiry*. As a rhetorical term, *superficial* is used pejoratively by Burke. Yet given his physiologically grounded aesthetic theory, *surface* must remain a key descriptive term in his account of the *mediation* of beauty.

Burke's way of resolving this figurative contradiction is to demonstrate that beautiful surfaces are not, in fact, superficial. The most beautiful surfaces turn out to incorporate (even if on a lesser scale) something of the depth, vertigo, and peril associated with the sublime. Accordingly, Burke's description of a "beautiful woman" brings figures of both surface and depth into play:

> Observe that part of a beautiful woman where she is perhaps the most beautiful, about the neck and breasts; the *smoothness*; the softness; the easy and *insensible swell*; the variety of the *surface*, which is never for the smallest space the same; the deceitful maze, *through which the unsteady eye slides giddily*, without knowing where to fix, or whither it is carried. Is not this a demonstration of that *change of surface* continual and yet hardly perceptible at any point which forms one of the great constituents of beauty? (3.15.115, my emphasis)

As in Burke's description of the ocean's terrible sublimity, depth is not literally articulated here, but the fear of sinking or of being immersed in a foreign element is unmistakable. A little farther on, in his discussion of beautiful sounds, Burke refers to *"that sinking,* that melting, that languor, which is the *characteristical effect of the beautiful,* as it regards every sense"* (3.25.123, my emphasis). Clearly then, and here is the paradox, the sensations—or at least the rhetorical figures—produced by the beautiful are not entirely distinct from those produced by the sublime.

Burke cannot represent depth as a unique property of the sublime without forfeiting the criterion by which beautiful surfaces ("through which the unsteady eye slides giddily") are distinguished from merely superficial ones (e.g., the "flat simplicity" of water or oil molecules, which are "insipid, inodorous, colourless, and smooth to the touch" [4.21.152–53)]). Though sensations of beauty may not involve the actual physiological alternation between contraction and relaxation that characterizes sensations of sinking or falling (and thus of the true sublime), beauty nevertheless mimics such sensations by inducing a relaxation of the nervous system closely enough allied to vertigo to require at least *some* rhetoric of depth for its description. Thus the "giddiness" produced by beautiful objects is an effect not unlike a gentle descent:

When we have before us such objects as excite love and complacency, the body is affected, so far as I could observe, much in the following manner. The head reclines something on one side; the eyelids are more closed than usual, and the eyes roll gently with an inclination to the object, the mouth is a little opened, and the breath drawn slowly, with now and then a low sigh: the whole body is composed, and the hands fall idly to the sides. (4.19.149)

The problem with such a description of the beautiful, for Burke, is that it threatens to collapse not only into a rhetoric of depth but into a trivialization of depth in general. Thus Burke immediately attempts to realign the sensation of sinking with the figure of *height* and to distinguish it from the vulgar bathos of mere lassitude: "These appearances are always proportioned to the degree of beauty in the object, and of sensibility in the observer. And this gradation from the highest pitch of beauty and sensibility, even to the lowest of mediocrity and indifference, and their correspondent effects, ought to be kept in view, else this description will seem exaggerated, which it certainly is not" (ibid.). Having made this distinction, Burke can now continue to describe the beautiful with a modified figure of depth[16] and as producing a modified sensation of sinking: "But from this description it is almost impossible not to conclude, that beauty acts by relaxing the solids of the whole system. There are all the appearances of such a relaxation; and a relaxation somewhat *below the natural tone* seems to me to be the cause of all positive pleasure" (149–50, my emphasis). In response to the beautiful, our nervous systems sink "below" their accustomed levels of stimulation, producing a "melting and languor" distinct from, though not precisely antithetical to, the sublime interplay of tension and slackness.

Burke's tendency to implicate figures of depth in his descriptions of the beautiful, and his conventional use of such figures as well in the self-reflexive passages of the *Enquiry* (e.g., getting "beyond the surface of things," "to descend far into the particulars" (2.10.77), denies to the sublime a unique association with depth. And just as figures of depth seem to assert themselves within descriptions of surface phenomena, so processes originally figured in terms of depth seem capable of being reconceived in terms of surfaces. Such is the case with the *Enquiry*'s metaphors of penetration and interiority (e.g., "turn[ing] the soul inward on

---

[16] Again, this foreshadows strategic distinctions in the gothic novel. Compare, for instance, the gradual descents into beautiful valleys, and the more threatening views from sheer precipices, in Radcliffe's *The Mysteries of Udolpho*.

itself," "work[ing] beyond the surface of things"). In endeavoring to demonstrate how the mind may be affected by the body, Burke relates the "curious story of the celebrated physiognomist Campanella," who

> had not only made very accurate observations on human *faces*, but was very expert in mimicking such, as were any way remarkable. When he had a mind to *penetrate into the inclinations* of those he had to deal with, he *composed his face*, his gesture, and his whole body, as nearly as he could into the exact similitude of the person he intended to examine; and then carefully observed what turn of mind he seemed to acquire by this change. So that, says my author, he was able to *enter into the dispositions and thoughts* of people, as effectually as if he had been changed into the very men. (4.4.132–33, my emphasis)

In this striking anecdote, Burke represents a rearrangement of surface features as a virtual act of penetration. Depths not only are signified by their surfaces but are in some way *functions* of those surfaces. More generally, gestures not only are signs of hidden reflections but are as well ways of representing and thus re-creating them.[17]

While from one perspective every description in the *Enquiry* seems to tend toward figures of depth, from another perspective everything tends toward surface. In fact, the apparent ubiquity of depths is matched by an ubiquity of surfaces. In discussing the "beautiful in sounds," Burke cites lines from Milton's "L'Allegro" and comments: "Let us parallel this with the softness, the winding surface, the unbroken continuance, the easy gradation of the beautiful in other things" (4.25.122). This "parallelling" of Miltonic sound with the "surface" of "the beautiful in other things" begs either a physiological description of acoustical "surfaces," or a figurative understanding of the "surface of things." No physiological explanation is forthcoming from Burke, though, and the implication of the passage is that *all things* have a surface in some sense—with that sense

---

[17] Ironically, the sympathetic conflation of observer and observed in this anecdote calls into question the very integrity of empiricist methodology. For a more traditional mid-eighteenth-century view of physiognomy, see Henry Fielding, "An Essay on the Knowledge of the Character of Men," in *Miscellanies by Henry Fielding, Esq.*, vol. 1, ed. Henry Knight Miller (Oxford: Wesleyan University Press, 1972), 153–78. Fielding sees the "skill" in interpreting "Character" through "Physiognomy" as consisting less in sympathetic identification or imitation and more in the *reading* of "Marks which Nature hath imprinted on the Countenance" (157, 178).

left unspecified. There is no Berkeleyan theory of analogy here to provide an account of how our "tactile ideas" may be transferred to nontactile or indeed nonsensory phenomenon. That is, there is no account of the nature and different *types* of analogy or of the distinction between true and false analogy. Though Burke will shortly provide a physiological justification for referring to "flat" or "smooth" tastes, the implication that *sounds* have surfaces hints at an entirely different understanding of surfaces and depths and, as well, a more generalized understanding of "analogy." We might say that Burke presents us with an even more literal, physiological account of sensation than Locke's or Berkeley's, but then he also hints at a world in which the distinction between "literal" and "figurative" designations is more problematic than ever.

Burke's belief in the essential "analogy" of the senses confounds the distinction between literal and metaphoric descriptions of our sensations. Though in the "Introduction on Taste" he describes as "metaphor[ical]" the application of the word "taste" to our non-oral sensory responses and aesthetic judgments, it becomes clear as the *Enquiry* progresses that the analogous structure and functioning of our various sense faculties imparts a considerable literality to all transferences and exchanges of our sense-faculty vocabulary. Here, as elsewhere in empiricist writing, we are confronted with the question of language's relation to sense perception: do physiological similarities among objects or sensations illustrate our concepts of metaphor and analogy, or do metaphor and analogy illustrate the principles of coordination among our physiological responses? Do empirical differences and relations condition our rhetorical categories, or do the rhetorical categories condition empirical relations? These are not questions that Burke's *Enquiry* answers, but he foregrounds them in instructive ways long before he arrives at his discussion of language in part 5. And they are particularly at issue when he attempts to account for the "modification" undergone by overwhelming sensations when translated into anecdotes, narratives, and "reflections."

EMISSARIES, MODIFICATIONS, AND REFLECTIONS

We have seen, both in Berkeley's and in Burke's writing, a certain group of figures consistently associated with depth: principally the figures of solidity (three-dimensionality), interiority, and height. Their close association is evident, for instance, in this passage from the *Enquiry* in which

Burke describes the virtues of "discovering" God's wisdom through an investigation of our own "passions":

> Whilst referring to him whatever we find of right, or good, or fair in our- selves, discovering his strength and wisdom even in our own weakness and imperfection, honouring them where we discover them clearly, and adoring their *profundity* where we are lost in our search, we may be inquisitive without impertinence, and *elevated* without pride; we may be admitted, if I may dare to say so, into the counsels of the Almighty by a consideration of his works. The *elevation* of the mind ought to be the principal end of all our studies, which if they do not in some measure effect, they are of very little service to us. But besides this great purpose, a consideration of the rationale of our passions seems to me very necessary for all who would affect them upon *solid* and sure principles. It is not enough to know them in general; . . . we should pursue them through all their varieties of operations, and *pierce into the inmost, and what might appear inaccessible parts of our nature.* (1.9.52–53, my emphasis)

We have already witnessed the association of depth with three- dimen- sionality and interiority in Berkeley's work, but the association of depth with height ("profundity" with "elevation") introduces a new twist. In "The Romantic Myth," Northrop Frye argues that the eighteenth-century sublime prepares the way for romanticism precisely by rewriting the tra- ditional, theologically inflected depth/height scheme as an interi- or/exterior scheme while retaining the conventionally positive connota- tions of height.[18] Though Frye does not elaborate on the extended figurative implications of this transition, it is clear that the translation of the older paradigm into the newer one does not yield a simple propor- tional analogy (i.e., depth:height = interiority:exteriority) at least in part because it involves the introduction of a new term—namely, the concept of surface.

According to the *Oxford English Dictionary*, the word *surface* does not even occur in English until the early seventeenth century. Prior to that point, the word *face* sufficed to designate the exterior aspect of an object

---

[18] See Frye, "The Romantic Myth," in *A Study of English Romanticism* (New York: Random House, 1968), 11–12, 33, 46–47. According to Frye, the simple translation of up/down to out/in is marked by several problems. First, the theme of *quest*, traditionally associated with *ascent*, is not reconceived as a centrifugal, externalizing project but rather as a simultaneously downward and inward process (33, 46–47). Second, the "old celestial imagery" is replaced by an emphasis on the "sublime," which strips height of its theological and mythological overtones without converting it into a bland, generalized exteriority (28).

(e.g., "and the Spirit of God moved upon the face of the water"). We might speculate that the process of deanthropomorphization implicit in the transition from "face" to "surface" corresponds to the superceding of theological discourse by the discourse of the natural sciences in the late seventeenth century. The increasingly abstract or theoretical nature of the very objects of study requires a terminology applicable across a wide range of natural phenomena, but without apparent dependence on, or direct reference to, an anthropocentric worldview. In any case, the empiricist emphasis on "impressions," and "imprints," and the optical and tactile properties of physical "surfaces" clearly introduces a new factor into the traditional spatial metaphors of philosophy. Yet the relationship of surfaces to depths (or other "fuller" forms of spatial dimensionality) can be narrativized in different ways: while Locke and Berkeley present a world in which visual three-dimensionality is continuously and spontaneously constructed from impressions of surface, Burke presents a world in which distance, height, and depth are constantly in danger of *collapsing* back into the diminished dimensionality of surface. This constant threat has both psychological and political overtones and teases new dramatic possibilities out of empiricism's central tropes. What sustains this drama (and sustains as well the "distance" that keeps heights and depths from "collapsing") is not one but rather a number of overlapping and conflicting figures, most importantly "modification" and "reflection." Burke refers to both these processes in order to account for the distinctive attentuation of "pain" or "power" that constitutes aesthetic response and sustains the requisite "distance" between us and figures of power or authority. But as we shall see, "reflection" confuses the very distinction it attempts to clarify, between rational introspection and the prereflective "modification" of striking or threatening impressions.

Both James Boulton and Walter Hipple have emphasized the originality of Burke's contention that pain may be a direct source of pleasure.[19] However, neither call attention to the curious and ambiguous notion of "modification" that Burke insists is necessary for any conversion of pain into sublimity. In his *Spectator* essays on the "Pleasures of the Imagination," Addison anticipates Burke in figuring a nonsublime pain as one in which "the Object *presses* too close upon our Senses."[20] But for

---

[19] See Boulton, editor's introduction, lvi; and Walter Hipple, *The Beautiful, the Sublime, and the Picturesque in Eighteenth-Century British Aesthetic Theory* (Carbondale: Southern Illinois University Press, 1957), 86–89.

[20] Addison, *Spectator*, no. 418.

Addison, the "reflection" that allows us to enjoy terror is a direct function of our "distance" from the source of pain, and in fact the "distance" becomes itself the subject and source of our enjoyment (as it does according to Johnson in his *Preface to Shakespeare*, as well). In Burke's more Humean scheme, distance can only *attenuate* the effect of pain (whether that distance is provided by time, space, langauge, or fiction), and the process of "modification" is more obscure. At first glance, Hume's account in "Of Tragedy" would seem to parallel Burke's "modification" theory, since Hume emphasizes the "convers[ion]" rather than the *distance* that determines the relationship between "melancholy passions" and "pleasure." However, Hume also insists that the "melancholy passion" is "effaced by something stronger of an opposite kind" in the process of conversion, and thus he envisions a much stronger *break* between the *source* and the *effect* of tragedy than is implicit in Burke's concept of "modification."[21]

The close relationship between the two "pressing" threats that so concern Burke—the social-political and psychological-aesthetic—is even more strikingly revealed in the passage where he first describes how anything that excites "pain" may be a "source of the sublime":

> I am in great doubt, whether any man could be found who would earn a life of the most perfect satisfaction, at the price of ending it in the torments, which justice inflicted in a few hours on the late unfortunate regicide in France. But as pain is stronger in its operation than pleasure, so death is in general a much more affecting idea than pain; because there are very few pains, however exquisite, which are not preferred to death; nay, *what generally makes pain itself, if I may say so, more painful*, is, that it is considered as an *emissary of this king of terrors*. When danger or pain *press too nearly*, they are incapable of giving any delight, and are simply terrible; but at

[21] Hume, "Of Tragedy," essay no. 12 in *Essays, Moral, Political, and Literary* (London, 1742), 235. Compare, as well, Hartley (*Observations on Man*), who explains the transformation of pain into pleasure simply in terms of "degree," "transit," "repetition," or "passage" in time: "The doctrine of vibrations seems to require, that each pain should differ from the corresponding and opposite pleasure, not in kind, but in degree only; *i.e.* that pain should be nothing more than pleasure itself, carried beyond a due limit. . . . It may be observed also, that some painful sensations, as they decrease by time, or the removal of the cause, pass into positive local pleasures, of the same species as the preceding pain" (22–23). "[The] transit of original pains into pleasures, and of vivid pleasures into faint ones, by frequent repetition, bears some relation to the above-mentioned transition of pains into positive local pleasures" (25).

certain distances, and *with certain modifications*, they may be, and they are delightful, as we every day experience. (1.7.39–40, my emphasis)

The regicide Damiens's crime is in pressing too near the king, both literally and figuratively. For this the king punishes him with death, the "king of terrors," but not before forcing him to experience *distance* in the form of torture—pain being the "emissary of this king." Pain is thus a trope of death much as the sublime is a trope ("modification") of pain. What appears at first as an anecdote illustrating how the elision of critical distance ("press[ing] too near" to a "source") is destructive of the sublime, turns out to be a corroborating demonstration of the "modification" or troping necessary to produce heightened effects, and of the political investment in maintaining such effects through brute physical, as well as rhetorical, means. The effectiveness of political authority, of physical torture ("what makes pain itself . . . more painful"), and of the sublime, respectively, all depend upon the figure of distance. Though the historical anecdote is introduced ostensibly as an arbitrary example, the political implication of this emphasis on distance is clearly central to Burke's aesthetic of "source" and "modification." What we are allowed to contemplate in this episode is the anarchic collapse of a vertical sociopolitical scale (figured by the immanent contact of king and subject-turned-regicide) but also at the same time a *prolongation* or *extension* of the distance between a different "king" and subject, mediated by an "emissary."

It is worth noting that the vicarious experience of a threat to the political order is implicit as well in Burke's description of the suspended lexical order necessary to the sublime in poetry. According to Burke the rhetorical sublime depends in part on the breaking down of normal syntactic relationships, a process of elision and condensation that confuses, "hurries," and "dazzles" the mind.[22] Yet it can hardly be coincidental that in the two examples of asyndeton cited by Burke as instances of sublime rhetorical anarchy, a *king* should be one of the objects of description suddenly suspended among others with no discernible system of relationships. The two passages cited are *Paradise Lost*, 1.589–99, and

---

[22] See n. 15, on "asyndeton." See also Weiskel's comments on "aggression" in Longinus (*The Romantic Sublime*, 5); and Neil Hertz's observations about Longinus's sublime "disintegration and figurative reconstitution" in "A Reading of Longinus," *Critical Inquiry* 9 (March 1983): 591.

King Henry IV, part 1, 4.1.97–109; and Burke's comments on the two, respectively, are as follows:

> Here is a very noble picture; and in what does this poetical picture consist? in images of a tower, an archangel, the sun rising through mists, or in an eclipse, *the ruin of monarchs, and the revolutions of kingdoms. The mind is hurried out of itself, by a croud of great and confused images; which affect because they are crouded and confused. For separate them, and you lose much of the greatness, and join them, and you infallibly lose the clearness.* (2.4.62, my emphasis)

> There are also many descriptions in the poets and orators which owe their sublimity to a richness and profusion of images, in which *the mind is so dazzled as to make it impossible to attend to that exact coherence* and agreement of the allusions, which we should require on every other occasion. I do not now remember a more striking example of this, than the description which is given of *the king's army* in the play of Henry the fourth. (2.13.78, my emphasis)

For a sublime effect to occur, the king must be neither "joined" to nor "separated" from the other elements in the poem. The reader must be "dazzled" by the powerful associations of kingship, yet unable to make this striking impression cohere with others. Like Spenser's or Milton's figure of "amazement," the figure of "dazzlement" here both levels and reprivileges the king.

As we noted above, the metaphoric model of surfaces and depths remains tangentially related to an older model in which heights are opposed to depths. From both an eschatological and a secular perspective, depth and height have a curious relationship. On the one hand they are ambiguously, even indeterminately related; on the other hand they are clearly antithetical, as in eschatological topography or evaluations of social rank. The confusion of these two schemes is clearly demonstrated in the following passage, in which Burke dicusses the relationship between pain and delight:

> The prosperity of no empire, nor the grandeur of no king, can so agreebly affect in the reading, as the ruin of the state of Macedon, and the distress of its unhappy prince. . . . Our delight in cases of this kind, is very greatly *heightened*, if the sufferer be some excellent person who *sinks* under an unworthy fortune. Scipio and Cato are both virtuous characters; but we are more

deeply affected by the violent death of the one, and the ruin of the great cause he adhered to, than with the deserved triumphs and uninterrupted prosperity of the other; for terror is a passion which always produces delight when it does not *press too close*. (1.14.45–46, my emphasis)

In terms of pure affect, depth and height are as one, signaling equally the vertiginous distance that separates them.[23] But in a different sense, "height" of fortune and of social rank are quite distinct from their opposites and must be kept so for the dynamic effects of heightened/deepened response to occur when a protagonist "sinks." The aesthetic risk articulated in this passage (the threat to the effect of sublimity) lies in two distinct potential collapses: a tragic character's lack of social *standing* (or even a too-easy identification with the hero on the reader's part) and the possibility of terror "pressing too close" to us as we listen or read. Similarly, in the passage on the regicide Damiens, the "emissary" referred to by Burke is not only the "pain," which signals approaching death to Damiens, but the anecdote itself, upon which we may safely reflect from a distance, with a heightened/deepened sense of violation and terror. What is necessary, according to this parable, is that truly painful feelings be kept at a distance and "modified."

Burke first discusses "modification"—distinguishing it implicitly from "reflection"—a few pages earlier in part 1, when he opposes "grief" to the "delight" that, as he will shortly demonstrate, is constitutive of true sublimity. In grieving, writes Burke, we dwell upon an irretrievably lost object of affection, suspended between pain and pleasure, but with pleasure uppermost. By contrast, sublime delight is not a qualified form of pleasure but rather an attenuated kind of pain:

> It is the nature of grief to keep its object perpetually in its eye, to present it in its most pleasurable views, to repeat all the circumstances that attend it, even to the last minuteness; to go back to every particular enjoyment, to dwell upon each . . . ; in grief, the *pleasure* is still uppermost; and the affliction we suffer has no resemblance to absolute pain. . . . The Odyssey of Homer,

[23] Weiskel notes that "height and depth are of course merely two perspectives within the same dimension of verticality," though he attributes differences of emphasis to differences of philosophical temperament: "What is 'lofty' for the idealist will be 'profound' for the naturalizing mind" (*The Romantic Sublime*, 24). My own reading of Burke stays closer to the physiological associations of "depth" and "height": I believe it is inevitably the *common* factor of verticality, in addition to any philosophical or social distinction, that is being invoked when height and depth are contrasted.

which abounds with so many natural and affecting images, has none more striking than those which Menelaus raises of the calamitous fate of his friends, and his own manner of feeling it. He owns indeed, that he often gives himself some intermission from such melancholy reflections, but he observes too, that melancholy as they are, they give him pleasure. . . . On the other hand, when we recover our health, when we escape an imminent danger, is it with joy that we are affected? The sense on these occasions is far from that smooth and voluptuous satisfaction which the assured prospect of pleasure bestows. The delight which arises from the modifications of pain, confesses the stock from whence it sprung, in its solid, strong, and severe nature. (1.5.37–38)

This passage presents us with two distinct, and yet overlapping, kinds of attenuated pain. In "reflecting" pleasurably on an irretrievable object, grief bears no *resemblance* to the pain it attenuates, despite the apparent resemblance between grief and pain. The "modification" essential to delight, however, preserves a direct, if distant, relationship to pain. The important, if subtle, distinction between reflection and modification is reinforced in part 2, where Burke emphasizes how the "modifications" of terror necessary to produce sublimity necessarily preclude rational reflection:

I know of nothing sublime which is not some *modification* of power. And this branch rises as naturally as the other two branches, from terror, the common stock of every thing that is sublime. . . . Strength, violence, pain and terror, are ideas that rush in upon the mind together. Look at a man or any other animal of prodigious strength, and what is your idea before reflection? Is it that this strength will be subservient to you, to your ease, to your pleasure, to your interest in any sense? No. . . . Now, though in a just idea of the Deity, perhaps none of his attributes are predominant, yet to our imagination, his power is by far the most striking. Some reflection, some comparing is necessary to sastisfy us of his wisdom, his justice, and his goodness; to be struck with his power, it is only necessary that we should open our eyes. (2.5.64–68)

The distinction between rational reflection (which destroys aesthetic effects) and those modifications of terror, pain, and power that constitute the sublime is carried over into Burke's discussion of language in part 5. In attempting to account for the "power they [words] may have on the passions," Burke argues that a rational analysis (figured as sustained visual attention, which brings an idea "to light") destroys all affect.

Words, he argues, gain their affective power by virtue of the spontaneous impressions they create, even if those impressions are but attenuated versions of *prior* immediate impressions:

> Put yourself upon analysing one of these words, and you must reduce it from one set of general words to another, and then into the simple abstracts and aggregates, in a much longer series than may be at first imagined, before any real idea emerges to light, . . . and when you have made such a discovery of the original ideas, the effect of the composition is utterly lost. . . . Such words are in reality but mere sounds; but they are sounds, which being used on particular occasions, wherein we receive some good, or suffer some evil . . . they produce in the mind, whenever they are afterwards mentioned, effects similar to those of their occasions. The sounds being often used without out reference to any particular occasion, and carrying still their first impressions, they at last utterly lose their connection with the particular occasions that gave rise to them. (5.2.164–65)

The affective power of words, according to this passage, is a function of impressions that have been modified ("carried" over, though with a "loss" of "connection") but have not yet lost their vitality through any sustained act of introspection. What Burke preserves here is a basic distinction between two degrees of attenuated feeling, represented as a difference in *distance* from an original feeling. Some modification or distance is clearly necessary for words to gain an affective power that may extend beyond their initial conditions of reference; yet too self-conscious or reflective a detachment from those words renders them powerless.

As in the parable of regicide and king (and the earlier opposition of grief to sublime delight), Burke presents a spatialized drama in which our distance from an initially—or potentially—overwhelming "impression" may produce spectacular effects or—if extended too far—may collapse back into a diminished spatial and psychic dimensionality. The means by which we sustain an appropriate distance from an impression (or from a potential source of impressions) is figured variously as "reflection," "modification," "emissary," "dwelling upon," "keeping in our eye," "emergence," "carrying," "loss of connection," "loss of force," "sympathy," and "substitution."[24] For an aesthetic effect to be produced the distance involved must be more than merely quantitative (some qualita-

[24] Burke describes the affective power both of representation in general and of language specifically as a function of "sympathy" and "substitution." See 1.13.44 and 5.5–6.172–73.

tive "modification" must occur), yet this process must stop short of self-conscious, rational reflection. We might place these variously figured processes along a spectrum, ranged from the least to the most self-conscious, and in that case "modification" and "reflection" would clearly appear at opposite ends. But it is equally clear that any estimate of the difference between modified and reflective feeling is itself a product of reflection.

Burke constantly exhorts us to "examine" our own minds for a confirmation of the difference between spontaneously "modified" and self-consciously "reflective" feelings. Such a paradox, as we have seen, is incipient in the rhetoric of both Locke and Berkeley. But in their work the paradox helps underscore an essential point regarding the inextricable relationship of attention to inattention; they are concerned with the way in which successive sedimentations of reflection and habit constitute the set of attitudes and dispositions we call common sense. For Burke, however, the paradox points to the ineluctability of perceptual distortion rather than to the strategic circularity of attention and inattention. "Reflection," in Burke's scheme, is both necessary and dangerous, and, as we shall see, it both produces and destroys aesthetic effects.

THE DANGERS OF REFLECTION

The stories of Cato and Damiens convey a sense of the sublime through figures of depth and height, both implicit and explicit. The figure of depth thus functions as the sublime "emissary" of a pain, which is itself in turn the emissary of death. But is it *through* our reflection, or only in the *absence* of any reflection, that the figure of depth achieves this mediation? In his chapter "Power," Burke suggests precisely the opposite—that reflection actually *destroys* the dynamic tensions of the sublime:

> Pain is always inflicted by a power in some way superior, because we never submit to pain willingly. So that strength, violence, pain and terror, are ideas that rush in upon the mind together. Look at a man, or any other animal of prodigious strength, and what is your idea before reflection? Is it that this strength will be subservient to you, to your ease, to your pleasure, to your interest in any sense? No; the emotion you feel is, lest this enormous strength should be employed to the purposes of rapine and destruction. (2.5.65)

Here, the power of a "superior" being impresses us with sublime (and thus deep) sensations, for as long as we can stave off "reflection." Reflection can thus *collapse*, as well as preserve, distinctions between height and depth and can confuse objects "reflected in the depth" with those "which there abide / In their true dwelling."[25] In Locke and Berkeley, such potential for perceptual illusion and confusion is countered by the suggestion that "reflection" is more like the activity of reading or processing language than it is like "seeing" something. Burke's physiological bias, however, does not lend itself as easily to the dissolution of optical models into linguistic ones.

Reflection, according to Burke, is crucial to the project of investigating the passions, yet the fact that our most basic passions themselves occur in the absence of reflection makes their original circumstances difficult to recall.[26] Though reflection may compromise the intensity of the passions, lack of reflection can prevent their being retraced:

> It is no small bar in the way of our enquiry into the cause of our passions, that the occasion of many of them are given, and that their governing motions are communicated at a time when we have not capacity to reflect on them; at a time of which all sort of memory is worn out of our minds. For besides such things as affect us in various manners according to their natural powers, there are associations made at that early season, which we find it very hard afterwards to distinguish from natural effects. (4.2.130)

Reflection here is linked to memory, and the absence of both is figured as the wearing away of a surface—resulting in the erosion of any clear distinction between "natural effects" and effects of "association." Burke implies that an ability to "reflect" on an "early" passion when it was "communicated" would have helped to impress the memory of its circumstances so deeply that it could not be worn away. Yet memory is still

---

25 William Wordsworth, *The Prelude* (1850), in *Poetical Works*, ed. Thomas Hutchinson (Oxford: Oxford University Press, 1969), book 4, ll.265–67. Hume makes a similar point in his *Treatise*, where reflection is acknowledged to create new impressions even as it allows us to preserve or recall old ones. Though reflection helps us "keep" certain impressions "in our eye" (1.1.7), it nonetheless "produces . . . new impressions . . . which may properly be called impressions of reflexion, because derived from it" (1.1.2).

26 Cf. a slightly different version of the mnemonic function of "reflection" in Locke's *Essay*. Locke claims that our ideas about the operations of our mind "pass [through the mind] continually; yet like floating Visions, they make not deep Impressions enough, to leave in the Mind clear distinct lasting *Ideas*, till the Understanding turns inwards upon it self, *reflects* on its *Operations*, and makes them the Object of its own Contemplation" (2.1.8). See as well Hume's remarks concerning original impressions: " 'Tis impossible perfectly to understand any idea, without tracing it up to its origin, and examining that primary impression, from which it arises" (*Treatise*, 1.3.2).

distinct from the effect of the passion. In the absence of reflection it is the memory only, and not the passion itself, which wears away; the passion still affects deeply, even if its origins are inscrutable.[27]

Just as our earliest passions are indissociable from their original "occasions" (the "occasions" themselves being, nonetheless, irrecoverable), so affective language is indissociable from the circumstances in which it is learned. In this latter case, the circumstances of origin are not worn away but simply fail to have any continued relevance. Although ethical terms that are impressed at an early stage on our "ductile" minds may continue to have an effect in later life, such moral affections may well fail to coincide with our moral ideas:

> Mr. Locke has somewhere observed with his usual sagacity, that most general words, those belonging to virtue and vice, good and evil, especially, are taught before the particular modes of action to which they belong are presented to the mind; and with them, the love of the one, and the abhorrence of the other; for the minds of children are so ductile, that a nurse, or any other person about a child, by seeming pleased or displeased with any thing, or even any word, may give the disposition of the child a similar turn. When afterwards, the several occurrences in life come to be applied to these words; and that which is pleasant often appears under the name of evil; and what is disagreeable to nature is called good and virtuous; a strange confusion of ideas and affections arises in the minds of many; and an appearance of no small contradiction between their notions and their actions. (5.3.165)

The reference here is to a number of related passages from Locke's *Essay* (1.3.22–23; 2.33.10; 4.20.9), and Burke not incidentally reproduces the Lockean configuration linking femininity, class inferiority, rhetoric, and false reflection. Burke, however, is more ambivalent about the consequences. Poorly grounded moral notions may nonetheless be satisfactory ones. Burke is not prepared to condemn categorically the cases in which moral affection is the result of purely rhetorical associations—where, far from being tied to "natural effects" (as was the case with our earliest passions), passion is tied contingently to a lexical sign, the connection having been instituted at a time when no concrete "occasions" had yet "c[o]me into view":

---

[27] This is fairly straightforward Humean doctrine concerning the passions: reason, in the form of reflection, is given us for the sake of teaching conformity with the passions, to which we are subject anyway. See Hume, ibid., 2.2.3–4; 3.1.1.

> There are many, who love virtue, and who detest vice, and this not from
> hypocrisy or affectation, who notwithstanding very frequently act ill and
> wickedly in particulars without the least remorse; because these particular
> occasions never came into view, when the passions on the side of virtue were
> so warmly affected by certain words heated originally by the breath of others.
> (5.3.165–66)

The inability to bring future contingencies "into view" when we learn our
ethical vocabulary suggests that language may be subject to our inca-
pacity for "reflection," rather than a resolution to it. On the other hand it
may suggest that reflection is inseparable from language and that reflection plays an ambiguous role in the preservation of our deepest feelings.

If lack of reflection allows the erosion of memory or confusion of our
impressions, it is still not clear in what sense reflection itself might preserve them. Language is clearly central to memory, but if language allows
us to reflect upon our sensations, it helps us not only to preserve and
recover deep impressions but to create them.

> Now, as words affect, not by any original power, but by representation, it
> might be supposed, that their influence over the passions should be but light;
> yet it is quite otherwise; . . . eloquence and poetry are as capable, nay indeed
> much more capable of making deep and lively impressions than any other
> arts, and even than nature itself in very many cases. . . . The influence of most
> things on our passions is not so much from the things themselves, as from
> our opinions concerning them; and these again depend very much on the
> opinions of other men, conveyable for the most part by words only. . . .
> There are many things of a very affecting nature, which can seldom occur in
> the reality, but the words which represent them often do; and thus they have
> an opportunity of making a deep impression and taking root in the mind,
> whilst the idea of the reality was transient. (5.7.173)

Previously, Burke had suggested that the absence of reflection early in life
allowed many of our earliest passions to be worn away, beyond retrieval.
But along with reflection comes language, and language is allowed in
"very many cases" to make *deeper* impressions than "transient" natural
effects, precisely through the force of repetition and iterability.[28]

---

[28] Burke claims not only that language may often strike "deeper" than "transient"
realities but that it also can make deeper impressions "than any other art." The latter has
much to do with what Hertz terms language's "peculiar agility"—the way in which language seems capable of fulfilling both our desires for figuration and our fears of disfigura-

In his essay "A Reading of Longinus," Neil Hertz argues that in the tradition of the Longinian sublime, style must be elevated enough to hide the rhetorical figures that accomplish the most fundamental fractures and reintegrations of psychological power in the text, that is, those that are necessarily involved in transfers of emotional energy between subject and object.[29] Thus, the "movement of disintegration and figurative reconstitution" that defines the "sublime turn" (591) can function persuasively only "when figurative language is concealed" (594)—when the stresses created by sublime energy are reconciled through rhetorical figures that go unnoticed. Sublime language is, in a sense, a sleight of hand, distracting from its own suasive intentions.

Reflection is the unnoticed figure of Burke's *Enquiry*. The *Enquiry* works to convince us that rational reflection has no essential connection to those figures in the text that embody and transmit energy and power (e.g., "heightened" delight or "deep" pain). In his single extended discussion of optical reflection, Burke draws a distinction between light reflected from various surfaces and the transmission of light "without opposition" *through* a transparent body:

> Suppose I look at a bottle of muddy liquor, of a blue or red colour: the blue or red rays cannot pass clearly to the eye, but are suddenly and unequally stopped by the intervention of little opaque bodies, which without preparation change the idea. . . . But when the ray passes without such opposition through the glass or liquor, when the glass or liquor are quite transparent, the light is something softened in the passage, which makes it more agreeable even as light; and the liquor reflecting all the rays of its proper colour *evenly*, it has such an effect on the eye, as smooth opaque bodies have on the eye and touch. So that the pleasure here is compounded of the softness of the transmitted, and the evenness of the reflected light. (4.25.159)

What we see when we look at a colored transparent body is both light passing "softly" *through* the body and light reflected "evenly" from the particles of the body. It is worth noting that even the light "transmitted" through the "transparency" without any "change [of] idea" undergoes

---

tion. Hertz notes the various characterizations of these "two poles" as "the divine and the human, the true and the false, the position of the father and that of the son, or whatever." See Hertz, "A Reading of Longinus," 594.

[29] Ibid., 579–610. Subsequent references to Hertz's essay will cite page numbers and will appear parenthetically within the body of the chapter.

some modification: it is "something softened" and made "more agreeable." We might suspect, then, that even ostensibly unmediated transmissions of light entail something of the effect of reflection, and that reflection is more ubiquitous and less distinctive a phenomenon than Burke allows. Nonetheless, Burke clearly interprets reflection as a quite special case of optical sensation, and distinguishes it from the transmission of light (or idea) through a "transparent" medium.[30]

Though Burke does not depend heavily on schematic optical analogies throughout the *Enquiry*, we can see that he pays some minimal empirical attention to the actual mechanics of reflected light. His meditations on the relationship between optics and aesthetic response are to be found primarily in the latter half of part 4 (4.9–24). It not surprising, then, that when we make the abrupt transition to part 5, with its explicitly antipictorial linguistic doctrine, Burke carefully avoids using the metaphor of reflection that had been common throughout the rest of the essay.[31] Burke does not want his theory of language to be confused in any way with his interest in optics. Throughout part 5, Burke consistently rejects the suggestion that words "raise" pictures or images in our minds, or that language allows ideas to "emerge." The reflective faculty, which enables us to bring our ideas or memories "into view," then, cannot be too closely aligned with language, since Burke cannot afford to figure language as an internally directed sight. Nonetheless, the figure of reflection is implicit throughout this chapter, even central to it. As we have

[30] On Burke's interest in Newtonian optics, see Nicolson, *Newton Demands the Muse*, 4, 123, 128–29.

[31] There is some ambiguity as to whether the antipictorial theory of language in part 5 pertains to all language or only to affective language. Burke initially describes the chapter as an "enquiry into the manner in which they [words] excite such emotions [of beauty and the sublime]" (5.1.163), but he immediately proceeds to challenge the notion that the "raising" of "ideas" is the proper "power of poetry and eloquence, *as well as that of words in ordinary conversation*" (5.2.163, my emphasis). There is also some ambiguity as to whether his attack on the notion that words stimulate pictures and concepts is an attack on the notion of verbal representation per se. He at first asserts of "compounded abstract" words that "whatever power they may have on the passions, they do not derive it from any representation raised in the mind" (5.2.164); but later he writes more generally that "words affect, not by any original power, but by representation" (5.7.173). I have assumed for the purposes of my discussion that Burke's antipictorial theory of language is indeed generalizable and does not refer exclusively to affective language. I have also assumed that his contradictory remarks about representation do not alter his general thesis about the failure of words to stimulate immediate visual or conceptual correlatives in the mind. For a fuller reading of Burke's antipictorialism, see W.J.T. Mitchell's chapter "Eye and Ear: Edmund Burke and the Politics of Sensibility," in *Iconology*.

seen, Burke's empiricism requires that he corroborate his theory of language precisely by examining what goes on in his own mind when he uses words:

> But I am of opinion, that the most general effect even of these words, does not arise from their forming pictures of the several things they would represent in the imagination; because on a very diligent examination of my own mind, and getting others to consider theirs, I do not find that once in twenty times any such picture is formed, and when it is, there is most commonly a particular effort of the imagination of that purpose. (5.4.167)

> But let anybody examine himself, and see whether he has impressed on his imagination any pictures of a river, mountain, watery soil, Germany, &c. (Ibid.)

> Strange as it may appear, we are often at a loss to know what ideas we have of things, or whether we have any ideas at all upon some subjects. It even requires a good deal of attention to be thoroughly satisfied on this head. (5.5.168)

The functioning of language, if not identical to the process of reflection, is nonetheless discovered through reflection. And the way in which language moves us remains connected to that peculiar form of "modification" that Burke elsewhere figures as reflection. Even in the closing paragraphs of part 5, Burke cannot resist figuratively attributing the effects of language to such qualities as its relative "polish" or its embodiment of a "fire already kindled in another" (5.7.175–76). If language and reflection are necessary to the preservation of our deepest memories, they also compete with those memories. Burke thus raises the possibility that reflection does not merely add a memory of passion's origins to passion itself but *imposes* its own depths ("conveyed" from the "opinions of other men") on remembered passion. If the ability to reflect helps us preserve and recall deep impressions, it is accompanied by the creation of *new* depths, producing anew the threat of a crucial disfiguration in the historical sedimentation of our passions.

Burke heightens the tensions implicit in empiricist rhetoric by employing even more consistently than Locke or Berkeley a single set of rhetorical figures to describe the respective structures of world, body, and mind. This follows from his belief in the essential analogy of the senses (e.g., 4.22.155), but it also indicates how far he has departed from Locke's and Berkeley's assumptions about the cognitive value of analogy and other rhetorical categories. For Locke and Berkeley, the coordination of our sense faculties is merely contingent—a pragmatic set of connections arrived at through experience—and this contingency illustrates the illegitimacy of rhetorical language. The application of terms proper derived from one sense faculty to the sensations received from another sense faculty can never be anything other than rhetorical. Locke describes such expressions as "marks" or "figures" and thereby affiliates them loosely with the functioning of *all* verbal signs; Berkeley works harder at establishing the degrees and kinds of rhetorical departure from "proper" speaking—true and false analogy, proportional and metaphorical analogy, metaphor and propriety of speech. But in either case rhetorical language is conceived of as marking the limits of empirical observation: language enters when reflection takes over from sensation, and *rhetorical* language indicates reflection that has become sedimented—reflection that is no longer aware of itself, unreflecting reflection.

Burke turns this formulation on its head. The observable patterns in our various sensory responses to the world both illustrate and validate the concept of analogy and thus establish the cognitive value of rhetoric. As in Locke and Berkeley, the relationship between sensation and language ultimately remains circular, but the emphasis has shifted considerably. Instead of *merely rhetorical* expressions illustrating the perilous contingency of our commonsense construction of the world, we have the "consent of all men" in certain "metaphors" (introduction, 14) illustrating the presence of natural connections and patterns in the phenomenal world.

What is still contingent in Burke's formulation, we might speculate, is the set of figures he chooses for describing world, body, and mind. Certainly he inherits particular figures, and a particular narrativization of their connection, from empiricist philosophy: that is, the figures of reflection, surface, and depth, and the myth of optical constructivism. But in bringing rhetoric to the foreground in his account of perceptual and aesthetic psychology, he makes possible the next step in the empiricist investigation of the world: the question of what the world might "look" like if we regarded more ironically the unreflecting "consent of all men" in our most familiar figures of speech. It is to this question that William Hazlitt turns, but with a further ironic twist. For Hazlitt's term for the activity of abstracting oneself from rhetoric—particularly the empiricist rhetoric of reflection, surface, and depth—is precisely the figure of "reflection."

5

The "Character" of Reflection:
Hazlitt on Depth and Superficiality

As one who hangs down-bending from the side
Of a slow-moving boat, upon the breast
Of a still water, solacing himself
With such discoveries as his eye can make
Beneath him in the bottom of the deep,
Sees many beauteous sights—weeds, fishes, flowers,
Grots, pebbles, roots of trees, 'and fancies more,
Yet often is perplexed and cannot part
The shadow from the substance, rocks and sky,
Mountains and clouds, reflected in the depth
Of the clear flood, from things which there abide
In their true dwelling; now is crossed by gleam
Of his own image, by a sun-beam now,
And wavering motions sent he knows not whence,
Impediments that make his task more sweet;
Such pleasant office have we long pursued
Incumbent o'er the surface of past time
With like success, . . .

—WORDSWORTH, *The Prelude*

REFLECTING, REFLECTING, REFLECTING

HAZLITT INHERITS from Burke and the romantic poets a world structured almost obsessively in terms of surfaces, heights, depths, and reflections. Landscapes, habits of speech, and character all seem to be organized around the pervasive figures of spatial dimensionality and optical
transmission. Yet as an empiricist, Hazlitt is also interested in determining precisely how it is that our impressions of "depth" are constructed—
how it is that we come to infer depth of field, depth of meaning, and
depth of character from those discrete and variable impressions of the

world with which our experience presents us. And it is in particular his interest in depth of character—or more generally in our conventional, spatial figurations of character—that distinguishes Hazlitt's rather unorthodox and ironic empiricism.

In Hazlitt's opinion, our conception of "character"—principally, though not exclusively, of human character—is arrived at by reflection. "Character" is composed by, reflected in, and a reflection upon, experience. Yet Hazlitt intentionally uses the figure of reflection in a number of different senses, corresponding to a number of distinct mental and rhetorical operations. One kind of reflection simply involves the narcissistic projection of our own prejudices and preconceptions, in a process compared by both Burke and Wordsworth to the transposing of optical images on one another. Another kind of reflection involves self-criticism, including a skeptical analysis of the role played by habit and figures of speech in our picture of the world. Finally, reflection may involve the ironic reversal or inversion of our habitual descriptions and figures of speech.

Hazlitt's emphasis on this last type of reflection constitutes one of his strong connections with—and developments of—the empiricist tradition that figures reflection as a turning away from metaphysical speculation. Hazlitt interprets reflection as a process of *reversal* and conceives of reversal and inversion as critical tools that throw the rhetorical component of perception and knowledge into relief. Like Berkeley, Hazlitt loves to push empirical methods until they produce counterintuitive claims (e.g., superficial knowledge is the best) and to insist that these are the logical consequence of our commonsense views, even if they require a revision of our commonplace figures of speech. Unlike Berkeley, however, Hazlitt intends ironic consequences to follow from this strategy. His concern, ultimately, is not only to expose the rhetorical construction of our commonsense view of the world but to insist as well on the rhetorical operations by which such an exposure is carried out.

Despite his fascination with figures of speech, Hazlitt criticizes rhetorical theories of knowledge that appear to reduce knowledge to "well speaking."[1] Hazlitt is more interested in the *mutual* pressures that language and experience exert on one another. Like a twentieth-century empiricist, Karl Popper, Hazlitt is interested in what we might call "perceptual prejudice"—the way in which empirical observation necessarily

---

[1] See p. 186.

anticipates patterns and shapes in experience.[2] But he also insists that prejudice and self-criticism are mutually conditioning. If our attribution of "depth" to certain experiences is a result of preconceptions rather than of spontaneous, unmediated perception, the reflection that produces depth is still of various sorts. In some cases language may condition sensation, and in other cases unanticipated sensations may force a reconsideration of our habits of speech. Hazlitt's metaphor for both these processes is "reflection." Reflection may confuse or delude us, it may foreground our illusions, and on rare occasions it may suggest changes in the way we talk. In the three essays that we shall examine here—"Mr. Wordsworth," "On the Knowledge of Character," and "On Depth and Superficiality"—Hazlitt gradually begins to examine the metaphoricity of "reflection" itself and to speculate about the limitations of the very figure that helps us explain the limiting and enabling functions of rhetoric.

REFLECTION AS INVERSION: THE "INTERNAL EVIDENCE" OF WORDSWORTH

The Prelude had not yet been published when Hazlitt sat down to write his essay "Mr. Wordsworth" in 1818.[3] Nevertheless, in a striking passage, Hazlitt managed to capture Wordsworth's peculiar sensitivity to the mediating function of reflections, exemplified in the famous "surface of past time" passage cited at the beginning of this chapter. Hazlitt's Wordsworth has his head bent to the ground yet remains attentive to the presence of objects above and around him:

> Nursed amidst the grandeur of mountain scenery, he has stooped to have a
> nearer view of the daisy under his feet, or plucked a branch of white-thorn
> from the spray: but in describing it, his mind seems imbued with the majesty
> and solemnity of the objects around him. . . . There is little mention of
> mountainous scenery in Mr. Wordsworth's poetry; *but by internal evidence*

[2] See Popper's remarks on the role of "custom," "habit," and the "expectation of regularity" in empirical observation (*Conjectures and Refutations*, 43–49).

[3] All citations from Hazlitt refer to *The Complete Works of William Hazlitt in Twenty-One Volumes*, centenary edition, ed. P. P. Howe (London: J. M. Dent, 1932). The Wordsworth essay, reprinted originally in *The Spirit of the Age*, appears in 11.86–95. All subsequent references to Hazlitt's work will cite volume and page numbers from this edition, with the titles of specific works indicated where necessary.

one might be almost sure that it was written in a mountainous country, from
its bareness, its simplicity, its loftiness and its depth! (89–90, my emphasis)

Two kinds of reflection are implied here, though neither is explicitly
identified. First, the process of visual and intellectual reflection by which
qualities of surface ("bareness"), of depth, and of height ("loftiness") are
reconciled. Second, the rhetorical process of reflection by which the
"daisy" and the "white-thorn" are "imbued" with sensations appropriate to a different perceptual and figurative scheme—in short, the process
by which a poem's "internal evidence" is made to supply a set of implied
figures quite distinct from its explicit figurative ornaments (the latter
being, appropriately enough, flowers). The tension thus is between the
implied and the ostensible subject matter. And "reflection" is in fact the
implicit answer to two questions raised by the passage: How is it that
impressions of surface, height, and depth can be made to cohere? And
further, how is it that these impressions can be transferred to, and then
inferred from, impressions of a flower?

Hazlitt is concerned to explain Wordsworth's sensations: how they
came about, whether they were received from his physical surroundings
or generated in some other way, how they were experienced by the poet.
But Hazlitt is also concerned with the way in which Wordsworth's language mediates these experiences, particularly with the way in which the
poet's rhetoric shapes in advance his "discovery" of nature. If Wordsworth is—as he presents himself—the most reflective of poets, Hazlitt
wants to know to what extent this is a fact about Wordsworth's way of
recuperating nature through language and to what extent it is a fact about
what Wordsworth actually "saw" in nature in the first place. Both the
naivete and the complexity of such a question are concentrated in the
figure that Wordsworth uses most frequently to describe the confusion of
renewed encounters with initial responses and that Hazlitt wishes, in a
quite different vein, to privilege as a critical term: the figure of reflection.

In the first half of the Wordsworth essay, Hazlitt attempts repeatedly
to explain the strange paradoxes of style and values he finds in Wordsworth's poetry. Each attempt begins by describing Wordsworth's poetic
contradictions in terms of depths and heights, then appears to follow
Wordsworth in resolving these contradictions through an ethos of humility figured in terms of surfaces, and concludes by describing the entire
process ambiguously as one of "reflection." In the essay's first paragraph,
Hazlitt sums up the paradox of Wordsworth's career in an ironic aphor-

ism: "With him 'lowliness is young ambition's ladder': but he finds it a toil to climb in this way the steep of fame." Reconciling depths and heights will thus be Wordsworth's challenge, and a few sentences later Hazlitt suggests that the poet's "household truths" have indeed managed to provide the desired resolution: "His style is vernacular: he delivers household truths. He sees nothing *loftier* than human hopes; nothing *deeper* than the human heart. This he probes, this he tampers with, this he poises, with all its incalculable weight of thought and feeling, in his hands; and at the same time calms the throbbing pulses of his own heart, by keeping his eye ever *fixed on the face* of nature" (86, my emphasis). The "face" of nature soothes both the heights of ambition and the depths of the simple heart. The prosopopoeia is clearly Wordsworth's, but this figure of a reconciling surface is given a new twist in Hazlitt's next paragraph, as its political implications are brought under consideration: "The political changes of the day were the model on which he formed and conducted his poetical experiments. His Muse (it cannot be denied, and without this we cannot explain its character at all) is a *levelling* one. It proceeds on a principle of equality, and strives to *reduce* all things to the same standard" (87, my emphasis). The mediation of surfaces and depths is once again presented as a surface, but now it is more disturbing than soothing, since it "reduces" as it reconciles. (Even given that in Hazlitt's usage "reduce" means to find a common denominator rather than to "diminish," the overtones are not reassuring.) Yet in turn, the two contrasting associations of surface imagery (the vital "face" of nature and the abstract politics of "leveling") are reconciled as Hazlitt concludes the first movement of the essay by referring to Wordsworth's poetic activity as a mode of "reflection": Wordsworth's "reflections are profound," Hazlitt writes, "according to the gravity and the aspiring pretensions of his mind." The figure of surface disappears into the figure of reflection, which seems to hold depths and heights together just as well, without the conflicting associations of nature and politics.

Though the first movement of the essay concludes by reconciling surface, depth, and height in the figure of reflection, Hazlitt begins the immediately ensuing paragraph by returning to Wordsworth's insistent rejection of heights and describing it once more as a kind of leveling:

> His popular, inartificial style gets rid (at a blow) of all the trappings of verse, of all the high places of poetry: "the cloud-capt towers, the solemn temples, the gorgeous palaces," are swept to the ground, and "like the base-

less fabric of a vision, leave not a wreck behind." All the traditions of learning, all the superstitions of age, are obliterated and effaced. We begin *de
novo*, on a *tabula rasa* of poetry. (87)

Here, Hazlitt associates surface imagery with the *tabula rasa* of both
empiricist and rationalist philosophy, and like Burke of *Reflections on the
Revolution in France*, he expresses suspicion of the entire trope. There is
no moment in which Wordsworth may begin "*de novo*, on a *tabula rasa*,"
argues Hazlitt, because the activity of "leveling" (or "effacing") leaves
behind the unique trace of the leveler: "The author [Wordsworth] tram-
ples on the pride of art with greater pride." Hazlitt then shifts the conceit
slightly and describes Wordsworth's temperamental affinity for surfaces
as a process of stripping or revealing rather than of leveling or reducing:
"The decencies of costume, the decorations of vanity are stripped off
without mercy as barbarous, idle, and Gothic." But this revelation of
surface, too, turns out to be mere preparation for further dressing up:
"He clothes the naked with beauty and grandeur from the stores of his
own recollections" (87–88).

In surveying Wordsworth's work, now, Hazlitt is confronted not only
with contrasting figures of depth, height, and surface but as well with
three different conceptions of surface: surface as the "face" of nature;
surface as the leveling-out of pretensions (whether of style or of politics);
and surface as the "stripping" or undressing of rhetorical ornament. The
resolution is once again found in the figure of reflection, as Hazlitt ends
the paragraph by describing how "Mr. Wordsworth's unpretending
Muse, in russet guise, scales the summits of reflection, while it makes the
round earth its footstool, and its home!" (88). It is through "reflection"
that Wordsworth is supposed to resolve his contrary tendencies toward
sublimity and bathos, toward the "unpretending . . . russet guise" and
the "stripping" of "costume." As a figure for mental activity, reflection
blurs the distinction between narcissistic self-projection and objective
analysis, while as a figure for Wordsworth's subject matter it mediates
between the pretentious heights and unknowable depths of human
thought and feeling. While the figure of surface mediates through a process of suppression that is at the same time a process of assertion (e.g., a
"russet guise," or pride trampling on pride), the figure of reflection mediates by denying its own constitutive role, by proposing to allow all figures
to speak, when in fact it is limited in the figures it can represent. Hazlitt
uses the figure of reflection to reconcile tensions in the figurative scheme

whereby the world is divided into surfaces, depths, and heights, much as Berkeley uses figures of surface in his *Treatise* to reconcile—and in fact to evade—what he takes to be a false distinction between interiority and exteriority.

It is at this point that Hazlitt begins to speculate on the odd disparity between Wordsworth's philosophical loftiness and the relative absence of literal references to heights in his poetry. In a passage I have already cited, Hazlitt writes:

> Nursed amidst the grandeur of mountain scenery, he has stooped to have a nearer view of the daisy under his feet, or plucked a branch of white-thorn from the spray: but in describing it, his mind seems imbued with the majesty and solemnity of the objects around him. . . . There is little mention of mountainous scenery in Mr. Wordsworth's poetry; but by internal evidence one might be almost sure that it was written in a mountainous country, from its bareness, its simplicity, its loftiness and its depth!

Considering the crucial role played by the figure of reflection in Hazlitt's argument about Wordsworth to this point, we might echo Hazlitt's own puzzlement here and ask why the term *reflection* does not appear in a passage so clearly describing a reflective process (i.e., the process by which Wordsworth's sense of loftiness is mediated through rhetorical figures of surface and depth)?

We might speculate that Hazlitt cannot name the rhetorical sleight of hand by which Wordsworth achieves his effects, precisely because it is the same trope by which Hazlitt has accomplished his own resolution of the disparate themes he finds in Wordsworth. If we take Hazlitt at his word, however, we must also say that the figure of reflection is not entirely self-effacing, since it is discoverable by its effects—"by internal evidence." What is the signature of reflection, then? What reveals its presence in a particular configuration of surfaces, depths, and heights? The character of optical reflection that most fascinates Wordsworth himself is the palimpsest—the transposition or overlay of images that results from the projection of reflected light on a surface, particularly a transparent one. But another notorious effect of optical reflection, and one that seems to interest Hazlitt more, is the inversion of images, or the reversal of their relationships. We can note this in his final explicit reference to "reflection" in the Wordsworth essay. Wordsworth's "later philosophical productions," writes Hazlitt, are either sublime or ridiculous (depending on the "class of readers"), but in any case they tend to "[repeat] the same conclusions till they become flat and insipid." This is because "Mr. Wordsworth's mind is obtuse, except as it is the organ and the receptacle of accumulated feelings; it is not analytic, but synthetic; it is reflecting, rather than theoretical" (91). Again, the reconciliation of height and depth (the sublime and the ridiculous) by means of a figure of surface ("flat and insipid") gives way in turn to the figure of reflection. But here, the trope of reflection is not characterized in terms of its relation to surfaces, depths, or heights, as it has been previously. It is implicitly defined as "synthetic" and as a kind of "receptacle." These qualities of reflection are inferred through a syntactical figure of reflection rather than through apposite or related tropes: it is the appositional structure of the final two clauses in the sentence that illustrates the way in which "reflection" works. Logically, "synthetic" is to "analytic" as "reflecting" is to "theoretical," but Hazlitt syntactically reverses the final two terms to yield a logical chiasmus: instead of a:b, A:B, we get a:b, B:A. The relationship of analysis to synthesis is a mirror (i.e., reverse) image of the relationship of reflection to theory. Thus, in its final appearance in the essay, "reflection" displays its nature as much through structural "internal evidence" as through any figurative qualities attributed to it.

Repeatedly in the first half of the essay, Hazlitt calls attention to the presence of both heights and depths in Wordsworth's poetry. Hazlitt is concerned not only with the figures of height and depth that actually appear in the poetry but with thematic heights and depths (philosophical and quotidian subjects) as well as rhetorical heights and depths (bombastic and pathetic styles). In each case, Hazlitt argues, Wordsworth's competing tendencies toward height and depth are successfully merged in tropes of surface, whether in the prosopopoeiac "face" of nature, in the political and philosophical ideal of a *tabula rasa*, or in "flatness" of style. In turn, the entire Wordsworthian project of articulating and reconciling extremes is described by Hazlitt as a process of "reflection." At first, reflection appears to be a process that necessarily privileges one of the terms it is employed to mediate. Thus in the first three instances in which he describes Wordsworth's poetry as reflective, Hazlitt at the same time implies that it is (respectively) profound, lofty ("the summits of reflection"), and superficial ("ingrafted . . . his reflections"). But the final reference to "reflection" suggests that it is capable of working more as a catalyst, neither appearing as an explicit figure itself nor privileging one of its objects; a reflection may simply reverse or invert the relationship of the terms it is called upon to mediate.

The traditional association of inversion with irony can hardly be lost on Hazlitt, and it is perhaps with a sense of irony that he refrains from using the term *reflection* any further in the essay once he has articulated its disruptive tendencies. Instead, the figure of reflection is present only through "internal evidence" in the second half of the essay, in a somewhat ironic comparison of Wordsworth to Rembrandt. Discussing the occasional "fair play" of Wordsworth's critical mind, Hazlitt gives as an example Wordsworth's appreciation of Rembrandt:

> His [Wordsworth's] eye also does justice to Rembrandt's fine and masterly effects. In the way in which that artist works something out of nothing, and transforms the stump of a tree, a common figure into an *ideal* object, by the gorgeous light and shade thrown upon it, he perceives an analogy to his own mode of investing the minute details of nature with an atmosphere of sentiment; and in pronouncing Rembrandt to be a man of genius, feels that he strengthens his own claim to the title. (93)

This passage is concerned with at least three kinds of reflection: first, and most obviously, the "gorgeous light and shade" that Rembrandt "throw[s] upon" a "common figure" to make it into an "ideal object"; second, Wordsworth's "investing the minute details of nature with an atmosphere of sentiment" (with "investment" here being a figure not only of reflection but of figuration itself); and finally, Wordsworth's perception of Rembrandt's genius as an "analogy to his own." The passage as a whole stands as an ironic counterpart to the repeated suggestions throughout the first half of the essay that Wordsworth's genius is an essentially "reflective" one. Though nothing is taken away from Wordsworth in the second half of the essay (indeed, Hazlitt continues to describe him as a man of "deep" feelings and "lofty" understanding), the poet's powers of appreciation and description are revealed chiefly as a function of temperamental affinity. They are limited to certain topics, or to topics structured in certain ways; they are not the powers of disinterested genius. But according to Hazlitt, Wordsworth does not so much impose his vision on a subject matter (or delve into it) as he registers similarities between his own temperament and that of the objects or persons around him. "Reflection" is thus understood more as a passive than as an analytic power; and for Hazlitt a power of the latter sort may be creative, in a way that Coleridge, for example, did not allow it to be.[4] At the same time, however, the passage is a tribute to Wordsworth, for it shows Hazlitt using the poet's own technique of "internal evidence" to engage in rhetorical strategies by means other than explicit figuration (in this case, the extended *narrative* trope of reflection, which we have encountered previously in Locke, Berkeley, and Burke).

According to Hazlitt, then, reflection in the Wordsworthian sense does not alter any of the figurative relationships it mediates. Furnished in his imagination with the heights, depths, and glassy surfaces of his native lake country, Wordsworth *reflected* on life by seeing the figures of height, depth, and surface wherever they occurred around him and by attempting to gather them together in mutually evocative or mutually implicating tropes. He did not reflect, however, in the second, critical sense suggested by Hazlitt: reflection as ironic inversion rather than as synthesis or reconciliation. The kind of ironic reflection that allowed Hazlitt to see Wordsworth's fondness for "depths" as an "inverted ambition" was (according to Hazlitt) foreign to Wordsworth's intellectual and rhetorical temperament. The fact that some of Wordsworth's most powerful poetic experiments with figures of surface and depth were written but unpublished at this time must remain for us a historical irony. Nonetheless, Hazlitt himself was to put this latter kind of reflection to good use in two of his most important essays and to question the relationships of surface, depth, and height so radically as to call into question their very referentiality.

CHARACTER, REFLECTION, AND PREJUDICE

At first glance the figure of reflection appears to be almost entirely absent from Hazlitt's "On the Knowledge of Character" (1821), an essay organized around figures of surfaces and depths. Nevertheless, the essay is about reflection—both the solipsistic and the critical kind. As Hazlitt

---

[4] See Bromwich, *Hazlitt*, 62, 255–57. See also Coleridge's remarks on the essentially passive nature of the "imagination" (as opposed to active "fancy"), in chaps. 5 and 6 of *Biographia Literaria*, 2 vols, ed. John T. Shawcross (Oxford: Clarendon Press, 1907), 70–74, 85–88. Hazlitt comments ironically on this passive aspect of Coleridge's "imagination" in the essay on Coleridge from *The Spirit of the Age*: "Mr. Coleridge is too rich in intellectual wealth, to need to task himself to any drudgery: he has only to draw the sliders of the imagination, and a thousand subjects expand before him, startling him with their brilliancy, or losing themselves in endless obscurity—" (11.30).

investigates a number of commonplaces concerning the depths and superficialities of human behavior, he consistently returns to two central observations: first, that our assessments of people's characters are generally
nothing more than projections of our own preconceptions and prejudices;
second, that the fullest understanding of character requires an *inversion*
of our usual assumptions about the relationship of depth to surface,
knowledge to judgment, and character to behavior. On the one hand,
superficiality of character seems but a product of the reflected light in
which we inevitably view it, while on the other hand, reflection allows us
to see character in a radically new context.

The essay begins with an apparent paradox: "The more I learn,"
declares Hazlitt, "the less I understand [character]" (8.303). Hazlitt thus
sees his task in the essay as twofold: both "getting at a knowledge of
character" and at the same time getting "at the bottom of this riddle"
(303). But if the "riddle" is the fact that "learning" vitiates "understanding," Hazlitt is confronted with a predicament. He characterizes his investigation as a plumbing of depths, yet what he is investigating is precisely the futility of such an enterprise. This is confirmed by his assertion in
the second paragraph that surfaces, and not depths, are the most trust-
worthy witnesses to character:

> There are various ways of getting at a knowledge of character—by
> looks, words, actions. The first of these, which seems the most superficial, is
> perhaps the safest, and least liable to deceive: . . . A man's whole life may be
> a lie to himself and others: and yet a picture painted of him by a great artist
> would probably stamp his true character on the canvas, and betray the secret
> to posterity. (303)

With his inquiry defined as the penetration of depths, and his most de-
pendable evidence defined as superficial, Hazlitt seems to be in need of a
reconciling metaphor. Yet he proposes no answer to the riddle of his
riddle and continues to assert that the clue to character lies both on and
beneath the surface.

Though we need to examine the intrinsic tensions in Hazlitt's view of
character, there is a subtle shift of categories early in the essay that
accounts for at least part of the apparent paradox. Hazlitt begins by
proposing to examine our "knowledge" of character, but a half-dozen
paragraphs into the essay he is already writing of our "*judging* by appearances" and of the "*judg[ing]* of character." The shift in concerns from

knowledge to judgment is important since, as Hazlitt will argue later in the essay, intimate knowledge of a person's character inhibits us from evaluating it impartially. Clearly, part of Hazlitt's paradox lies in the simple fact that we mean different things by the "knowledge" and the "judgment" of character and that we might not presume or care to "judge" those whom we "know" best. Nonetheless, the implicit division of personality into "deep" characteristics that we can "know," and "superficial" characteristics that we can "judge," does not by itself explain the figurative distribution or balance of the essay.

Having distinguished in the opening paragraphs among the various surface layers of character (with visual appearance being the most superficial and "actions" the least so), Hazlitt is quick to unsettle the distinction between surface and depth by suggesting that they are identical extremes. The most superficial personality traits, he argues, are those that we perceive first; and they are thus likely to be the most idiosyncratic; thus the most distinctive; and thus the most revealing:

> We are struck at first, and by chance, with what is peculiar and characteristic; also with permanent *traits* and general effect; these afterwards go off in a set of unmeaning, common-place details. This sort of *prima facie* evidence, then, shows what a man is, better than what he says or does; for it shows us the habit of mind, which is the same under all circumstances and disguises. (304)

The value of *prima facie* or surface evidence here is precisely that it expresses what "is the same *under all circumstances and disguises*," and the truthfulness of surface is thus revealed as a function of its relationship to depth. If, as Hazlitt claims a few paragraphs later, "[e]xtremes meet," then the deepest and the most superficial aspects of a person's character will perhaps be found to be congruent, regardless of the contradictions and variations that person's behavior.

For Hazlitt, the difficulty of judging character (like the difficulty of reading) is that one must sort out various kinds of surface evidence in order to determine which is the most superficial and thus the deepest. He illustrates this paradox with reference to the relationship between innocence and seduction:

> The greatest hypocrite I ever knew was a little, demure, pretty, modest-looking girl, with eyes timidly cast upon the ground, and an air soft as enchantment; the only circumstance that could lead to a suspicion of her *true*

character was a cold, sullen, watery, *glazed* look about the eyes, which she bent on *vacancy*, as if determined to avoid all explanation with yours. *I might have spied in their glittering, motionless surface, the rocks and quicksands that awaited me below*! (305, my emphasis)[5]

Once again, the point of interpreting surfaces is precisely to understand what they conceal. Yet we suspect that the attribution of dangerous depths ("rocks and quicksands below") to this girl is not an accusation of design or deceit but rather a reminder that her surface *goes all the way down*—that the vacant, "cold, sullen, watery glaze" does *not* conceal anything warmer or deeper. Convention demands that "true character" be figured as something *beneath*, and distinct from, surface expression, yet Hazlitt is articulating a different paradox: that the most superficial characteristics of this girl's behavior would have been sufficient to warn him if convention had not insisted that they be discounted. Ironic reflection here consists not so much in seeing a depth of character *different* from its surface expression as in seeing that the oppositional surface/depth paradigm must be dissolved.[6]

If the "rocks and quicksands . . . below" are not a figuration of the girl's deeper character, then presumably they have something to do with Hazlitt's own psychological investments. And, in fact, Hazlitt does suggest in the essay that the entire notion of "depth" of character owes something to (what we assume to be) the uniqueness and fragility of our own feelings and motivations. In explaining his assertion that "looks" are a more accurate guide to character than are words, Hazlitt cites the fact that true eloquence requires considerable effort and pains but that the evidence of this can be registered only in a speaker's or writer's *face*. He gives himself and Coleridge as contrasting examples:

What is it to me that I can write these TABLE-TALKS? It is true I can, by a reluctant effort, rake up a parcel of half-forgotten observations, but they do not float on the surface of my mind, nor stir it with any sense of pleasure, nor even of pride. Others have more property in them than I have: *they* may reap the benefit, *I* have only had the pain. Otherwise they are to me as if they had never existed: nor should I know that I had ever thought at all, but that I am reminded of it by the strangeness of my appearance. . . . Look in C——'s

---

[5] We might suspect here a parody of Burke's famous and equally anxious passage on the "gradual variation" of the female body (*Philosophical Enquiry*, 3.15.115).

[6] This is also the moral of *Liber Amoris* (9.95–162, particularly 157–62).

face while he is talking. His words are such as might "create a soul under the ribs of death." His face is a blank. Which are we to consider as the true index of his mind? Pain, languor, shadowy remembrances are the uneasy inmates there: his lips move mechanically! (305)

To the reader or listener, the words of a Hazlitt or a Coleridge seem to possess a spontaneous life (if this were not the case, the words would not be considered eloquent); yet Hazlitt's and Coleridge's faces clearly register drastically different costs for the marshaling of thoughts into words. Coleridge's face is a "blank": the relationship, in him, between depth and surface, is even more starkly ironic than in Hazlitt (hence the almost sinister contrast between Coleridge's "uneasy inmates" and "mechanical" lips in the final line, separated by the implacable syntax of the colon).[7] Ironically, it is only by having read Coleridge's mind that Hazlitt is able to credit him with the same paradoxical sincerity that he finds in himself. Though Hazlitt may, by looking in the mirror or noticing his own clumsiness, deduce that he is mentally preoccupied, he has no need of such evidence, for he is already experiencing "effort" and "pain" as he "rakes" up his observations—sifting the surface ashes to find the living embers beneath. Once again extremes meet, as the most superficial aspect of character (facial expression) mimics accurately what is going on beneath "the surface of [the] mind," while both are at odds with the intermediate evidence of language. Furthermore, Hazlitt's example suggests why it is that we *think* of character as a deep rather than a superficial thing: because we must strain to construct the evidence, from which others, including ourselves at another moment, will spontaneously reconstruct our characters.

In Hazlitt's view, when we attribute depth of character to someone, we seem to be constructing that depth partly from a reading of their surface characteristics and partly from a projection of our own sense of self-division. But if some form of egoistic self-projection is necessary to suggest to us the ineffable dimension of another person's character, is it possible that what we project is not merely dimensionality or depth in the abstract but specific motives as well? In short, our attribution of depth of character to another person may be an act of self-deception, based on our own preconceptions, associations, and prejudices. This is precisely the

---

[7] See also a similar passage in *The Spirit of the Age*, where Coleridge is described as having "sunk into torpid, uneasy repose, tantalized by useless resources, haunted by vain imaginings, his lips idly moving, but his heart for ever still" (11.34).

phenomenon that Hazlitt now proceeds to examine, as he moves into a discussion of the principles guiding our knowledge of the character of other nations, other social classes, and the "opposite" sex.

The concept of national "character" would seem to be a perfect example of "depth" as the projection of our own preconceived notions onto a subject. As a way of undercutting the putatively empirical claims buttressing cultural stereotypes, Hazlitt demonstrates how many contradictions are manifest in the various commonplaces concerning French and English "character," and concludes that "the whole is an affair of prejudice on one side of the question, and of partiality on the other. . . . The commonest facts and appearances are distorted, and discoloured. [Travelers] go abroad with certain preconceived notions on the subject, and they make everything answer, in reason's spite, to their favourite theory" (307). The strategy of the essay up until this point has been to proceed through figures of reversal, by ironizing familiar distinctions, particularly those conventionally figured in terms of surface and depth. However, this passage returns us to the more familiar notion of reflection (reflection as the superimposition of patterns on one another during the process of mediation or transmission), a process Hazlitt describes as "prejudice." This passage reminds us of Hazlitt's Wordsworth, reflectively "ingrafting" his own thoughts on peasants, and is implicitly opposed to Hazlitt's own favored mode of reflection, demonstrated in his description of Wordsworth's "depth" as "inverted ambition."

If Hazlitt's purpose is to expose the narcissistic role generally played by reflection in our assessments of character, and to replace it with a more disinterested and ironic kind of reflection, then we might expect him to follow his critique of "national character" with equally skeptical comments about the notion of "class" character. He begins his discussion of class character skeptically enough, asserting that "we are ignorant of [the characters] of our own countrymen in a class a little below or above ourselves." Yet quite suddenly misprision becomes misrepresentation, and the responsibility shifts from subject to object: "Persons . . . in a higher or middle rank of life know little or nothing of the characters of those below them, as servants, country people, &c. I would lay it down in the first place as a general rule on this subject, that all uneducated people are hypocrites. Their sole business is to deceive" (307).[8] Unlike the rela-

---

[8] Cf. a more general, if equally ironic, indictment of human character in Fielding's "Essay on the Knowledge of Men": "Thus, without asserting in general, that Man is a deceitful Animal; we may, I believe, appeal for Instances of Deceit to the Behavior of some

tionship between the French and English, the relationship between the lower and middle (or upper) classes is not presented as one of "prejudice on one side . . . and of partiality on the other"; instead, the motive for misrepresentation seems to be one-sided. Yet if deceit on the one side seems to eclipse or absolve self-deception on the other, Hazlitt is quick to acknowledge that *responsibility* for the uneasy situation is evenly divided. Of the "servant" classes, he writes: "Their betters try all they can to set themselves up above them, and they try all they can to pull them down to their own level." If individual members of the middle and upper classes are less inclined to act a part than their "inferiors" (so the argument goes), still, as *groups*, both classes have an equal interest in characterizing one another to the other's disadvantage.

But how, precisely, do servants misrepresent their "superiors" in characterizing them? Hazlitt contends that they "turn the qualities of their masters and mistresses inside out," perversely refusing to accept favorable treatment or to "come to equal terms" and slandering any superior who "condescends" to do them a good turn (308). But in the figure of *turning qualities inside out*, there is an odd shift from the conventional vertical metaphors of "class" discourse back to an interior/ exterior model more compatible with the essay's pervasive figures of surface and depth. In fact, the phrase constitutes a perfect figure for Hazlitt's own mode of arguing, which is to proceed by paradoxes and to turn conventional assumptions "inside out." The effect of this is to bring Hazlitt's rhetorical strategy into alignment with the political and rhetorical strategy of the servant class—precisely that class whose character he supposes himself to be ignorant of, owing to their deceit and his good will.

In discussing the "knowledge" of national character, Hazlitt admits no possibility of a neutral perspective (it being a question of "prejudice on one side" and "partiality on the other"), but his discussion of class seems at first to violate this principle. Individuals from the middle and upper classes are apparently less susceptible to prejudice and partiality in their social intercourse with the lower classes than vice versa. But the descrip-

---

Children and Savages" (*Miscellanies*, 1.154). "Thus while the crafty and designing Part of Mankind, consulting only in their own separate Advantage, endeavour to maintain one constant Imposition on others, the whole World becomes a vast Masquerade, where the greater Part appear disguised under false Vizors and Habits; a very few only shewing their own Faces, who become, by so doing, the Astonishment and Ridicule of all the rest" (ibid., 1.155).

tion of servant-class strategy as one of "turning qualities inside out" functions as a *caveat*, both for the reader and for the ironist himself. No strategy of inversion is neutral, or without motivation. The idea that reflection- as-inversion constitutes a more disinterested strategy of analysis than that reflection that projects a (preconceived notion of) depth onto a surface is itself ironically qualified by the revelation that inversion can be a motivated, and even combative, rhetorical strategy.

Hazlitt's next subject is the knowledge of character in personal relationships, and here, as in his discussion of "national" character, he emphasizes the constitutive role of prejudices and preconceptions:

> I do not think that what is called *Love at first sight* is so great an absurdity as it is sometimes imagined to be. We generally make up our minds beforehand to the sort of person we should like, . . . and when we meet with a complete example of the qualities we admire, the bargain is soon struck. . . . The idol we fall down and worship is an image familiar to our minds. (310–11)

From romantic relationships, Hazlitt proceeds to the question of friends and family, and the degree to which familiarity compromises our ability to assess character:

> Familiarity confounds all traits of distinction: interest and prejudice take away the power of judging. . . . We do not see the features of those we love, nor do we clearly distinguish their virtues or their vices. . . . We hardly inquire whether those for whom we are thus interested, and to whom we are thus knit, are *better* or *worse* than others—the question is a kind of profanation—all we know is, they are *more* to us than any one else can be. Our sentiments of this kind are rooted and grow in us, and we cannot eradicate them by voluntary means. (311–12)

> Natural affection is not pleasure in one another's company, nor admiration of one another's qualities; but it is an intimate and deep knowledge of the things that affect those, to whom we are bound by the nearest ties, with pleasure or pain. (315)

In these passages, Hazlitt begins to develop his distinction between knowledge and judgment and to associate it with the distinction between depth and surface. When our affections are strong, and our familiarity with someone considerable, surface "features" begin to disappear, and our feelings for a person begin to grow "rooted" in us. Judgment may require that we "abstract" or distinguish the various qualities that compose someone's character, but "depth" and "rootedness" make such abstraction impossible. When we know someone "deeply," we know so *much* about them—have developed so many associations and noted so many connections—that we are overwhelmed by the "contradictoriness of the evidence":

> The chain of particulars is too long and massy for us to lift it or put it into the most approved ethical scales. The concrete result does not answer to any abstract theory, to any logical definition. There is black, and white, and grey, square and round—there are too many anomalies, too many redeeming points in poor human nature, such as it actually is, for us to arrive at a smart, summary decision on it. . . . We suspend our judgments altogether. (313)

The point here is not only that the deepest character traits of an individual are inter*connected* (and thus potentially self-contradictory) but that they are concrete. "Depth" thus constitutes the antithesis of "abstraction," which would on the contrary involve the stripping away of particular and concrete qualities. Yet it is important to keep in mind that "depth of character" is really a figurative measure of how well a person is *known* rather than a description of the character in question. As in Locke's *Essay* (1.1.6–7), when "depth" is interpreted as a quality to be sought for, it is already in danger of becoming an abstraction; it is only the depth of our own "lines" that we may safely aspire to gauge. "Depth" simply indicates a degree of familiarity. People are not so much "deep" or "superficial" as they are *known* deeply or superficially, that is, concretely or in the abstract. Our knowledge of character is a function of the degree to which we "suspend" that which can never be put entirely on a "scale."

As with Locke's figure of depth and Burke's figure of reflection, Hazlitt's "depth" is used to depict both a specific content and a specific *relationship* to content. Because of this, *abstraction* has a double relationship to the surface/depth distinction: on the one hand, knowledge of character "in the abstract" is opposed to knowledge of the "depth" of specific characters; on the other, abstraction is contrasted with the surface/depth distinction altogether, since it involves considering how character might be understood *apart from* the figurative distinctions conventionally imposed upon it. Hazlitt seems implicitly to accept that all understanding is rhetorical and that attempts to comprehend character without any figurative aid are doomed. Thus "abstraction" itself must ultimately be given a figure—that of reflection, or inversion.

It is only recently that the central role of "abstraction" in Hazlitt's work has been fully appreciated. In *Hazlitt and the Spirit of the Age*, Roy Park argues that Hazlitt rejected "abstraction"—whether of the empiricist or the metaphysical variety—as a "closed system": "Hazlitt's objection to abstraction . . . was specifically an objection to all closed systems of thought in which the whole of human experience was interpreted in the light of the system's initial premiss, empirical or metaphysical, with scant regard to the individuality, complexity and diversity of 'the truth of things.' It was a rejection of closed systems as such."[9] More recently, however, David Bromwich has argued that Hazlitt's objection is only to the conventional notion of abstraction as a lifeless "system" and that "abstraction" is in fact crucial, and closely related, to Hazlitt's ideas about creativity, moral disinterestedness, and the imagination.[10] According to Hazlitt, argues Bromwich, "we formulate a principle only by an effort of abstraction. . . . No great result is ever attained by the imagination, whether in art or in action, but by means of some such effort."[11]

Hazlitt indeed objects to the conventional understanding of abstraction as something a movement away and apart from "experience"—whether sensual, intellectual, or moral. In the essay "On Abstract Ideas" (written in 1812 and published in 1836), he writes that abstraction has generally been considered by philosophers "as a sort of artificial refinement upon our other ideas, as an excrescence, no ways contained in the common impressions of things" (2.191). Hazlitt takes it upon himself to refute both Locke—who had argued for the existence of such abstract ideas—and the subsequent philosophers who had either revised or rejected the Lockean concept of abstraction (principally Condillac, Berkeley, and Hume). According to Hazlitt, all traditional arguments either for or against the existence of abstract ideas derive from attempts to explain how the mind *synthesizes* the particularity of its experiences. Thus for Locke, the particular ideas suggested by experience are analyzed and then combined into new (general) ideas that do not themselves refer to any particular experience, whereas for Berkeley, this process of separation and recombination yields only new *particular* ideas that have no

---

[9] Roy Park, *Hazlitt and the Spirit of the Age: Abstraction and Critical Theory* (Oxford: Clarendon Press, 1971), 35.

[10] Bromwich, *Hazlitt*, 27–29, 52–53, 75–76.

[11] Ibid., 62.

different epistemological status from the ideas impressed on us directly by our experience.[12] Locke thus affirms, while Berkeley denies, the existence of "abstract" ideas distinct from the concrete and particular ideas suggested by experience.

As we saw in Chapter 1, however, Hazlitt argues that our synthesis of experience occurs *as we are experiencing* and that we never experience absolute particularity to begin with.[13] Abstraction is that human faculty which *selects* impressions from a hypothetically infinite field of sensations, connecting some of those sensations, while at the same time establishing limits to those connections:

> The real foundation of all our knowledge, is and must be general, that is, a mere confused impression or effect of feeling produced by a number of things, for there is no object which does not consist of an infinite number of parts, and we have not an infinite number of distinct ideas answering to them. Yet it cannot be denied that we have some knowledge of things, that they make some impression on us, and this knowledge, this impression, must therefore be an abstract one, the natural result of a limited understanding, which is variously affected by a number of things at the same time, but which is not susceptible itself to an infinite number of modifications. (206)

"Abstraction" is thus as much a part of our immediate sense impressions as it is of those moral and intellectual notions we conventionally call "abstract": "Every idea of a sensible quality . . . implies the same power of generalization, of connecting several impressions into one sort, as the most refined and abstract idea of virtue and justice" (192). Abstraction is constituted by both our synthetic capacity for *connecting* and our analytic capacity for *limiting* and is present in "every act of the mind of whatever kind, and in every moment of its existence" (191). Furthermore,

---

[12] See Locke, *Essay*, 2.11.9–10; and Berkeley, *Treatise*, introduction, §§6–10.

[13] See Bromwich, *Hazlitt*, 75–77. In the essay "On Abstract Ideas," Hazlitt gives as an anti-Berkeleyan example the abstraction implied by the word *army*: "Those who say we cannot conceive of an army of men without conceiving of the individuals composing it, ought to go a step further, and affirm that we must represent to ourselves the features, form, complexion, size, posture, and dress, with every other circumstance belonging to each individual" (2.209). According to Hazlitt, it would be absurd to suppose that our comprehension of particularity does not come to an end. His defense of abstraction as the necessary limit to empiricism is prompted by thinking about words as formative of ideas, as well as the other way around. In this respect, Hazlitt's argument closely resembles Wittgenstein's remarks on "simple" and "composite" ideas in *Philosophical Investigations*, part 1, §§46–49, 59–60.

without the faculty of abstraction we would be unable to make judgments or comparisons:

> If there is no such comparison or perception of resemblance, or idea of abstract qualities, then there can be no idea answering to the words "of the same sort"; but these particular ideas will be left standing by themselves, absolutely unconnected. As far as our ideas are merely particular, *i.e.* are negations of other ideas, so far they must be perfectly distinct from each other: there can be nothing between them to blend or associate them together. Each separate idea would be surrounded with a *chevaux de frise* of its own, in a state of irreconcilable antipathy to every other idea, and the fair form of nature would present nothing but a number of discordant atoms. . . . [O]ne colour could no more resemble another colour, or suggest its idea, than it could that of a sound, or a smell; there could be no clue to make us class different shades of the same colour under one general name, any more than the opposite. . . . There must be a mutual leaning, a greater proximity between some ideas than others . . . or there could not be in the mind more ideas of same or like, or different, or judgment, or reasoning, or truth, or falsehood, than in the stones in the fields, or the sands of the seashore. (213–14)

Far from being a mere *associative* power, abstraction is that faculty which enables us to *compare* and thus to *judge*.[14] Abstraction is the first step in the imaginative plotting out of possible futures, because only when we understand that our various impressions exist *in relationships* can we entertain the possibility of those relationships being changed.

I have argued that, given Hazlitt's recognition of the rhetorical constraints upon all understanding, abstraction itself must ultimately be identified with a rhetorical figure. The identification of abstraction with the surface/depth scheme, and with "reflection" in particular, is the subject of the next section in this chapter, but first we must consider Hazlitt's own critique of the notion that all knowledge can be resolved into rhetoric. In the essay "On Abstract Ideas," Hazlitt finds fault with Condillac and the Abbé Du Bos for leaving no reasoning power to the mind except that of "well speaking." He quotes Du Bos as follows: "If we reason only

---

[14] The importance for Hazlitt of the distinction between "association" and "abstraction" is emphasized by Bromwich, who argues that the "defense of abstract ideas" is the "pivot on which Hazlitt's dismissal of Hartleyan associationism must turn, before it can justify the imagination of the *Essay*" (*Hazlitt*, 72). Bromwich is referring here to Hazlitt's 1805 *Essay on the Principles of Human Action* (1.1–91).

by means of words this is a new proof that we can only reason well or ill, according as the language, in which we reason, is well or ill made. . . . [T]he whole art of reasoning is thus reduced to well speaking." But just what, Hazlitt wants to know, "in this supremacy of words is to be the criterion of well speaking" (198)? If Roy Park is right that Hazlitt's objection to abstract reasoning is really an objection to the determinism implicit in any reasoning from first principles, then we might say that Hazlitt's problem with Du Bos is precisely the latter's postulation of language as a *determining* rather than a dialectically *constitutive* element in thought.[15]

For Hazlitt, to dissolve reasoning into rhetoric is still only to identify the ground on which reasoning takes place; it cannot explain the *choice* of one reason over another. That choice is admittedly circumscribed by habits, prejudices, and preconceptions, and these in turn have their life in language, but one of the functions of rhetoric is, after all, to get people to change their minds. If, in a particular circumstance, the figure with which Hazlitt illustrates the nature of abstraction turns out to bear a close affinity to the rhetorical practices that abstraction is itself intended to help clarify and investigate, this is as much a liberating as a determining discovery: for it only reminds us that there are potentials for rearrangement within any configuration of language or thought.

ABSTRACTION AS RHETORICAL INVERSION

Hazlitt begins his essay "On Depth and Superficiality" by announcing both his subject matter and his method, and from the start there is a close, even ironic, relationship between the two:

> I wish to make this Essay a sort of study of the meaning of several words, which have at different times a good deal puzzled me. Among these words, *wicked, false* and *true*, as applied to feeling; and lastly, *depth* and *shallowness*. It may amuse the reader to see the way in which I work out some of my conclusions underground, before throwing them up on the surface. (12.346–47)

The slipperiness of Hazlitt's argument in this essay is signaled immediately by two shifts. No sooner is the distinction between surface and

[15] Aarsleff, in turn, has found fault with Hazlitt's reading of Condillac. See *From Locke to Saussure*, 28–31, 120–40.

depth announced as one of the essay's topics than it reappears in the articulation of the essay's methodology as well. The relationship between "depth" and "shallowness" will be worked out "underground" before being brought to the "surface." If the essay solves the "puzzle" of depth and shallowness, then, it will not be by situating them within a different figurative paradigm; the intractability of these particular figures is suggested already by the terms of the inquiry. Yet the reduplication of topical distinctions at the level of method is imperfect, or rather hides a further shift, since the depth/surface scheme is not a perfect reproduction of the depth/shallowness scheme. It is not only the distinction between subject matter and methodological framework that is being called into question here but the inevitable reliance of rhetorical argumentation on imperfect analogies and slight figurative shifts as well. The extent to which such shifts can be both a source of insight and a limiting condition is the topic of Hazlitt's essay.

Hazlitt's first puzzle is to distinguish "natural wickedness" from mere "childish humour":

> A great but useless thinker once asked me, if I had ever known a child of a naturally wicked disposition? and I answered, "Yes, that there was one in the house with me that cried from morning to night, *for spite*." I was laughed at for this answer, but still I do not repent it. . . . I was supposed to magnify and over-rate the symptoms of the disease, and to make a childish humour into a bugbear; but, indeed, I have no other idea of what is commonly understood by wickedness than that perversion of the will or love of mischief for its own sake, which constantly displays itself . . . in early childhood. (347)

Though Hazlitt does not analyze "spite" in terms of surface and depth until later in the paragraph, it is clear that what he sees himself ridiculed for here is attributing a morally analyzable depth of motive to the child's cries instead of accepting them as morally insignificant (and thus superficial) manifestations of a simple distress. Hazlitt's mistake thus supposedly lies in his seeing depth where he should see simply surface. Yet neither of these constitutes the terms by which Hazlitt chooses to describe the baby's behavior, at least initially. The dominant theme in this anecdote concerns not surfaces and depths but rather *perversity*—what Hazlitt later in the paragraph will call the human "spirit of contradiction." It is neither depth nor superficiality but perversity that Hazlitt accuses the baby of, and the description is clearly intended to apply to Hazlitt as well for making the very accusation. Hazlitt hints broadly at his own perversity by beginning the anecdote with the provocative phrase, "A great but useless thinker" and proceeding to describe himself as a man of "jealous" temper and "morbid" preoccupations, more disconcerted by things that in "no ways concern" him than he is at personal slights or offenses. Like the surface/depth distinction in the opening paragraph, the concept of perversity appears simultaneously as a topic and as a rhetorical strategy.

It may defy conventional sense to blame a baby for crying, Hazlitt seems to suggest, but then it defies sense for the baby to cry without ostensible motive. And it is precisely the absence of any detectable motive that Hazlitt finds so deeply threatening:

> If the child had been in pain or in fear, I should have said nothing, but it cried only to vent its passion and alarm the house, and I saw in its frantic screams and gestures that great baby, the world, tumbling about in its swaddling-clothes, and tormenting itself and others for the last six thousand years! The plea of ignorance, of folly, of grossness, or selfishness makes nothing either way: it is the downright love of pain and mischief for the interest it excites, and the scope it gives to an abandoned will, that is the *root of all evil*, and the original sin of human nature. (348, my emphasis)

If both his subject and his treatment of it run counter to sense, Hazlitt argues, that is because there *is* a strong counterintuitive strain in human behavior, a "spirit of contradiction," and it can be put to mischievous or speculative ends—though in either case it will be labeled "perverse." Hazlitt goes on to describe some of the other habitual perversities of human behavior, such as the arbitrary "hankering" for trouble or the insistence on straining our own principles of credulity. The contradiction in each case lies in the absence of even a rational selfishness to explain the malice or perversity of the will:

> The griefs we suffer are for the most part of our own seeking and making; or we incur or inflict them, not to avert other impending evils, but to drive off *ennui*. . . . We had rather be the victims of [an] absurd and headstrong feeling, than give up an inveterate purpose, retract an error, or relax from the intensity of our will, whatever it may cost us. (349)

> There seems to be a love of absurdity and falsehood as well as mischief in the human mind. . . . A lie is welcome to it, for it is, as it were, its own offspring;

and it likes to believe, as well as act, whatever it pleases, and in the pure spirit
of contradiction. . . . *Credo quia impossibile est* is the standing motto of
bigotry and superstition; that is, I believe, because to do so is a favourite act
of the will, and to do so in defiance of common sense and reason enhances
the pleaure and the merit (ten-fold) of this indulgence of blind faith and
headstrong imagination. (351)

The perversity of the will in these cases lies in the fact that there is not
even a rational principle of self-interest guiding it—nothing to be gained
to the subject's advantage. The conventional moral and psychological
categories of depth and surface are inadequate here, because the tension is
not between ostensible and hidden motives, but between conventional
and perverse (or intuitive and counterintuitive) motivations. Nonetheless,
traces of a surface/depth rhetoric can be found in Hazlitt's description of
the crying baby's character: the "abandoned will, that is the root of all
evil"; the "character [that] implies the fiend at the bottom of it"; and the
"craving after what is prohibited . . . [that] frets and vexes the surface of
life with petty evils, and plants a canker in the bosom of our daily enjoyments" (348). Yet if the traditional figures of ethical and theological
discourse are difficult to escape, they still provide no principle for distinguishing motives or morals. If the baby is innocent, that is not because it
is free of deep motives but because there is an obvious context for its cries.
If the baby is wicked, that is not because it has hidden, malevolent motives but because it is manifestly contradicting its own best interests.

In order to demonstrate the inadequacy of the surface/depth scheme
in moral matters, Hazlitt not only must replace it with the category of
contradiction (which has yet to be given a trope or a figure itself) but
must also reveal the confusion inherent in the surface/depth relationship
itself. Hazlitt does this by concluding his discussion of "wickedness" with
an odd and complex figure of depth:

> If we wish a thing to be kept secret, it is sure to transpire; if we wish it to be
> known, not a syllable is breathed about it. This is not meant; but it happens
> so from mere simplicity and thoughtlessness. No one has ever yet seen
> through all the intricate folds and delicate involutions of our self-love, which
> is wrapped up in a set of smooth flimsy pretexts like some precious jewel in
> covers of silver paper. (352)

Self-love is the inscrutable motive or explanation for self-contradictory
behavior, according to Hazlitt, yet it is figured both as a depth and as the

set of surfaces by which that depth is mediated. Self-love is both the "precious jewel" *and* the "intricate folds," the "set of smooth flimsy pretexts," and the "covers of silver paper" surrounding the jewel. As we have seen previously in Hazlitt, and in Burke as well, a single figure is allowed to stand both for a content and for a relationship to that content as well. Though the contradiction within this figure might have been predicted given Hazlitt's initial acknowledgment that the surface/depth distinction would constitute his method as well as his topic, this particular passage initiates the *figurative* working-out of that narrative predicament.

If Hazlitt is to generate a new paradigm with which to comprehend human motives and behavior, he must generate it from the commonplaces of moral discourse. His temperamental perversity or unorthodoxy must locate itself in a figure that is at the same time a critique of those figures he wishes to supersede. I have argued all along that the most tempting figure for this purpose is that of *reflection*. The rest of Hazlitt's essay, and the rest of this chapter, plot out the way in which the figure of reflection allows us to "consider things only in their abstract *principles*" while maintaining a "spirit of *contradiction*," all in the course of critiquing the distinction between surfaces and depths.

In discussing the perverse and self-contradictory motives for violent or "wicked" behavior, Hazlitt cites the anecdote of the woman who "whipp'd two 'prentices to death, / And hid them in the coal-hole" and offers the following explanation:

> I do not know that hers is exactly a case in point; but I conceive that in the well-known catastrophe here alluded to, words led to blows, bad usage brought on worse from mere irritation and opposition, and that, probably, even remorse and pity urged on to aggravated acts of cruelty and oppression, as the only means of *drowning reflection on the past in the fury of present passion.* (350, my emphasis)

The passage contains a number of rhetorical oddities (not least of which is the obscure syntax), but of principal interest to us here is the phrase "drowning reflection." Reflection in this context is clearly associated with memory and judgment and is thus opposed to "present passion." But the idea that reflection might be "drowned" suggests that it is an activity usually to be found at the surface (which would accord with the actual physical phenomenon of reflection), while its association with memory and its opposition to "present" sentiments would align it more traditionally with the figure of depth. Though the catechrestic apposition of "drowning" and "reflection" obscures the relationship of the latter to the surface/depth scheme in this passage, Hazlitt proceeds farther on in the essay to clarify the dual relationship of reflection to both surface and depth.

Hazlitt's subject in the ensuing paragraph is the relationship between "true" and "false" moral feelings. Although the discussion is dominated by figures of interiority and exteriority, Hazlitt refers to reflection at two crucial points: at first in the context of "true" feelings and then later in that of "false" ones. In the first case, Hazlitt associates reflection with the activity of surveying or examining: "That then is *true* or *pure* pleasure that has no alloy or drawback in some other consideration; that is free from remorse and alarm; and that will bear the soberest reflection; because there is nothing that, upon examination, can be found acting indirectly to check and throw a damp upon it" (352). The distinction between truth and falsity of feeling, like that between innocence and wickedness, turns out to be more a distinction between self-consistency and self-contradiction than between interiority and exteriority (or, presumably, depth and surface). True feelings are not so much deep as they are "unalloyed" and "unchecked," and the process of distinguishing between self-consistency and contradiction is figured conventionally as a "reflection." Reflection, in this context, is a surface phenomenon, a process of "examining" that which is "borne" up. Yet only a few sentences later, reflection takes on quite a different function. As Hazlitt proceeds to describe "false" feelings, he returns to the figure of "drowning," and once again "reflection" is to be found at the *bottom* of the matter:

> On the other hand, we justly call those pleasures *false* and *hollow*, not merely which are momentary and ready to elude our grasp, but which, even at the time, are accompanied with such a consciousness of other circumstances as must embitter and undermine them. For instance, putting morality quite out of the question; is there not an undeniable and wide difference between the gaiety and animal spirits of one who indulges in a drunken debauch to celebrate some unexpected stroke of good fortune, and his who does the same thing to drown care for the loss of all he is worth? The outward objects, the immediate and more obvious sensations are, perhaps, very much the same in the latter case as in the former, . . . but the still small voice is wanting, there is a reflection at bottom, that however stifled and kept down,

poisons and spoils all, even by the violent effort to keep it from intruding. (352–53)

Here, reflection no longer examines that which lies on the surface but rather something "at bottom," something "stifled and kept down" that "undermines" our conscious circumstances. As with the earlier cate-chresis of "drowning reflection," we are confronted with somewhat of a logical anomaly. Optical reflection takes place on surfaces, and in the case of water, at least, reflected images are precisely those that *interfere* with our perception of what is at "bottom." Though there are esoteric ways of picturing the figure of "a reflection at bottom" so as to make it logically consistent (e.g., light refracted by the water's surface can sometimes be seen reflected on the bottom of a clear pool), Hazlitt does not in fact intend "reflection" here to be related schematically to the figures of sur-face and depth. "Reflection" in this passage is simply a synonym for self-criticism, even skepticism. Though the figure traditionally implies a rela-tion to both surfaces and depths—and even a way of articulating the relationship between the two—Hazlitt is not as interested in determining the specific relationship between superficial and deep feelings as he is in establishing the hypothetical interconnectedness of *all* feelings. At the same time, however, he wishes to indicate the necessary limits to such interconnectedness: "The difficulty is not so much in supposing one men-tal cause or phenomenon to be affected and imperceptibly moulded by another, as in setting limits to the everlasting ramifications of our impres-sions, and in defining the obscure and intricate ways in which they com-municate together" (354). The kind of reflection that is to be found at the "bottom" of false or hollow feelings is thus characterized by its infinite qualifications and ramifications rather than by some inadequacy or dis-tortion in its relation to surface expression and behavior. Hazlitt's asso-ciation of such reflection with the figure of depth is not unimportant, as we shall see, but it is no basis for a schematic distinction between "deep" and "superficial" moral traits.

Hazlitt presents us with essentially two kinds of reflection in the passages we have just considered, one associated with "true" moral feel-ings and the other with "false" ones. The former, active reflection in-volves requires that we "examine" individual feelings and determine whether they are being "indirectly" influenced. The latter, passive reflec-tion is not an activity (i.e., a process of examination) but an associative relationship actually subsisting among a given number of feelings. Thus one consists in a process of individuation and analysis, while the other is a product of synthesis; the former associated with figures of surface, the latter with figures of depth.[16] For Hazlitt, neither of these two kinds of reflection alone provides an adequate picture of the way in which our feelings function and are related. The two must be combined; we must try to "[set] limits to the everlasting ramifications of our impressions," even as we are "defining the obscure and intricate ways in which they communicate together."

Performing both these tasks simultaneously is a critic's real challenge, and in its most accomplished form it is called "abstraction." To abstract is to single out an *aspect* in the object we are contemplating—to highlight certain of the object's internal relations at the expense of others. Far from ignoring an object's concreteness, abstraction involves selecting certain of its concrete relations for special consideration.[17] Abstraction thus highlights rhetorical figures, indeed the rhetorical nature of perception itself; and a corollary to this is that the way in which abstraction itself is figured

---

[16] Cf. Locke's "wit" and "judgment" (*Essay* 2.11.2).

[17] Hume, too, figured this kind of abstraction (the attention to *aspects*) as a "reflection." See, for instance, book 1 of the *Treatise*: "When we wou'd consider only the figure of the globe of white marble, we form in reality an idea both of the figure and colour, but tacitly carry our eye to its resemblance with the globe of black marble: And in the same manner, when we wou'd consider its colour only, we turn our view to its resemblance with the cube of white marble. *By this means we accompany our ideas with a kind of reflexion, of which custom renders us, in a great measure, insensible.* A person, who desires us to consider the figure of a globe of white marble without thinking on its colour, desires an impossibility; but his meaning is, that we shou'd consider the colour and figure together, *but still keep in our eye* the resemblance to the globe of black marble, or that to any other globe of whatever colour or substance" (1.1.7, my emphasis). Hume notes that we are "insensible" to this process of reflection in ourselves, and on Hazlitt's construction this is because the process of abstraction does not have an inherent affinity for specific "figures"— an affinity we might be able to stand outside of, and note. Rather, it is *people* who have affinities for certain subjects, and *subjects* that may have certain figurative constitutions. The figurative aspect of our perceptions, then, is difficult for us to *compare* with anything, so long as we continue paying attention to the same subject. Again, Hazlitt anticipates Wittgenstein here. See the discussion of "aspects" in part 2 of *Philosophical Investigations* (193–216), where Wittgenstein makes the following observation: "I suddenly see the solution of a puzzle-picture. Before, there were branches there; now there is a human shape. My visual impression has changed and now I recognize that it has not only shape and colour but also a quite particular 'organization.'—My visual impression has changed;—what was it like before and what is it like now?—If I represent it by means of an exact copy—and isn't that a good representation of it?—no change is shewn" (196). Wittgenstein concludes that the difference such differences make can only be determined by subsequent *behavior*: "For when should I call it a mere case of knowing, not seeing? . . . (Fine shades of behaviour.— Why are they *important*? They have important consequences.)" (204).

in a particular discourse will determine in turn the particular figures that
the discourse "throws up."

The possibilities and limitations of abstraction—in its characteristic
Hazlittian form of "reflection"—are beautifully demonstrated in the essay's final anecdotes, all of which are devoted to an investigation of the
essay's final, "hardest question": "What is *depth*, and what is *superficiality?*" Hazlitt's initial, half ironic answer reminds us that the rhetorical figures within a question or an investigation tend to reinscribe themselves within the text of the "answer": "It is easy to answer that the one is
what is obvious, familiar, and lies on the surface, and that the other is a
recondite and hid at the bottom of a subject. The difficulty recurs—What
is meant by lying on the surface, or being concealed below it, in moral
and metaphysical questions?" (355). Hazlitt's first attempt to define the
surface/depth distinction nontautologically leads him to explain it as a
distinction between "cause" and "effect," or between the "abstract" and
the "concrete":

> *Depth* consists . . . in tracing any number of particular effects to a general
> principle, or in distinguishing an unknown cause from the individual and
> varying circumstances with which it is implicated, and under which it lurks
> unsuspected. It is in fact resolving the concrete into the abstract. Now this is
> a task of difficulty, not only because the abstract naturally merges in the
> concrete, . . . but being scattered over a larger surface, and collected from a
> number of undefined sources, there must be a strong feeling of its weight and
> pressure, in order to dislocate it from the object and bind it into a principle.
> The impression of an abstract principle is faint and doubtful in each individu-
> al instance; it becomes powerful and certain only by the repetition of the
> experiment. (355–56)

As in the essay on character, Hazlitt here suggests that our metaphor of
depth is an attempt to describe the feel of a process rather than of a
content. And even if an "abstract principle" is a content that "lurks"
beneath, the *process* of abstraction nevertheless involves the consolida-
tion of "surface" details. Abstraction is not so much an act of penetration
as it is an act of "resolving" or "impressing." Like the figure of reflection,
abstraction is associated with *both* surfaces and depths, and like reflection it both "dislocate[s]" and "bind[s]."

This process of simultaneously dislocating and binding impressions is
essentially one of constructing "analogies," of recognizing not only patterns, but similarities between different patterns. It involves the associa-

tive connection of certain elements in a perceptual field both with each other and with a similar configuration of elements recalled from some previous experience. This is entirely in keeping with the economizing impulse identified by Locke and Berkeley as a part of the mind's essentially practical tendencies. It is a process of "abridging" impressions into *figures* rather than one of plunging beyond impressions to some depth that is incapable of figuration:

> Both knowledge and sagacity are required, but sagacity abridges and antici-
> pates the labour of knowledge, and sometimes jumps instinctively at a con-
> clusion; that is, the strength or fineness of the feeling, by association or
> analogy, sooner elicits the recollection of a previous and forgotten one in
> different circumstances, and the two together, by a sort of internal evidence
> and collective force, *stamp any proposed solution with the character* of truth
> or falsehood. Original *strength of impression* is often (in usual questions at
> least) a substitute for accumulated weight of experience; and *intensity of
> feeling is so far synonimous with depth of understanding.* (356–57, my
> emphasis)

Hazlitt attempts to relate surface to depth in conventional empiricist fashion by describing intense experiences as those that have been "stamped" or "impressed" more incisively on the mind. However, this only replicates the metaphors of surface and depth without explaining them. Recognizing that his explanations so far have been either tautological or tangential, Hazlitt finally proposes to "give an illustration or two of this very abstruse subject" and, in fact, proceeds to give three.

The three anecdotes that follow attempt to describe, respectively, the meaning of a single word, the explanation of a particular physical phenomenon, and the motive for a peculiar instance of human behavior, all as the resolutions of surface into depth. Unlike Hazlitt's previous explanations, these anecdotes are remarkably successful as *illustrations* of the relationship between surface and depth. But once again, much of this has to do with the fact that the surface/depth distinction *is in some senses already inscribed* in the subject matter selected for discussion, so that the subsequent analysis in terms of surface and depth does not produce a revelation of anything that was hidden or obscure.

Hazlitt's first illustration has to do with the precise meaning of the word *elegance*. Hazlitt is concerned to distinguish *elegance* from a number of related terms: "*Elegance* is a word that means something different from ease, grace, beauty, dignity; yet it is akin to all these; but is seems more particularly to imply a sparkling brilliancy of effect with finish and precision" (357). If we keep in mind that the larger point of this particular example is to illustrate "surface" and "depth" of meaning, then we may feel that the choice of the word *elegance*—already associated with surface qualities such as "finish"—is likely only to confuse or reproduce the stakes of the argument before the analysis even gets under way. Yet Hazlitt insists that his purpose in this anecdote is to get *beneath* the superficial meaning of the word (a meaning that fails to distinguish it sufficiently from a number of other related terms) and to identify its abstract, unique meaning:

> Sparkling effect, finish, and precision, are characteristic, as I think, of elegance, but as yet I see no reason why they should be so, any more than why blue, red, and yellow, should form the colours of the rainbow. I want a common idea as a link to connect them, or to serve as a substratum for the others. Now suppose I say that elegance is beauty, or at least *the pleasurable* in little things: we then have a ground to rest upon at once. For elegance being beauty or pleasure in little or slight impressions, precision, finish, and polished smoothness follow from this definition as matters of course. . . . [B]y getting the primary conditions or essential qualities of elegance in all circumstances whatever, we see how these branch off into minor divisions in relation to form, details, colour, surface, &c. and rise from a common ground of abstraction into all the variety of consequences and examples. (357)

Hazlitt is clearly working with a Burkean vocabulary of "beautiful" sensations here ("smoothness," diminutiveness, "elegance"), but his intention is to reveal the arbitrariness of such a rhetoric. Hazlitt wishes to demonstrate that an aesthetic term may be more "deeply" understood by deducing the "substratum" of qualities (in this case, the "beauty, or at least the pleasurable in little things") common to its various applications in diverse circumstances, a substratum that may then be recognized in every "branch" of the word's use ("precision, finish, and polished smoothness follow from this definition as a matter of course"). Hazlitt concludes the example, however, with a curious caveat: "The Hercules is not elegant; the Venus is simply beautiful. The French, whose ideas of beauty or grandeur never amount to more than an elegance, have no relish for Rubens, nor will they understand this definition" (357–58). If a reader's preconceived ideas of elegance ultimately dictate the degree to which he or she accepts Hazlitt's analysis of "elegance," then it is fair to assume that ideas about "surface" and "depth" will also prejudice the analysis, determining in part the choice of suitable subject matter for proofs and demonstrations. If the word *elegance* is easy to analyze in terms of surface and depth of meaning, then this is partly because it is a word whose discursive conventions *entail* talk about surface and surface qualities.

Hazlitt's second and most powerful illustration concerns the proverbial discovery of gravity in the fall of an apple. Once again, if we keep in mind that the point of the anecdote is to illustrate the distinction between superficial and deep understanding, then we will be "struck" by the degree to which the topic is already articulated in terms of depths and heights, even before it is analyzed:

> When Sir Isaac Newton saw the apple fall, it was a very simple and common observation, but it suggested to his mind the law that holds the universe together. What then was the process in this case? In general, when we see any thing fall, we have the idea of a particular direction, of *up* and *down* associated with the motion by invariable and every day's experience. . . . Sir Isaac Newton by a bare effort of abstraction, or by a grasp of mind comprehending all the possible relations of things, got rid of the prejudice, turned the world as it were on its back, and saw the apple fall not *downwards*, but simply *towards* the earth, so that it would fall *upwards* on the same principle, if the earth were above it. . . . [T]his view he arrived at by a vast power of comprehension, retaining and reducing the contradictory phenomena of the universe under one law, and counteracting and banishing from his mind that almost invincible and instinctive association of *up* and *down* as it relates to the position of our own bodies. (358)

According to Hazlitt, Newton discovered the deep explanation for the phenomenon of "attraction" not by penetrating beyond the surface appearances of the phenomenal world but by "abstracting" away the very metaphors of surface, depth, and height from his common experiences and habitual associations. And he did this specifically by "turn[ing] the world" upside-down—by inverting a metaphorical configuration already within his vocabulary rather than by discarding, supplementing, or translating it.[18]

---

[18] Bromwich has also noted the relation between abstraction and inversion in Hazlitt's construction of the Newton anecdote: "This [inversion] he [Newton] accomplished by abstraction, but an effort of abstraction when sufficiently strange has the power to invert the former relationship of depth to surface" (*Hazlitt*, 356).

In a sense it is not even proper to talk of a removal of metaphor here—since there is no more primary, proper, or original use of the figures "up" and "down" to which the terms may be returned once stripped away from our notions of visual space. Hazlitt's account of a world abstracted from rhetoric is far more radical than Locke's, Berkeley's, or Burke's speculations concerning the relationship of visual space to rhetorical language, exemplified in their common trope concerning a *blind man's language*. In those cases, the problematic dependence of language on *sight* is examined. In Hazlitt's example, far more is being bracketed than mere optical sensations; it is not simply the individual referents of "up" and "down," respectively, that are being suspended but the entire structural paradigm or vision of the world constituted by the interrelation of those terms.

With this anecdote, Hazlitt implicitly gives the phenomenon of abstraction a *figure*—that of *reflection*, in one of its most literal senses (as an inverted mirror-image). Like the ironist, Newton resolves "contradictory phenomena" by turning things upside down; he tries to see a few selected things the *opposite way*, as a prelude to seeing all things in a *genuinely different* way. In earlier passages of the essay, Hazlitt had identified "reflection" alternately with surface and with depth, and it was unclear how reflection was supposed to mediate between the two. Whether it was understood as the careful examination and distinguishing of surface appearances or as the deep principle of association connecting and confusing our ideas, reflection had little to do with the overall vertical model of surface and depth: it explained only the relationship of superficial characteristics to one another, or of deep characteristics to one another, and not the relationship of surface to either depth or height. But with the figuring of intellectual reflection as a visual inversion of the world, reflection manifests itself precisely as the imaginative process that highlights conceptual relationships by abstracting them and allowing us to *imagine them differently* (as Newton "comprehend[ed] *all the possible relations of things*").[19] Reflection is thus no longer simply a figure for the content of an analysis or for our relationship to that content, but for our ability to imagine *change*.

With his Newtonian anecdote, Hazlitt literalizes the conventional empiricist trope of reversal, of reflection as the humble retreat from philosophical inquiry. The figure of retreat from sublime speculation—

[19] Bromwich describes this as Hazlitt's ability "to conceive of a thing as abstract and not stripped of every relation" (ibid., 76).

literalized in the fall of Newton's apple—is simultaneously ironized and authorized. The sensory figure buried within a philosophical trope turns out to suggest an extension rather than a constriction of the trope's range of applications. Literalizing turns out to be but a prelude to finding new metaphoric descriptions: new uses for old metaphors, a new way of arranging old facts, and a new way of "seeing" the world. The process of rhetorical investigation is indeed one of "reflection," oscillating between literal and figurative interpretations and discovering the continual mutual adjustments demanded by language and sensation.

For his final illustration, Hazlitt returns to the question of analyzing character in terms of deep and superficial motives. He relates the anecdote of an "American lady . . . who married young and well" but who "died at length of pure envy," apparently because her sister had "married . . . a richer husband, and had a larger (if not finer) family" (358). Hazlitt then offers a commentary on the anecdote (putatively related by an anonymous observer) in which the underlying explanation for the woman's death is attributed to the *absence of social heights and depths* in American culture:

> Some one said on hearing this, that it was a thing that could only happen in America; that it was a trait of the republican character and institutions, where alone the principle of mutual jealousy, having no *high and distant objects* to fix upon, and divert it from immediate and private mortifications, seized upon the happiness or outward advantages even of the nearest connexions as its natural food, and having them constantly before its eyes, gnawed itself to death upon them. I assented to this remark, and I confess it struck me as shewing a *deep insight into human nature.* . . . The *democratic level,* the *flatness of imagery,* the *absence of those towering and artificial heights* that in old and monarchical states act as conductors to attract and carry off the splenetic humours and rancorous hostilities of a whole people, and to make common and petty advantages *sink* into perfect insignificance, were full in the mind of the person who suggested the solution; . . . Now this solution would not have been attained but for the *deep impression* which the operation of certain general causes of moral character had recently made, and the quickness with which the consequences of its removal were felt. (358–59, my emphasis)

Once again, the resolution of superficial clues into "deep" explanations is an intellectual activity performed on anecdotal material already inscribed with surfaces, depths, and heights. In all three of his anecdotes, Hazlitt has attempted to demonstrate how "surface" details may be analyzed to yield "deep" explanations, and in each case the demonstration seems facilitated by the fact that tropes of surface and depth are already present in the rhetorical or narrative articulation of the topic, whether in the "finish" and "smoothness" implicit in the word "elegance," the figures of height and depth essential to Newton's thoughts about motion, or the demographic and topographical distinctions between American and European culture. Taken together, the anecdotes suggest that the application of explanatory figures such as surface and depth is limited to situations and topics that are already conceived of in terms of those very figures. At the same time, though, the Newton anecdote suggests that this rhetorical and epistemological constraint is not rigidly determining. If the rhetorical structure of an analytic method must have some figurative affinities with its subject matter, the analysis is hardly limited to a static reduplication or reiteration of the subject's structure. Newton's discovery itself did not involve an absolute break with a previous scheme but rather an inversion of one part of the scheme, highlighting the potential independence of certain terms within it from their conventional contexts and associations, while retaining the relationship of those terms relative to each other.

The inversion or reversal of an anecdote's central figures may help to isolate the function of these figures and, in doing so, enable us to imagine things in a different light or a different context. This is essentially a process of abstraction, since it involves imagining a phenomenon stripped of one (or some) of its particular attributes, without imagining it devoid of *all* attributes. The implied irony is that inversion and "reflection" are themselves contextually dependent methods of abstracting, being precisely those figures appropriate for the critique and revision of phenomena already articulated and narrativized in terms of surfaces and depths.

Hazlitt does not entirely relativize the distinction between surfaces and depths. Although he demonstrates that the traditional configuration can be turned on its head, Hazlitt still finds something of value in the surface/depth distinction that may be isolated and defined, even if this ultimately involves casting it in different figurative terms. Hazlitt concludes that at the most general level depth and surface represent "intensity" and "diffusion," respectively. An impression of depth involves the "collection" and "binding" of sensations "scattered over a larger surface" (356), and this gives to depth the quality of relative intensity or condensation. "Intensity of feeling" is "synonymous with depth of understanding," and "intense continuity of feeling . . . forms the depth of sentiment." Hazlitt concludes the essay, then, by recasting the distinction between surface and depth as one between "strong" and "diffused" impressions. The final sentence reads: "In a word, I suspect depth to be that strength, and at the same time subtlety of impression, which will not suffer the slightest indication of thought or feeling to be lost, and gives warning of them, over whatever extent of surface they are diffused, or under whatever disguises of circumstances they lurk" (360). This definition of depth as simply strength of impression deprives the concept of some of its imaginative interest, perhaps because the figurative contrast between intensity and diffusion is not nearly so striking as that between depth and surface. Nevertheless, the definition has an appeal in its very broadness—it would seem (initially, at least) to be much less susceptible to ironic inversion than the figure of depth itself.

We began this chapter by highlighting the set of questions implicit in Hazlitt's investigation of Wordsworth's metaphoric schemes: how does Wordsworth manage to scale the heights of contemplation while plumbing the depths of the human heart, reading the face of nature, and leveling vain institutions? Hazlitt's answer is that Wordsworth accomplishes this through "reflection." But reflection itself is manifested in several different ways: as internal representation, as irony, and as the "internal evidence" of a verbal structure implicit in its syntactical figures and its ironic strategies, if not in its local tropes. Hazlitt implies, however, that the rhetorical strategy of "reflection" is perhaps *too* powerful in Wordsworth's work, dividing or doubling all that it reconciles and making the entire world over in Wordsworth's own image.

The tension between representation and irony, implicit in the figure of reflection, is played out in the rhetorical scheme of Hazlitt's essay "On the Knowledge of Character." Here, our understanding of character is conceived of as a process of reflection in two senses: first, as the mirroring or projection of our own prejudices and preconceptions onto other people's characters; second, as the perversely *inverted* or paradoxical fact that character becomes more self-contradictory and incoherent the better we know it. We find it difficult to accept the irony that "deep" knowledge impairs our ability to judge character, because this would call into question the very concept of depth of character and thus contradict our strongly felt sense of a distinction between our own motives (or capacities) and actual behavior. Hazlitt's conclusion is that our private sense of a distinction between what is deep and what is superficial within ourselves can be misleading and that we are liable either to overrate or to underrate ourselves and our efforts. In order to counteract this tendency in our assessments of character (whether our own or that of others) it is important to *reflect* on the distinctions we are making between important and trivial characteristics, that is, to hypothesize those distinctions as dissolved, suspended, or inverted.

The association of paradox and irony with the figure of reflection is made explicit in the essay "Depth and Superficiality." Hazlitt's opening strategy of calling attention to an ironic rhetorical conflation of method and subject gradually gives way to his conviction that there must *always* be a figurative congruency between the two. Though this seems at first to establish constraints upon the essayist's task of analyzing and explaining, Hazlitt suggests that irony itself may reveal ways out of the subjectivist bind. In terms of the specific figures of the essay, irony in the form of "reflection" may invert the relationship of surface and depth (or background and foreground) and, in doing so, "abstract" them from their immediate circumstances, revealing the places where new figures might take hold (where, for instance, the trope of "attraction" might replace the trope of "falling"). In Hazlitt's work "reflection" not only *mediates* between surface and depth but helps isolate them from their surrounding contexts as well. Hazlitt thus contributes to empiricism by demonstrating the curious ways in which the tropes of reflection, surface, and depth not only *impose* themselves on our account of the world but might also be abstracted from it.

In the essays of Hazlitt's that we have considered, a tension arises between different figurative applications of the surface/depth scheme. Whether criticizing qualities of poetry, aspects of human character, or his own rhetorical and polemical strategies, Hazlitt generally uses *surface* and *depth* in a figurative sense, to describe abstract characteristics rather than concrete physical ones. Reflection is thus the name for a purely rhetorical motion—though the power of such a motion to structure thought and perception is insisted upon throughout. When we turn to Ruskin, however, we encounter a writer concerned with surfaces, depths, and reflections in a much more literal and graphic sense. As a critic of painting, Ruskin is concerned primarily with the negotiation between two concrete worlds, one three-dimensional and the other two-dimensional; he is interested equally in the "deep" spatial and perspectival mysteries of the three-dimensional world and in the two-dimensional representation of those mysteries. As the consummate technician of painting, Ruskin finds himself consistently analyzing the *surface* effects by which the canvas is made to render the illusion of depth-of-field, and acknowledging that depth is inaccessible except through the mediation of surfaces. Since for Ruskin, however, the mysteries of three-dimensionality are in themselves only *representations* of the more spiritual mysteries of creation, a certain ironic tension is created between his pejorative rhetoric of surfaces and his valorizing rhetoric of depths.

For Ruskin, optical reflection is a phenomenon that must be captured and yet "seen through"; it must be at once demystified and yet left to its own mysterious workings. This double perspective on optical reflections in turn thematizes Ruskin's ambivalence concerning the function of mental reflection—an ambivalence we have seen increasingly in the works of the writers we have looked at so far. Like Hazlitt, Ruskin contemplates the relationship between the surface/depth distinctions within his subject matter and the inescapable surface/depth distinctions of his own conceptual framework. But whereas for Hazlitt the tension between the two schemes results in irony, and ultimately in abstraction, Ruskin's unwillingness to part with either his moral or his technical vocabulary commits him to a rhetorical contradiction that, as we shall see, remains largely unresolved—lodged in the figure of reflection.

6

Ruskin's "Truth of Space": The Technique of Surface and the Ethics of Depth in *Modern Painters*

Now the fact is that there is hardly a road-side pond or pool which has not as much landscape *in* it as above it. It is not the brown, muddy, dull thing we suppose it to be; it has a heart like ourselves, and in the bottom of that there are the boughs of the tall trees, and the blades of the shaking grass, and all manner of hues of variable pleasant light out of the sky. Nay, the ugly gutter, that stagnates over the drain-bars in the heart of the foul city, is not altogether base; down in that, if you will look deep enough, you may see the dark serious blue of far-off sky, and the passing of pure clouds. It is at your own will that you see, in that despised stream, either the refuse of the street, or the image of the sky.

—RUSKIN, *Modern Painters*, vol. I

HEARTSIGHT DEEP AS EYESIGHT

NO LITERARY writer has ever been more attentive to the surfaces of things than John Ruskin. But where are we to find those surfaces? Everywhere in *Modern Painters* we are confronted with detailed empirical observations alongside vexing questions of reference: are his "surfaces" the surfaces of landscapes (of rocks, foliage, water, and clouds), of a painted canvas, or of something altogether more metaphorical—say, experience, meaning, or life? Ruskin's rhetoric tends to reproduce all the ambiguities of representation and illusion that he sorts out so magnificently in his discussions of landscape painting. Everywhere throughout his writing the figures of "surface," "depth," and, above all, "reflection" are applied bewilderingly to both landscape and canvas, to both "eyesight" and "insight," and to both the physical qualities of objects and the affective impressions they produce. And yet in exemplary empiricist fashion, Ruskin holds fast to his faith in surfaces—not only to the surfaces of the phenomenal world but to "impressible" surfaces of the mind on which the world is recorded.[1] Artists who have failed to observe accurately the details of nature's "surfaces" are consistently condemned by Ruskin, while the exemplary modern painter, Turner, is lauded for his ability to depict light and space in terms of "round" and "retiring" surfaces.

Yet what precisely are the terms of the extraordinary praise accorded to Turner? The "master," Ruskin tells us, strides "farther and deeper" than any previous painter and does this because he has "heart- sight deep as eyesight."[2] Despite the pervasive emphasis on surfaces in Ruskin's technical criticism of art, his work is suffused with a rhetoric of depth. Ruskin uses the figure of depth to describe processes and qualities of mind more elusive than the initial "impression" of sensations and ideas. Thus, "deep knowledge," "deep feeling," and "deep thought" are consistently identified as signs of greatness and truth, and they constitute the key figures of praise in Ruskin's vocabulary. Though Ruskin formally adheres to the empiricist credo of a constructed visual third dimension, the figure of depth seems increasingly to take on qualities of innateness in his work. This valorization of depth does not necessarily conflict with the considerable estimation of surfaces in Ruskin's discussions of aesthetic technique, though as we shall see, the two figures are uneasy companions.

Paul Sawyer has suggested that the distinction between figurative depths and literal surfaces, far from being a problem in Ruskin's work, represents the *solution* to a problem: "*Modern Painters* I implicitly reconciles the contradiction between the language used by practicing artists and the language of philosophical empiricism, and it does so by a descrip-

[1] On the influence of classic British empiricist psychology on Ruskin, see Landow, *The Aesthetic and Critical Theories of John Ruskin*, 62, 74–76; Elizabeth K. Helsinger, *Ruskin and the Art of the Beholder* (Cambridge: Harvard University Press, 1982), 52–53, 169, 182–96; and Gary Wihl, *Ruskin and the Rhetoric of Infallibility* (New Haven: Yale University Press, 1985), 1–5. All three critics agree that Ruskin's impressionism is essentially Lockean. However, according to Landow and Helsinger, Ruskin considered the impressionistic force of sight and language to be equivalent, a significant departure from both the Lockean emphasis on the primacy of sight and the Burkean emphasis on the superior force of language. Wihl, operating under de Manian assumptions about the close relation between rhetoric and sensation in Locke's *Essay*, sees Ruskin's work as falling more squarely within the Lockean tradition.

[2] The quotations are from *Modern Painters*, vols. 1 and 5, respectively, in *The Works of John Ruskin*, 39 vols., ed. E. T. Cook and Alexander Wedderburn (London: George Allen, 1903–12), 3.15; 7.377. All subsequent references to Ruskin's work will cite volume and page numbers from this edition, with the titles of specific works indicated where necessary.

tive technique that enacts a fiction of 'deep seeing,' a fiction by which surfaces disclose essences and the factual becomes effective."[3] This is an exemplary Ruskinian argument, because it follows Ruskin in blurring the line between the figurative and the literal: "deep seeing" is presumably a figure, but is it clear that the "surfaces" beyond which "deep seeing" penetrates are *literally* surfaces? Sawyer argues that an implicit conflict between Ruskin's aesthetic and empirical attitudes toward the surfaces of the phenomenal world presents a problem and that the figure of depth is Ruskin's solution to that problem. But the surfaces that Ruskin expresses a desire to *get beyond* (in occasional phrases such as "a more essential truth than is seen at the surface of things" [4.284], "the surface of all human phenomena" [10.345], or "it is always easier to see the surface than the depth of things" [12.230]) are not at all the same as the "surfaces" that dominate his descriptions of nature and his theories of visual perception. "Surfaces" are not entirely the empirical entities or "depth" entirely the "fiction" in Ruskin's work that Sawyer suggests. "Surface" and "depth" play equally constitutive roles in a "truth of space" that is at once both figurative and literal.

Nevertheless, Sawyer's argument *is* Ruskinian, for Ruskin, like Burke, believes implicitly in a correspondence between the sensations of spatial depth obtained in and from landscape, and those aspects and qualities of human experience that we figuratively describe as "deep." In the chapter of *Modern Painters*, vol. 4, entitled "Mountain Glory," Ruskin asserts a direct connection between physical altitude and "deep feeling": "While we mourn over the fictitious shape given to the religious visions of the anchorite, we may envy the sincerity and the depth of the emotion from which they spring: in the deep feeling, we have to acknowledge the solemn influences of the hills" (6.427). If such a correspondence is generally tenable, as Ruskin clearly believes it is, then it becomes clear that "deep seeing" (Turner's "heartsight deep as eyesight") *does* offer itself as a way beyond surfaces, regardless of whether the latter are regarded literally as the empirical surfaces of the phenomenal world or figuratively as the "surface" of "life," "experience," or the "mind." Yet if

[3] Paul L. Sawyer, *Ruskin's Poetic Argument: The Design of the Major Works* (Ithaca: Cornell University Press, 1985), 38. See also a similar estimation by Patricia M. Ball in *The Science of Aspects: The Changing Role of Fact in the Work of Coleridge, Ruskin, and Hopkins* (London: Athlone Press, University of London, 1971). Ball argues that Ruskin refuses to subordinate "fact" to "feeling" and that he insists on the ultimate compatibility of subjectivity and factuality (55).

the figure of depth can indifferently designate mental and spatial categories, then we are indeed confronted with a potential conflict when we turn back to Ruskin's painterly praise of surfaces and his philosophical praise of depths, for a distinction between literal and figurative usages no longer separates these two discursive modes.

Unwilling to argue (as does Burke) that impressions of surface are less striking than impressions of depth, and further unwilling to argue (as does the ironist Hazlitt) that superficial perceptions and judgments may be more useful than "deep" ones, Ruskin finds it difficult to enforce the highly specific set of distinctions between empirical surfaces and depths upon which his technical criticism and theories of landscape depend so heavily. In effect, Ruskin presents his reader with a number of paradoxes that create perilous resonances within an ostensibly referential discourse.[4] First among these is the paradox of chiaroscuro. Ruskin believes that the chiaroscurist's delight in creating illusions of spatial depth on the canvas results at best in mere "projection," and at worst in making the viewer uncomfortably conscious of the painting's *surface*; while conversely, a modern "master's" loving attentiveness to the surface details of the natural world produces deeply studied and deeply felt works of art. Here we have both the Burkean fear of the *collapse* of aesthetic space and the Hazlittian belief in the essential constructedness of our impressions of depth.

Second, and proceeding from this, there is the paradox implicit in the art of painting itself, a two-dimensional medium representing a three-dimensional subject. The surface of the canvas is at once the most obvious and the most suppressed subject in Ruskin's writing. Though ostensibly a series of treatises on painting, *Modern Painters* often dispenses with the

---

[4] Wihl argues that Ruskin's "theoretical texts comment upon his own figurative texts in such a way that the latter become unreadable" (*Ruskin and the Rhetoric of Infallibility*, xii). My own reading of Ruskin is not based on such an axiomatic distinction between theoretical and figurative texts, but I would certainly agree that the overlapping figures of Ruskin's various projects and discourses (philosophical, psychological, aesthetic, empirical, and moral, at the very least) call the stability of these various discourses into question. For yet a different view of the self-disrupting nature of Ruskin's rhetoric, see Jay Fellows (*Ruskin's Maze: Mastery and Madness in His Art* [Princeton: Princeton University Press, 1981]), whose own work is an attempt both to duplicate and to exhaust Ruskin's rhetorical mode. Fellows describes his own project as the attempt to locate "the point where coherence, as if under a terrible burden, breaks down" and explains that his "phenomenological explorations of a consciousness at work will have occasions to refer back to both theory and biography, but the language will essentially have a life of its own—often a collective life, for Ruskin's texts, no matter how contradictory, overlap" (xviii).

medium of painting and gives the impression of treating landscape direct-ly.[5] The illusion upon which much of Ruskin's criticism depends is that painters paint directly onto (or over) the surfaces of nature itself, not over the surface of a canvas; references to the canvas are in fact almost entirely absent from Ruskin's writing except for those instances in which he is describing incompetent or merely illusionistic painterly effects. If the sur-face of the canvas is a paradoxical entity for Ruskin then the printed page is all the more so—particularly as the act of reading is Ruskin's model for deciphering God's hieroglyphic world. Ruskin's typological symbolism demands that reading be granted at least equal status with vision as a model for understanding.[6] This allegorical hermeneutic, though at a gen-eral level compatible with empiricism's dual visual/verbal model, pro-vides some of the rhetorical extravagance that constantly threatens to carry Ruskin beyond empiricism.

The final paradox concerns reflection. Of all the writers we have studied, Ruskin is in a certain sense the most radically empiricist: he purports simply to look at things and tell us what he sees. Furthermore, Ruskin pays far greater attention to—and develops a far more precise vocabulary for—the optical processes by which the visual world is pre-sented to our consciousness. He gives us perhaps the most intricate exam-ination of reflected light that we possess. Though Ruskin occasionally uses "reflection" in the conventional empiricist sense, as a rhetorical figure for the mental processes of memory, self-criticism, and self-adjustment, he has a much greater interest in the optical phenomenon of reflected light and its various consequences. Specifically, Ruskin is fasci-nated by the fact that almost everything we see is light reflected from surfaces, except for the antithetical and absolute extremes of direct light from the sun, and the black vacancy of shadows so "deep" that no light is reflected at all. These two crucial exceptions give to natural landscapes an extreme spectrum of light and color that the painter cannot hope to rival. The painter, working only with reflected light (and, in fact, almost inev-itably displaying his canvases in a light that is itself already reflected), must thus submit to the optical laws of reflection even while re-creating effects of light that are not properly reflections.

[5] Paul Sawyer writes: "His [Ruskin's] conception of . . . nature depends upon the most childlike suspension of disbelief: the canvas should always seem a real place to be entered." See *Ruskin's Poetic Argument*, 42.

[6] On Ruskin's typology, symbolism, and allegory, see Landow, *The Aesthetic and Critical Theories of John Ruskin*, chap. 5. See also n. 11.

In addition to this, reflection is responsible for certain illusions of "depth." Images reflected on the surface of water appear to be beyond, and in a sense *beneath*, that surface. The paradox created by this false depth has to do with the fact that we cannot focus optically on both the surface and the reflection at the same time even though they occupy the same space. As Ruskin puts it, the reflection "destroys the surface." As we have seen in both Locke and Burke, whereas prereflective judgments help construct our impressions of spatial depth, reflection itself may destroy those impressions. For Ruskin, the mediating role of optical reflection itself is so completely constitutive of our perceptions of both surface and depth that it threatens to overwhelm them and break down their distinctive characteristics. This confusing effect would presumably be at odds with the role played by mental reflection, but as we shall see in Ruskin's later work, the optical phenomenon of reflection comes to be a paradigmatic figure for the loss of faith in his own intellectual and spiritual reflections.

THE FALSE DEPTHS OF CHIAROSCURO

The transformation of depth into surface lies at the heart of painting, and early in *Modern Painters* Ruskin addresses the special problems of representation, illusion, and the construction of three-dimensional visual space that the medium raises. Representation in painting is pleasing, argues Ruskin, because it depends on deception while at the same time announcing itself as a deception. He then proceeds to offer a paradigmatic example of such deception:

> The most perfect ideas and pleasures of imitation are, therefore, when one sense is contradicted by another, both bearing as positive evidence on the subject as each is capable of alone; as when the eye says a thing is round, and the finger says it is flat: they are, therefore never felt in so high a degree as in painting, where appearance of projection, roughness, hair, velvet, etc., are given with a smooth surface, or in wax-work, where the first evidence of the senses is perpetually contradicted by their experience. (3.100–101)

Berkeley had made the fortuitous coordination of our various sense faculties into the basis of a theory of communication (e.g., visual sensations were signs for tactile experiences). And for Berkeley, counterexamples demonstrating the failure of coordination served to remind us of the essentially arbitrary nature of the signifying process. For Ruskin, however—a critic of representations as well as of sensations—such failure of coordination confesses "trickery and deception" rather than the principle of arbitrariness. Far from being an intrinsic advantage of the medium, painting's special potential for deceptive imitation constitutes a peril to be avoided at all costs. The "sensation of trickery and deception" intrinsic to imitations makes them "contemptible" in Ruskin's eyes (101–2). As it turns out, a painting that seemed to give us both "surface" and "projection" gives us, figuratively speaking, neither: we are left with neither "high" thoughts nor "impressions" but only with a self-conscious "reflection" that situates itself between the two:

> Ideas of imitation, then, act by producing the simple pleasure of surprise, and that not of surprise in its *higher* sense and function, but of the mean and paltry surprise which is felt in jugglery. These ideas and pleasures are the most contemptible which can be received from art. First, because it is necessary to their enjoyment that the mind should *reject the impression* and address of the thing represented, and *fix itself only upon the reflection* that it is not what it seems to be. All *high* or noble emotion or thought is thus rendered physically impossible, while the mind exults in what is very like a strictly sensual pleasure. (101–2, my emphasis)

The illusion of three-dimensionality (what we now call "depth-of-field," and what Ruskin refers to variously as "depth," "aerial perspective," "tone," "projection," "relief," and "retirement") is clearly central to painting's claims as a representational form yet also perhaps destructive of that form. This paradox is expressed most immediately in the consistent conflict between Ruskin's class-inflected rhetoric of evaluation, in which "high" and "low" effects are antithetical, and his rhetoric of spatiality, in which height, depth, and projection are problematically related to one another (and to surface). As we can see in the passage just cited, any reflection on the tension between medium and content becomes an obstacle to those "higher" thoughts that are ostensibly the purpose of the artwork.

It is entirely appropriate that Ruskin should designate as "reflection" that faculty of mind that reveals the chiaroscurist's effects of relief to be a deception. For the effects of depth-of-field that the chiaroscurist tries to produce *are reliant upon reflected light*, unlike nature's own "depths," which are defined precisely by the total *absence* of reflection:

Not only does nature surpass us in power of obtaining light as much as the sun surpasses white paper, but she also infinitely surpasses us in her power of shade. Her deepest shades are void spaces from which no light whatever is reflected back to the eye; ours are black surfaces from which, paint as black as we may, a great deal of light is still reflected, and which, placed against one of nature's deep bits of gloom, would tell as distinct light. Here we are, then, with white paper for our highest light, and visible illumined surface for our deepest shadow, set to run the gauntlet against nature, with the sun for her light, and vacuity for her gloom. (261, my emphasis)

The artist can only present by means of reflected light what nature presents as a vacuity: "depth." "Depth" in this case signifies both spatial recess and an extreme effect of lighting (in fact, its total absence), and it is thus a register on two different scales. As we shall see, these two referential modes of "depth" are neither identical nor entirely distinguishable; there are certain unsurpassable ambiguities in the figure of depth even when it is used literally to designate empirical effects in the visual world. It is unclear both from Ruskin's examples and from his discursive statements whether the term is being used synecdochically as a measurement of distance—in which case he is offering an empirical theory that explains the relative absence of light in terms of the relative distance of reflecting surfaces—or whether "depth" is a more obscure, perhaps metaphorical, figure for darkness.

Since a painter's depictions of spatial perspective and relative distance are largely dependent upon the contrasts between deep gloom and high illumination (as well as the contrasts among an almost infinite variety of intervening "tones"), and since the two extremes of vacuity and direct light are unavailable, it is necessary that all painting should substitute reflecting surfaces for genuine depth. But the particular charge against the "meanness" of chiaroscuro is that in sacrificing too many "truths" of surface reflection and tonal relationship for the suggestion of spatial depth, it produces an effect of projection that is, in Ruskin's eyes, only an *inverted* depth.[7] Ironically, however, the vertical configuration of Ruskin's social and ethical rhetoric realigns the figure of projection with that of depth even as he attempts to distinguish the two:

---

[7] See, for instance, Ruskin's remarks on "mean and false chiaroscuro" in *The Elements of Drawing*: "Even when, as by Correggio, exquisite play of hue is joined with exquisite transparency, the delight in the depth almost always leads the painter into mean and false chiaroscuro" (15.138).

Finally, far below all these come those particular accuracies or tricks of chiaroscuro which cause objects to look projecting from the canvas, not worthy of the names of truths, because they require for their attainment the sacrifice of all others; . . . And thus he who throws one object out of his picture, never lets the spectator into it. Michael Angelo bids you follow his phantoms into the abyss of heaven, but a modern French painter drops his hero out of the picture frame.

This solidity or projection, then, is the very lowest truth that art can give; it is the painting of mere matter, giving that as food for the eye which is properly only the subject of touch. (164)[8]

Ruskin's ostensible argument is that true effects of depth in painting make us feel as if we were entering an "abyss," while mere effects of projection leave us in exile outside the painting's mise-en-scène. But the assimilation of the depth/projection distinction to the interior/exterior distinction is disrupted on two accounts.[9] First, Ruskin's moral rhetoric reintroduces the figure of depth on the wrong side of the equation, as effects of projection are designated as "low." Second, the theme of exclusion is dramatized not only by figures of exteriority (e.g., "out of the picture") but by the figure of *depth* as well: "A modern French painter *drops* his hero out of the picture frame."

The oxymoronic term *chiaroscuro* captures perfectly for Ruskin the paradoxical effects that proceed from techniques of contrast. And just as an exclusive concentration on depth-of-field results in the destruction of depth (or at least its parodic transformation into a "low" effect), so the perfection of "flat" tones may help the artist to outdo "depth." Ruskin notes that the painter—working on a more abbreviated scale of light and darkness than nature has at its disposal—must choose between two principles of contrast. He may use his darkest color and his brightest color wherever the deepest gloom and highest illumination actually appear in the landscape he is painting. He will then retain *in relative proportion* all the intermediate tones, while scaling down their absolute incremental distinctions. In this case, the darkest and brightest points in the picture

[8] One might almost suspect some conscious irony in this passage, given Ruskin's conspicuous description of good painting as "food for the eye" in the same sentence where he depreciates all emphasis on tactility in painting.

[9] That the interior/exterior distinction is always a morally loaded one is emphasized by Paul de Man in both "Semiology and Rhetoric" (*Allegories of Reading: Figural Language in Rousseau, Nietzsche, Rilke, and Proust* [New Haven: Yale University Press, 1979], 3–19) and "The Epistemology of Metaphor."

will not necessarily represent different distances from the viewer's position, nor will they necessarily occur in juxtaposition. If this method is followed, the pattern of light in the painting will not intensify depth-of-field by reinforcing constrasts of distance with sharp contrasts in lighting, *but the total set of perspectival relations will be highly accurate.* Such was Turner's approach to contrast. But the Old Masters chose a different strategy, using their very brightest and very darkest colors to represent the difference of lighting at the landscape's greatest point of contrasting light, even though both brighter and darker points occurred elsewhere within the prospect. This required them to distort all differences of tone elsewhere in the painting. The effect, Ruskin claimed, was to "flatten" the parts of the landscape not containing any dramatic contrasts:

> They [the Old Masters] chose those steps of distance which are the most conspicuous and noticeable, that for instance from sky to foliage, or from clouds to hills; and they gave these their precise pitch of difference in shade with exquisite accuracy of imitation. Their means were then exhausted, and they were obliged to leave their trees flat masses of mere filled-up outline, and to omit the truths of space in every individual part of their picture by the thousand. (262)

The chiaroscurism of the Old Masters thus produces an effect quite the opposite of what they intend, and they employ a principle of contrast that ultimately destroys depth-of-field. Conversely, writes Ruskin in his chapter on *chiaroscuro*, the most vivid effects of contrast are achieved by a "flat" rendering of the "deepest" shades in a landscape:

> Now, this may serve to show you the immense prominence and importance of shadows where there is anything like bright light. They are, in fact, commonly far more conspicuous than the thing which casts them; for being as large as the casting object, and altogether made up of a blackness deeper than the darkest part of the casting object, while that object is also broken up with positive and reflected lights, their large, broad, unbroken spaces tell strongly on the eye . . . And hence, if we have to express vivid light, our very first aim must be to get the shadows sharp and visible; and this is not to be done by blackness . . . but by keeping them perfectly *flat*, keen, and even. A very pale shadow, if it be quite *flat*, if it conceal the details of the objects it crosses, if it be grey and cold compared with their colour, and very sharp-edged, will be far more conspicuous, and make everything out of it look a great deal more like sunlight, than a shadow ten times its depth, shaded off at the edge. (304–5)

Shadows, as the absence of "reflected light," are both "deep" and "prominent," and the painter best captures this paradox by rendering them as *flatly* as possible.

Ruskin's comments on chiaroscurism occur early in *Modern Painters* and are meant to illustrate a central principle of the work as a whole. Without a continual activity of self-scrutiny that is moral as well as empirical, the chiaroscurist will try to "pass off" effects that, on a first impression, are strikingly accurate but that prolonged attention will reveal to be incomplete, even deceitful. One must not only record one's impressions as accurately as possible but also review them as skeptically as possible.

KNOWABLE AND UNKNOWABLE DEPTHS

Part of the difficulty in deciphering Ruskin's attitude toward chiaroscuro has to do with the fact that contrasts of light and contrasts of distance are not the same thing, despite being designated by one and the same figure. Ruskin consistently uses the term *depth* to signify extremes of both spatial recess and pitch of color. On the one hand, Ruskin likes to use *depth* as a technical term for intensity of color. Thus he refers to "deep and quiet yellows" (274), to "transparent and deep azures" (292), to a "blackness deeper than . . . the casting object" (304), and to the "deep stagnant blue" of the sky in classical painting (408). (All this is complicated by the fact that Ruskin is referring sometimes to qualities of light, sometimes to qualities of pigmentation). On the other hand, he cautions that "depth" is *not* purely a function of color or a measure of color intensity. The darkness of the clouds in Turner's *Long Ships Lighthouse, Land's End*, for instance, is "a gloom dependent rather on the enormous space and depth indicated, than on actual pitch of color" (404). We are at a crux of Ruskin's figurative usage here, for *depth* seems to refer to something located *between* the category of extension and those of color and light. Depth is not merely pitch of color or intensity of light, but neither is it merely spatial extension.[10]

This may help to explain the rather astounding fact that in the two chapters entitled "Of Truth of Space," the figure of depth is almost entire-

[10] See, for instance, Ruskin's distinctions between "extension of space" and "deep melodies of tone" (3.269), between "depth" and "pitch" (3.404), and between depth of color and depth of shade (*Elements of Drawing*, 15.42).

ly absent. In these chapters—two of the most crucial for an understanding of Ruskin's empiricist aesthetics—depth-of-field is transformed into the figure of the *subtext*, and space becomes not so much a depth as a mysterious hieroglyph. The fault of painters who cannot adequately capture space, claims Ruskin, lies not in their failure to depict luminous depth-of-field in his paintings but in their failure to hint at the existence of distinct characteristics "underneath" the playful "writing" of nature's light and shadows:

> Take one of Poussin's extreme distances, such as that in the Sacrifice of Isaac. It is luminous, retiring, delicate and perfect in tone. . . . But we must remember that all these alternate spaces of grey and gold are not the landscape itself, but the treatment of it; not its substance, but its light and shade. They are *just what nature would cast over it, and write upon it with every cloud*, but which she would cast in play, and without carefulness, as matters of the very smallest possible importance. *All her work and her attention would be given to bring out from underneath this, and through this, the forms and the material character* which this can only be valuable to illustrate, not to conceal. (332, my emphasis)

In the next paragraph the relationship between the surface "play" of nature's writing and the "lesson" beneath is likened to a distinction between "adjunct" and "essence," a comparison that invokes the traditional Platonic depreciation of script as mere supplement. Yet we cannot help but notice that in the passage quoted, Ruskin describes the hidden essence underneath nature's writing as a "material character," which would seem to align it perilously with the graphic nature of writing, quite in keeping with the Lockean figures of "impression, "imprint," and "character," so central to the tradition of empiricist psychology. (Indeed, in vol. 2 of *Modern Painters*, when Ruskin outlines his theory of "types" of beauty, he defines "type" as "any *character* in *material* things by which they convey an idea of immaterial ones" [4.76n, my emphasis].)[11]

---

[11] Jeffrey L. Spear also draws attention to this passage, though his discussion of it focuses more on Ruskin's version of Christian typology. See Spear, *Dreams of an English Eden: Ruskin and His Tradition in Social Criticism* (New York: Columbia University Press, 1984), 35–38. On Ruskin's evangelical interest in typology, see also Robert Hewison, *John Ruskin: The Argument of the Eye* (London: Thames and Hudson, 1976), 25–26. For the purposes of this essay I am more concerned with the implicit analogy between "type" as image and "type" as an element of printing and thus of language. With this connection in mind it is interesting to note that Ruskin refers at several points to the "grammatical" accuracy of Turner's tones and colors (3.273, 326).

It is significant that Ruskin's more explicit figures of depth are re-placed in this chapter by the figure of a subtext; the latter has the advan-tage of a visible distinctness not possessed by the shadowy figure of depth, but the disadvantage of being less distinguishable from its own antithesis (text, or "writing") than depth is from surface. That the subtext as a substitutive figure of depth should seem inherently more decipherable than "deep" colors or "deep" spaces is important because these are the chapters in which Ruskin argues most forcefully for Turner's (and na-ture's) provision of detailed truths beneath or beyond appearances. Turner's work "suggest[s] more than it represents," writes Ruskin, but these "suggestions" are always empirically verifiable:

> Abundant beyond the power of the eye to embrace or follow, vast and various beyond the power of the mind to comprehend, there is yet not one atom in its whole extent and mass which does not suggest more than it represents; nor does it suggest vaguely, but in such a manner as to prove that the conception of each individual inch of that distance is absolutely clear and complete in the master's mind, a separate picture fully worked out: but yet, clearly and fully as the idea is formed, just so much of it is given, and no more, as nature would have allowed us to feel or see; just so much as would enable a specta-tor of experience and knowledge to understand almost every minute frag-ment of separate detail, but appears, to the unpractised and careless eye, just what a distance of nature's own would appear, an unintelligible mass. (335)

Central to Ruskin's conception of great painting is the paradoxical notion that representation might be mysterious without being vague, and precise without being entirely clear.[12] Ruskin is at some pains to defend this paradox, which he explains with the help of two examples. First he asks the reader to imagine himself moving farther and farther away from an object—in this case, the front of a house. Until the distant object actually blurs so completely that it becomes "a mere spot," it still possesses obser-vable details, which, "though totally merged and lost in the mass, have still an influence on the texture of that mass" (328). "Its shadows and lines and local colors are not lost sight of as it retires; they get mixed and indistinguishable, but they are still there, and there is a difference always perceivable between an object possessing such details and a flat or vacant space" (329). Next, Ruskin asks the reader to imagine a friend approach-

---

12 Cf. Burke's valorization of "obscurity" and relative depreciation of "clarity" (*Philo-sophical Enquiry*, 2.3–4.58–64; and book 5, passim).

ing from a distance. Even after the friend's face has become recognizable, argues Ruskin, "there are a thousand things in his face which have their effect in inducing the recognition, but which you cannot see so as to know what they are" (329). "Every object," Ruskin proceeds to generalize, "however near the eye, has something about it which you cannot see, and which brings the mystery of distance even into every part and portion of what we suppose ourselves to see most distinctly (337).

We have reached the limits of empiricism, the most anti-empiricist moment in the tradition of empiricist writing. According to Ruskin, great painting directs us beyond immediate details to those details that are distant, mysterious, perhaps unseen. The categories of ineffable, transcendent truth that empiricism appears to work so hard to refute, reappear now with a vengeance. There is always an unseen side to things, asserts Ruskin; even more surprisingly there are also *ways of pointing to the unseen* that preserve its unique mystery while rendering it with precision. What may be mysterious in presentation is, as he says, "absolutely clear and complete in the master's mind," not unlike the details of a familiar face seen from a distance—or a subtext that "always tells a story, however hintedly and vaguely" (335).

It is curious that Ruskin should abstain so conspicuously from references to "depth" in the very chapters in which he sets forth his theory of the "meanings" hidden in the recesses of visual space. Depth is apparently no more synonymous with *hidden meaning* than it is with spatial extension or intensity of color, though it is related to all these.[13] Depth is something more than sensation and yet less than a language or subtext. Throughout *Modern Painters*, vol. 1, Ruskin insists that despite the empirically verifiable qualities of visible depth, depth is nonetheless a figure for ineffable aspects of experience. "There is no part nor portion of God's works in which the delicacy appreciable by a cultivated eye, and necessary to be rendered in art, is not beyond all expression and explanation," he writes, and thus, "I have been entirely unable . . . to demonstrate clearly anything of really deep and perfect truth" (253). It is not entirely possible to resolve the tension between Ruskin's references to the ineffable spiritual effects of "deep" perspectives, lighting, and coloration on the one hand and the theme of a hidden, but legible, "material character" beneath the visible language of nature on the other hand—since the latter theme is

---

[13] See Landow (*Aesthetic and Critical Theories*), who argues that Ruskin inherits essentially romantic assumptions about the connection between "intensity" and the figure of depth (71–72).

clearly not independent of figures of depth. To some extent, we might speculate, it is precisely the function of the figure of depth to keep in suspense the relationship between legibility and ineffability.[14]

Of the putatively nonlinguistic qualities mediated by the figure of depth, one of the most important is a sense of the past.[15] The past gives us depth, or rather *appeals* to what is "deep" in us: "Fortunately for mankind, as some counterbalance to that wretched love of novelty which originates in selfishness, shallowness, and conceit, and which especially characterizes all vulgar minds, there is set in the deeper places of the heart such affection for the signs of age that the eye is delighted even by injuries which are the work of time" (203–4). Early personal experiences provide within us a "ground" (237) or "depth" to which future experiences may appeal. Thus Ruskin can advance it as a rule that the styles and sympathies of all great artists are determined in their childhood:

> It is a fact more universally acknowledged than enforced or acted upon, that all great painters, of whatever school, have been great only in their rendering of what they had seen and felt from early childhood; . . . no man ever painted, or ever will paint, well, anything but what he has early and long seen, early and long felt, and early and long loved. (229)

It is unclear, however, what kind of constraints this "necessity" imposes (or "stamps") upon practicing artists. Ruskin acknowledges that no nation or "field" is proscribed to any painter, since "impressions first received amongst the rocks of Cornwall [may] be recalled upon the precipices of Genoa," and thus "the law of nationality will hold with him only so far as a certain joyfulness and completion will be by preference found in those parts of his subject which remind him of his own land" (232). Nevertheless, continues Ruskin, there is certainly a danger in failing to establish the proper relationship between one's own historical or autobiographical depth and the depth of the landscape. Ruskin describes this danger first as an "impression" and then as a "reflection": "But if he attempt to *impress* on his landscapes any other spirit than that he has felt, and to make them landscapes of other times, it is all over with him, at

---

[14] This indeterminacy in the figure of depth leads Fellows to suggest that the figure represents Ruskin's rhetorical strategy for obliterating self-consciousness (*Ruskin's Maze*, 39–40).

[15] Fellows suggests that there is a close connection between Ruskin's figure of depth and his interest in the past. See Fellows, *The Failing Distance: The Autobiographical Impulse in John Ruskin* (Baltimore: Johns Hopkins University Press, 1975), 74–77.

least, in the degree in which such *reflected moonshine takes the place of the genuine light of the present day"* (232, my emphasis). "Reflection" is clearly the emblem here for a false mediation, one that "takes the place of the genuine light" and disrupts the "present." Yet what precisely is being mediated in this false gesture? What is it that displaces the "present" and the "light"? The answer can be nothing other than the "depths" of the artist's subjective memories. The lesser artist, Ruskin argues, tries to "impress" on new landscapes the "spirit" of the past, a spirit that Ruskin earlier in the chapter had linked to the "deeper places of the heart." As we have seen before (100–102), the figure of reflection "explains" how surfaces are modified to give an impression of depth, but once again (as with the previous case of chiaroscuro's illusionistic "relief"), such a process is taken to be inauthentic.

Ruskin's rejection of "reflected moonshine" in this passage is not unlike Hazlitt's critique of associationist psychology. For both Hazlitt and Ruskin, too mechanistic an account of our tendency to assimilate new experiences to previous ones simply short-circuits the subject-object dynamic and leaves no room for individual acts of selection, judgment, or appreciation. Though in his "Wordsworth" essay, Hazlitt suggests that the source for this short-circuiting is Wordsworth's power of "reflection," that hypothesis is revised in the essay "Depth and Superficiality," where the abstracting power of reflection is offered precisely as a way of overturning or overriding habitual associations. For Ruskin, however, "reflection" remains a figure for the imposition rather than the abstraction, of associations. "Deep" sympathies and "deep" meanings are ineffable because they cannot be mediated without distortion, and "reflection" thus offers to mediate that which can only be intuited. Ironically, Ruskin emphasizes in this same passage that after "grounding" himself on the landscapes of his native Yorkshire, Turner was still able to "acquire" a "depth and solemnity" from European scenery. Ruskin wants to assert an ineffable correspondence between Turner's depth and the depth of European landscape, even while insisting that any attempt to *create* such a correspondence (e.g., through the mediation of "reflection") is illegitimate.

We have seen Ruskin equivocate frequently about the role of mental "reflection" in accurate or "truthful" visual perception. This apparent ambivalence toward reflection is complicated by the fact that the relationships among surface, depth, and reflection, considered as optical phenomena, are analogous to, but *not identical with*, the relationships among "depth," "superficiality," and "reflection" considered as qualities of mind. It is additionally complicated by the fact that the figure of reflection is used by Ruskin—as by Locke, Berkeley, Hume, Burke, and Hazlitt—precisely to mediate between figures of spatial extension and figures for operations of the mind, the latter figured alternately as a "seeing" and as a "reading" machine. The mind conceived in terms of surface and depth *is* in some sense a reflection of visual space—though even this description contains a further recess of figurative implication in this use of the term *reflection*. The question of the epistemological status of this *third* use of reflection remains unresolved for Burke and Hazlitt, and they are able to ignore it because the phenomenon of optical reflection plays a relatively minor and inconsistent role in their work. In their work, the metaphor of reflection is possessed of a conveniently ambiguous vehicle, whether it is used as a figure for a specific kind of mental activity or for the phenomenological interplay between mind and world. Reflection is conceived sometimes as a reliable process of optical doubling, sometimes as a pale copy, sometimes as an uncannily inverted image—depending on the rhetorical use to which it is being put and the analogy (optic or linguistic) upon which it is modeled. Ruskin's work, however, is intensely concerned with *precise* optical principles and relationships and with the highly complex but empirically specifiable characteristics of surfaces, depths, and reflections.[16] It is impossible that his figurative use of "reflection" should suddenly lose all the complexities that he takes pains to draw out in the optical phenomenon of reflection.

One of Ruskin's most subtle critics, Gary Wihl, has suggested that in *Modern Painters*, vol. 1, Ruskin is able to exploit *both* of "two antithetical properties of the sign: its narrow referentiality as a token for a single idea, or perception, and its far-ranging significance when placed within an elaborate system, where it may trade places with neighboring signs."[17] The presence of a rhetorical tension in Ruskin's work is unmistakable, but is it a tension between literal and allusive reference? Perhaps we should pause before attributing a "narrow referentiality" even to Ruskin's technical vocabulary of optical effects. The more detailed Ruskin's analysis of optical effects becomes, the more difficult it becomes for him to give

[16] George L. Hersey quite rightly observes that Ruskin is "not merely a visual but an optical thinker," a thinker fascinated with the physical details of sight. See Hersey, "Ruskin as an Optical Thinker," in *The Ruskin Polygon: Essays on the Imagination of John Ruskin*, ed. Faith M. Holland and John Dixon Hunt (Manchester: Manchester University Press, 1982), 51.

[17] Wihl, *Ruskin and the Rhetoric of Infallibility*, 29.

a single definition of visual "depth" or to distinguish depth categorically from either surfaces or reflections (we will see this even more clearly when we turn to Ruskin's discussions of sky and water). And what if the numerous passages of *Modern Painters* in which Ruskin describes nature as a painter who *uses* depth and light for effect are to be taken as more than casual anthropomorphizations (e.g., 3.261, 310–11)? What if nature's visual depths are themselves material figures for a more abstract spiritual truth? If it should turn out that Ruskin's vocabulary of "depth" and "reflection" is figurative even at the level of naturalistic description (i.e., even when he is describing optical qualities of landscape), then we would have to question whether Ruskin's work really involves a tension between literal and figurative description or between empirical and aesthetic judgments.

The putative tension between Ruskin's delight in empirical detail and his delight in figurative language has provided a fruitful problematic for contemporary criticism, as we have seen in both Sawyer's and Wihl's emphasis on Ruskin's antithetical rhetorical modes. Wihl and Sawyer, both of whose studies are informed by poststructuralist assumptions about rhetoric, tend to focus on the aspect of the tension already inscribed in language, but we can also see a concern with the same categories and tensions traced out in a different way by more traditional critics. Elisabeth Helsinger, for example, points to the conflict between visual and verbal modes of cognition in Ruskin's work: "He describes the proper relation of thought to sight, characteristically, through a visual metaphor: a garland of thoughts and fancies grouped and fastened about a natural object."[18] Helsinger's argument is that Ruskin expresses the relationship between images and thoughts first of all by providing a figure for thought, and second by giving a figure to the relationship *between* image and idea. This differs from Sawyer's and Wihl's accounts by treating figuration neither as a technique of assimilation nor as willful misprision but rather as a testament to the compatible teleologies implicit in different modes of cognition. However, what underlies all three of these critical elaborations of Ruskin's method is an assumption that Ruskin's use of figurative language is intended to bring into a single configuration language that refers literally to the visible world and language that figuratively describes properties or activities of mind. But as we shall see, the distinction between these two categories becomes increasingly problemat-

[18] Helsinger, *Ruskin and the Art of the Beholder*, 55.

ic as Ruskin probes further into nature's dramatic play of surfaces, depths, and reflections.

THE DESTRUCTION OF SURFACE

Surfaces are the most pervasive and yet the most elusive objects of Ruskin's criticism. In a sensuously textured passage from *Praeterita* he celebrates, ironically, the mysterious absence of nature's surfaces, writing: "For all other rivers there is a surface, and an underneath, and a vaguely displeasing idea of the bottom. But the Rhone flows like one lambent jewel; its surface is nowhere, its ethereal self is everywhere, the iridescent rush and translucent strength of it blue to the shore, and radiant to the depth" (35.326). As a naturally occurring optical illusion, the "disappearance" of the water's surface when we stare at it is epiphanic, revealing the "ethereal self" of nature. As a painterly effect, however, the destruction of surface is a perilous matter, leaving the viewer no place to rest in the picture:

> I believe it is a result of the experience of all artists, that it is the easiest thing in the world to give a certain degree of depth and transparency to water: but that it is next to impossible, to give a full impression of surface. If no reflection be given, a ripple being supposed, the water looks like lead: if reflection be given, it, in nine cases out of ten, looks *morbidly* clear and deep, so that we always go down *into* it, even when the artist most wishes us to glide *over* it. (3.537)

In this second passage, cited from *Modern Painters*, vol. 1, we are confronted with an interpretive dilemma: is it really the surface of the water represented in the painting, or rather the painted surface of the canvas itself that the "artist most wishes us to glide over"? This question arises consistently when Ruskin uses the term *surface* in describing a painter's representation of a landscape. The painting's surface mediates between the physical surfaces and depths of nature on the one hand and "deep" or superficial experiences on the other, but it is clearly distinct from all of these categories. The surface of the canvas is not a subject Ruskin particularly wishes to dwell on, yet his emphasis on painterly technique makes it almost impossible that this embarrassing material condition of painting should be ignored. Ruskin's solution is to describe the act of painting as if it were a reproduction *of* surfaces rather than a reduction *to* surface. Thus Ruskin writes of a particular "mountain" in a Turner painting: "There is not a quarter of an inch of its surface without its suggestion of increasing distance and individual form" (3.461). It is *Turner* who "suggests" distance to us by way of the "surface" of his canvas, yet the fiction here is that the mountain's surface itself is doing the suggesting. Certainly it is one of the tenets of the "Truth of Space" that nature *does* "suggest" things to us visually, but to dissolve the painter's suggestion back into the landscape's, and the painting's surface back into nature's, is to suppress an important moment of mediation and to make a very particular kind of surface disappear.

The tension between focusing on a surface itself and focusing on something else (even a different surface) *in* or *beyond* it is a central paradox in the phenomenon of water reflections, and a crucial element in Ruskin's discussions of water in general. The discussion is empiricist not only in its close attention to the minutest optical details and processes but in its very acknowledgment of the shifts and divisions within our *attention* that constitute our ordinary experiences of the visual world. The passage on water reflections cited previously (3.537) proceeds to demonstrate this paradox by way of an example:

> Go to the edge of a pond in a perfectly calm day, at some place where there is duckweed floating on the surface, not thick, but a leaf here and there. Now, you may either see in the water the reflection of the sky, or you may see the duckweed; but you cannot, by any effort, see both together. If you look for the reflection, you will be sensible of a sudden change or effort in the eye. . . . the focus you adopt is one fit for great distance; and, accordingly, you will feel you are looking down a great way under the water . . . Hence it appears, that whenever we see plain reflections of comparatively distant objects, in near water, we cannot possibly see the surface, and *vice versâ*; so that when in a painting we give the reflections with the same clearness with which they are visible in nature, we presuppose the effort of the eye to look under the surface, and, of course, destroy the surface, and induce an effect of clearness which, perhaps, the artist has not particularly wished to attain, but which he has found himself forced into, by his reflections, in spite of himself.
> (537–38)

Reflections create the illusion of depth, of seeing beyond the surface, and the laws of optics require that we choose between a deep focus and a surface focus, sacrificing either the vertiginous reflection or the mediating surface. However, the two kinds of focus are not entirely reciprocal; reflections appear to exercise a greater power of fascination, and to demand more dramatic descriptions, than do surfaces. In fact, "reflection" is given quite extraordinary powers in this passage, not only "destroy[ing] the surface" but in addition producing a kind of specular inversion, as the subject of the sentence changes from "we" to "the artist." Of what possible significance is this shift from second-person plural to third-person singular? Why is the "artist" suddenly objectified in the moment of his unfortunately perspicacious reflection (a reflection he is "forced into . . . in spite of himself")?

This overt shift and doubling of perspective may be taken as a symptom of the suppressed double entendre that haunts the final sentence of the passage. For the phenomenon of mutually exclusive focuses—one of which "destroys" the surface to get beyond it—applies as fully to the canvas and its represented scene as it does to the surface of water and its reflected images. The almost inevitable reference of the passage to the phenomenology of *viewing a painting* points to the mental "reflection" necessary for us to see a canvas as a landscape rather than as a pattern of colors or brush strokes on a flat surface. Such "reflection" may be a natural habit for those familiar with the conventions of painting, but it is no less "destructive" of "surface" for that, and by virtue of such "destruction" it subverts one of Ruskin's foremost principles: that truthful seeing is initially impressionistic, and devoid of reflection, association, or the analytic reconstruction of perspective.

Ruskin is not unaware of the paradox involved here. And from a strictly logical point of view there is no contradiction in claiming that true-seeing for the artist requires some retention of a surface perspective while true-seeing for the viewer of a painting requires a suspension of surface perspective—since these are two different situations or moments of perception. Yet the peculiar intensity with which Ruskin cautions against the painter's neglect of surface (e.g., "morbidly clear"; "destroy the surface") cannot help but *suggest* that similar perils of self-abandonment and subjectivity attend the illusionistic pleasures of looking at painting.

Ruskin's strategy throughout *Modern Painters* is to emphasize constantly the attention that practicing artists must pay to the surface features of landscape, while distracting the reader's attention from the material surface of the canvases being described (again, with the exception of paintings by the various "faulty" landscapists whose work Ruskin con-

trasts with the truthfulness of Turner and nature).[19] Descriptions of particular landscape paintings merge into descriptions of landscape itself,
and at times it is difficult to tell whether Ruskin is focusing our attention
on a canvas or beyond it. The canvas itself seems to become most prominent (e.g., "pure staring . . . paint" [456]) when the painter has paid least
attention to surface details in his subject. Of the hills in a particular
landscape by Claude, Ruskin writes: "There is no detail nor surface in
one of them; not an inch of ground for us to stand upon; we must either
sit astride upon the edge, or fall to the bottom" (466). By contrast,
Turner's creation of depth-of-field is achieved primarily through his faithful representation of surfaces. In Turner's work, writes Ruskin,

> The eye is kept throughout on solid and retiring surfaces, instead of being
> thrown, as by Claude, on flat and equal edges. You cannot find a single edge
> in Turner's work; you are eveywhere kept upon round surfaces, and you go
> back on these you cannot tell how, never taking a leap, but progressing
> imperceptibly along the unbroken bank, till you find yourself a quarter of a
> mile into the picture, beside the figure at the bottom of the waterfall. (491)[20]

The sense of descent and "retiring" space conjured up here by Ruskin is
not the only possible effect producible by the emphasis on surface detail.
In a similar passage a chapter earlier, Ruskin describes the effect of the
"expression of retiring surface" in Turner's paintings of mountain ranges:
"We never get to the top of one of his hills without being tired with
our walk; not by the steepness, observe, but by the stretch; for we are
carried up towards the heaven by such delicate gradation of line, that we
scarcely feel that we have left the earth before we find ourselves among

---

[19] Patricia Ball argues that "while Ruskin underestimates the psychological complexities of the observing mind, he insists on a proper regard for the complexities of the object"
(*The Science of Aspects*, 73). Although this is not the same distinction as I would like to
make between an emphasis on the complexity of the represented object and one on the
complexity of the representational medium, I believe that Ball is correct in pointing to
Ruskin's reluctance to spend as much time discussing the phenomenology of art as he does
discussing "pure" optical phenomena. My argument at this point obviously borders on the
whole question of the materiality of "reading" in its widest sense (reading paintings as well
as reading script)—a question that is beyond the scope of this particular essay.

[20] Cf. Helsinger, *Ruskin and the Art of the Beholder*, on the difference between
Ruskin's and Hazlitt's ideas of how the viewer is brought to enter the imaginative space of a
painting (175–82). According to Helsinger, Hazlitt believes that we enter the painting
imaginatively by re-creating its scene in our minds, whereas Ruskin believes that we quite
literally "see" into the mise-en-scène and experience it realistically rather in a dreamlike
way.

the clouds" (467). Detailed surfaces lead us *into* paintings, but they are hardly confined to leading us *downward*. Though the "destruction of surface" creates a perilous perch or tumble, the evocation of surfaces allows the viewer to move about safely in the mise-en-scène.

Turner's genius for detail, claims Ruskin, proceeds from a "depth of knowledge" that enables him to "fill" all space: "Nothing could more strikingly prove the depth of that knowledge by which every touch of this consummate artist is regulated, that universal command of subject which never acts for a moment on anything conventional or habitual, but fills every corner and space with new evidence of knowledge, and fresh manifestation of thought" (489). But is Ruskin referring here to the "space" of the canvas or the "space" of nature? The emphasis on "corner" suggests that Turner's depth consists in the filling of the canvas. Certainly, in order to capture every detail in the landscape being represented, a painter presumably *has* to paint detail into every inch of the canvas. Yet even if filling the scene and filling the canvas are identical in practice, they refer nonetheless to different focuses, and not only visual but conceptual focuses. The evocation of depth would seem to proceed, then, as much from a suppressed tension between different categories of surface as from the faithful representation of nature's surfaces.

We have seen that in earlier chapters of *Modern Painters*, vol. 1, Ruskin associates depth with a sense of history. In the present chapter, he demonstrates that the depth achieved by a painter's attention to *surfaces* is equally connected to temporal consciousness:

> The great quality about Turner's drawings which more especially proves their transcendent truth is, the capability they afford us of reasoning on past and future phenomena, just as if we had the actual rocks before us; . . . so that we can pick and choose our points of pleasure or of thought for ourselves, and reason upon the whole with the same certainty which we should after having climbed and hammered over the rocks bit by bit. (487–88)

Though the specific figure associated with "past and future" here is that of *transcendence*, there is little question that Turner's deep knowledge and transcendent truth are isomorphic. In both cases, the saturation of the painting with detail opens up a dimension in which the viewer can move about and for which he or she can both project a future and trace a past.

Ruskin equivocates as to whether our choice of focus—our decision about how far to enter into the landscape of a painting—is really ours or is determined by the artist's coercive powers. In some instances he claims that our passage into the represented landscape is "imperceptible" and that we are "carried" along until we suddenly "find ourselves" at some distant point in the painting (e.g., 467 and 491, quoted in the preceding); in other instances, though, he insists that we "can pick and choose our points of pleasure or of thought for ourselves" (488, quoted in the preceding). Yet when it comes to our perception of actual landscapes, Ruskin is unambiguous: we have the opportunity, and in fact the responsibility, of choosing our focus. Specifically, our obligation is to search for "reflections" in nature, reflections that allow us to see "deeply" in both a physical and a moral sense:

> Now the fact is that there is hardly a road-side pond or pool which has not as much landscape *in* it as above it. It is not the brown, muddy, dull thing we suppose it to be; it has a heart like ourselves, and in the bottom of that there are the boughs of the tall trees, and the blades of the shaking grass, and all manner of hues of variable pleasant light out of the sky. Nay, the ugly gutter, that stagnates over the drain-bars in the heart of the foul city, is not altogether base; down in that, if you will look deep enough, you may see the dark serious blue of far-off sky, and the passing of pure clouds. It is at your own will that you see, in that despised stream, either the refuse of the street, or the image of the sky. (496–97)

In this passage we see Ruskin playing off a conventional moral and social rhetoric of verticality (e.g., the "baseness" of the city gutter) against an equally conventional but *contrasting* moral rhetoric employing the same figure (e.g., the "bottom" of nature's "heart," and the "deep" focus that reveals "serious" and "pure" images). The tension between the two connotations of depth here is an intentional irony. That which we call "base" has in it the potential to convey "pure" and "serious" impressions, if only we look "deep enough" into it. Yet this is *not* a case of learning to see with a more spiritual and less literal-minded or empirical eye, for the figure of deep-seeing here is not metaphorical (or at least not entirely so). Reflected images, as Ruskin points out time and time again, really *do* appear to exist beneath the water's surface. We really do adjust our eyes to the same angle for such images as we would if we were looking directly at the object, at its true distance. Our perception of the city gutter as "base," then, is a result of our not seeing empirically enough, of our "tak[ing] the ugly, round, yellow surface for granted" (497) and failing to perceive its reflected images in their precision of detail. If we chose to pay closer attention to the surface, we would be inspired to focus more deeply and would see things "above" as well as below. Of course the deep-seeing here is really a trick of reflection. Once again, reflection seems to enable us to resolve surfaces, depths, and even heights, in a comprehensive act of seeing. Yet at the same time, as we have seen earlier, the phenomenon of reflection raises questions about the clarity and *distinctness* of optical sensations, and this may in turn raise questions about the application of such figures as surface, depth, and reflection to the mind itself.

REFLECTING ON REFLECTIONS

Though Ruskin's most fascinating and extended discussions of reflection in *Modern Painters* occur in his chapters on the painting of water, he consistently reminds his reader that landscapes too are mediated almost entirely by reflected light. The phenomenon of reflection does not create a superimposition of images or duality of focus in landscapes as it does in water, but its effects are no less problematic. Light is reflected not only from natural objects directly to us but as well from object to object. Except for shadows (which are in any case the absence of reflection rather than a type of reflection), reflected light does not project patterns or form onto objects; it does however, project color:

> If we look at nature carefully, we shall find that her colours are in a state of perpetual confusion and indistinctness, while her forms, as told by light and shade, are invariably clear, distinct, and speaking. The stones and gravel of the bank catch green reflections from boughs above; the bushes receive greys and yellows from the ground; every hair's breadth of polished surface gives a little bit of the blue of the sky, or the gold of the sun . . . ; and the confusion and blending of tint are altogether so great, that were we left to find out what objects were by their colours only, we could scarcely in places distinguish the boughs of a tree from the air beyond them, or the ground beneath them. (3.161–2)

The blending and confusion of reflected colors is so complete and so variable as to make the exact determination of tint in a landscape almost impossible. "Every object will cast some of its own colour back in the light that it reflects," writes Ruskin in *The Elements of Drawing*; "it is therefore impossible to say beforehand what colour an object will have at any point of its surface, that colour depending partly on its own tint, and partly on infinite combinations of rays reflected from other things" (15.56).

If mental reflection cannot remedy the instability of optical effects, at least it prevents us from being misled by our memories of such phenomena: "It needs but a moment's reflection to prove how incapable the memory is of retaining for any time the distinct image of the sources even of its most vivid impressions" (3.287).[21] Our memories are not distinct, but then neither are our sensations, as the phenomenon of optical reflection demonstrates. Mental reflection reveals to us a certain slippage in our impressions (in both their reception and their retention), and perhaps it is not merely coincidental that the same rhetorical figure should designate not only a distortion of perception but also a way of recognizing that distortion. Is there according to Ruskin a logical congruency or analogy underlying the fact that our "reflections" demonstrate to us the indeterminacy of "reflected" light? Ruskin seems to imply this when he uses the figure of a "Venice glass" to describe *mind* and *sight* simultaneously. The "unreflecting" public, he writes, must be disabused of the notion that their minds are transparent:

> "Cannot we," say the public, "see what nature is with our own eyes . . . ?"
> . . . [M]y first business, before going a step further, must be to combat the nearly universal error of belief among the thoughtless and unreflecting, that they know either what nature is, or what is like her; that they can discover truth by instinct, and that their minds are such pure Venice glass as to be shocked by all treachery. (3.140)

On the one hand "Venice glass" is a figure for "their minds," while on the other it is a figure for *unmediated* visual perception ("cannot we see what nature is with our own eyes?"). Ruskin is writing here specifically about the education of the eye but also about the prejudices that stand in the way of that education, and the optical model of reflection registers, as it does generally in empiricist writing, a moral as well as a perceptual judgment. The fact that the "Venice glass" is a figure for both eye and mind suggests that the complementary rhetorical figure in the passage—

---

[21] Ruskin's argument here is distinctly Humean, with its emphasis on the vivacity and strength of the sense impressions relative to reflections or memories.

"unreflecting"—must also bear a double reading. In short, there is an appropriateness to the fact that "unreflecting" people believe they see natural forms without any mediation; only mental "reflection" can recognize its own double in the optical world.

We need to reflect on reflections. This tautological and ironic description of the relationship between mind and world is precisely what Ruskin must prevent from becoming explicit if he is to retain a rhetorical purchase on his subject; and yet it is a tautology that empiricist writing constantly verges on. *Modern Painters* continually hints at this and like paradoxes. Consider Ruskin's discussion of the reflections of clouds in water:

> In many cases of this kind it will be found rather that the eye is, from want of use and care, *insensible to the reflection* than that the reflection is not there; and a *little thought and careful observation* will show us that what we commonly suppose to be a surface of uniform colour is, indeed, affected more or less by an infinite variety of hues, . . . and that our apprehenshion of its lustre, purity, and even of its surface, is in no small degree dependent on our feeling of these multitudinous hues, which the continual motion of that surface prevents us from *analysing or understanding* for what they are. (507, my emphasis)

We need only to substitute the synonym "reflection" for phrases such as "thought and observation" or "analysing or understanding" in this passage in order to see the underlying empiricist tautology emerge—and in fact Ruskin proceeds only a few paragraphs later to refer to the "great spiritual refracted sun of . . . truth" that "bursts" through great works of art (509). Though this particular passage comes even closer than most to revealing the implicit tautology behind the dual registers of the surface/depth/reflection model, the tautology exists as a constant possibility throughout *Modern Painters*. The almost unprecedented detailing of nature's surfaces, depths, and reflections, with their problematic relationships and distinctions, virtually guarantees that Ruskin's rhetoric of cognitive depths, superficiality, and reflections will appear to have shifting and overlapping meanings.

If the mental process of reflection cannot be distinguished categorically from the phenomenon of optical reflection, we are led to the question of whether mental reflection follows nature in mirroring *images* (as in the case of reflections in water) or in blending and transposing *hues* (as in the case of light reflected from one solid object to another). Here again, Ruskin equivocates. In the chapter of *Modern Painters*, vol. 2, defining the "Three Forms of the Imagination," Ruskin states that works of art do not represent their subject matter "in a form of pure transcript" but rather "receive the *reflection* of the mind under whose *influence* they have passed, and are *modified or coloured* by its *image*" (4.223, my emphasis). Leaving aside the questionable "purity" of "transcript," we note that Ruskin draws on both modes of optical reflection for his analogy. The art work is said to receive the color rather than the image of the artist's mind, yet that coloring is received from the mind's "image" rather than its hue. In the first five editions of *Modern Painters*, vol. 2, the passage reads "shadow" for "influence," which would reinforce the idea of the imagination casting a definite form or image on its subject. But the change from "shadow" to "influence" in the 1883 edition seems to favor the less definite reading of "reflection" as the transposition of hue rather than the mirroring of form.

Ruskin's reluctance to accept the analogy between mental reflection and the mirroring of images goes back to the potential for narcissism and solipsism that Hazlitt detected in Wordsworth's poetic vision. Ironically, the epigraph that appears at the beginning of all five volumes of *Modern Painters* comes from Wordsworth's *The Excursion* and cautions against the philosophical belief that either the soul or the universe is simply a mirror "reflecting" the "self":

> Accuse me not
> Of arrogance, ...
> If, having walked with Nature,
> And offered, far as frailty would allow,
> My heart a daily sacrifice to Truth,
> I now affirm of Nature and of Truth,
> Whom I have served, that their Divinity
> Revolts, offended at the ways of men,
> Philosophers, who, though the human soul
> Be of a thousand faculties composed,
> And twice ten thousand interests, do yet prize
> This soul, and the transcendent universe,
> No more than as a mirror that reflects
> To proud Self-love her own intelligence.

The passage rails against solipsism even as it tries to forestall a similar charge against itself.[22] As if compelled to defend against his own reflection, the poet pleads that his decrial of "Self-love" not be attributed to his "arrogance."

Closely connected with this fear of solipsistic narcissism is the fear of alienation. For reflections, Ruskin begins to realize, *divide* at the same time as they *repeat*. In *The Elements of Drawing* (1857), Ruskin equates optical reflection with the principle of "Repetition," yet when he proceeds to give an example, the reflections multiply beyond his original intent:

> Symmetry, or the balance of parts or masses in nearly equal opposition, is one of the conditions of treatment under the law of Repetition. For the opposition, in a symmetrical object, is of like things reflecting each other: . . . Stand before a mirror; hold your arms in precisely the same position at each side, your head upright, your body straight; divide your hair exactly in the middle and get it as nearly as you can into exactly the same shape over each ear; and you will see the effect of accurate symmetry: you will see, no less, how all grace and power in the human form result from the interference of motion and life with symmetry, and from the reconciliation of its balance with its changefulness. Your position, as seen in the mirror, is the highest type of symmetry as understood by modern architects. (15.169–70)

The "position" of the subject "as seen in the mirror" is given as a model of "symmetry," but is this symmetry not a reflection of a reflection? The left half of the mirror-image "reflects" the right half of the mirror-image, but it reflects as well the left half of the subject standing before the mirror—and then must it not reflect too the *right* half of the subject? The image of the specular self is the closest that the phenomenon of reflection approaches to a condition of unmediated knowledge. Yet the self is both divided and multiplied in this paradigmatic instance of "reflection."

The implications of this division and multiplication are recognized only retrospectively by Ruskin, but in a way that shakes his faith in the

[22] Cf. Paul de Man's contention that romanticism is, at its symbolist extreme, "a subjective idealism, open to all the attacks of solipsism that, from Hazlitt to the French structuralists, a succession of de-mystifiers of the self have directed against it." Conversely, the allegorical pole of romanticism constitutes a renunciation of such idealism. Ruskin's citation of Wordsworth would signal, in this context, both his own and Wordsworth's awareness of the potential for self-delusion not only in symbolism and analogy in general but in the figure of reflection specifically. See de Man, "The Rhetoric of Temporality," in *Blindness and Insight*, 198.

entire empiricist enterprise. In a poignant passage at the beginning of the second volume of *Praeterita* (1886), he returns to the figure of a writer facing a mirror, only to recognize how the trope of reflection may have led him astray: "As I look deeper into the mirror, I find myself a more curious person than I had thought. I used to fancy that everybody would like clouds and rocks as well as I did, if once told to look at them; whereas after fifty years of trial, I find that it is not so" (35.243). Two kinds of seeing that previously Ruskin had assumed to be reliable and unproblematic are recognized now to contain uncertainties. Whereas before the exemplary immediacy of the specular image had been treated as a guarantee or proof of Ruskin's accurate principles of sight, here the uncertainty of self-reflection stands for the writer's inability to predict or control *how people see*. Despite Ruskin's intentions, in the passage from *The Elements of Drawing* the very presence of the figure of reflection had seemed to alter the larger analogy. But in *Praeterita* Ruskin goes even further and concedes that the figure of reflection cannot control or resolve the ambiguities of perception—that reflecting on reflection does not cancel out uncertainty but may only multiply it.

Ruskin's dilemma reflects perhaps more a *mise-en-abyme* of empiricist rhetoric than any necessary consequence of empiricism's perceptual models, yet the two are not entirely separable. From Locke through to Hazlitt, empiricism engages itself with questions both of perception and of rhetoric and representation. But the interest of each empiricist writer tilts more in one direction than the other: Locke's, for instance, in the direction of perception, Hazlitt's in the direction of rhetoric and self-representation. Only in Ruskin is the balance between issues of perception and those of representation so perfectly poised as to create a kind of mirroring effect that verges on unconscious irony. Whether the historical development of empiricist rhetoric (which reaches an impasse in Ruskin) can be disengaged from empiricism's meditations on the relationship between language and perception is an important question—and one that literary theory remains to address.

EPILOGUE

From Ruskin to I. A. Richards: The End of Empiricism and the Beginning of Empiricist Literary Criticism

RUSKIN'S CLOSE attention to the painted canvas brings out perhaps more fully than ever before in English writing the tendency of figures of surface, depth, and reflection to refer equally to visual and to mental phenomena. The conflation of sensory and mental references in the key rhetorical figures of the empiricist tradition thus finds its exemplary analogue in the condition of (representational) painting: a surface that represents depth-of-field by means of reflected light. Ruskin brings to a climax the tradition of empiricist aesthetics (initiated by Burke) that attempts to correlate empirical description with the rhetoric of aesthetics—to account for the relationship between the sight of "deep" chasms and the production of "deep" sensations or effects. Since the rhetoric of aesthetic effects and sensations is inevitably speculative and metaphoric, Ruskin thus seeks to identify a "truth of space" that is at once literal and figurative. Often it is simply impossible to tell whether Ruskin's "space" refers to the observable natural world, to the painter's canvas, or to something altogether more abstract and spiritual.

It would be tempting to see this tension as the result of competing discursive styles. Ruskin is the most floridly rhetorical of all the empiricist writers we have examined; and at the same time no other writer makes closer or finer observations about the natural world and its effects on us. Yet we would be wrong to conclude that the paradoxes and ambiguities of Ruskin's descriptive vocabulary are simply a rhetorical liability of empiricism's central tropes (i.e., "reflection," "surface," and "depth") or a result of the notorious tension in empiricism between the depreciation of rhetoric and reliance upon it. What complicates Ruskin's account of perception is no simple tension between figurative and expository usages or between aesthetics and natural science but rather the tremendous diversity of technical uses to which he puts a relatively small group of figures: "depth," for instance, is a measurement of color pigmentation, of light, of visual space, and of tactile space; it may indicate, variously, *solidity, intensity, palpability,* or *extension.*

Even in its literal, expository applications, the figure of depth is overdetermined and refers to experiences derived from different sense faculties. Since Ruskin does not believe, with Berkeley, that our sense faculties are logically and categorically distinct from one another or, with Burke, that an underlying "analogy" links them, the various sensory experiences and judgments assimilated in Ruskin's key figures remain ambiguously related. It is when we come to Ruskin's figure of reflection that this difficulty becomes most pronounced. Although Burke and Hazlitt had retained the optical empiricism of Locke and Berkeley—according to which visual three-dimensionality is a prereflective construction out of surface impressions—they also emphasized the power of reflection to confuse or dissolve a world systematically articulated in terms of surfaces and depths. An awareness of the alternately constructive and skeptical effects of mental "reflection" had always been central to empiricist philosophy, but Burke and Hazlitt hand on to Ruskin a systematic rhetoric of depths and surfaces to go along with the theoretical account of sensations and reflections. The empiricist narrative tracing the development of three-dimensional from two-dimensional visual impressions of the world—a process at once aided and threatened by reflection—becomes increasingly the model for our construction of "depth" in other realms: depth of meaning, depth of character, depth of affection.

For Ruskin, reflection is at once the most necessary and the most dangerous of phenomena. Optical reflections outline the surfaces of the visible world, allow us to construct our impressions of spatial depth, and help us to notice nature's spiritually resonant effects of contrast and transposition. But reflection also "destroys" visible surfaces, and here it is not so clear whether the process is optical, intellectual, or spiritual. According to Locke, when we reflect on our own experiences and sensations, we find our impressions to be essentially *legible.* But for Ruskin, the visible world is essentially "illegible" and "unintelligible," and our task is to recognize this illegibility in order to see in it evidence of deeper truths.[1] In some cases this involves focusing on surfaces to the exclusion of depths

---

[1] See the passages in *Modern Painters*, vol. 5 ("Of Turnerian Mystery") in which Ruskin illustrates his claim that "we never see anything clearly" by reference to what we actually *see* when we look at a printed page or a book binding on a library shelf (6.75–79).

and reflections (e.g., paying attention to the water's surface rather than to the images reflected by it); but in other cases it involves seeing beyond surfaces (e.g., not seeing mere painted canvas but a scene from nature when we look at a painting).

The ambiguities of Ruskin's "surfaces," "depths," and "reflections" highlight the central paradox of empiricist aesthetics: that ordinary perception involves not only the mediating influence of prereflective judgments and inferences (which are themselves the consequences of previous reflections) but as well the focusing of *attention*—and attention is inevitably, inextricably related to *in*attention. While perceiving, we are led from one sign to another; one sign slips out of focus as another sign passes into focus. Empiricism has two basic models for illustrating this process: our construction of a three-dimensional visual world from optical sensations that extend in only two dimensions; and the various diadic relationships that comprise and describe our linguistic practices (e.g., word and idea; sound and printed character; proper and metaphoric meaning). But these two models cannot be understood apart from each other. Thus the analogies offered by empiricism to account for the relationship of our actual sensations to our commonsense views are, variously, the relationship of "words" to the "ideas" for which they stand, of the literal meanings of words to their metaphoric extensions, and of material signifiers ("characters," "sounds") to virtually any other unit or dimension of verbal signification.

From Locke's inaugural distinction between ideas of sensation and those of reflection through to Ruskin's "innocence of the eye," empiricism has seen in our construction of visual depth an exemplary instance of the way in which sensation is supplemented by judgment. The analogy between this process and the workings of language receives different emphases in different empiricist writers, but the relationship always remains one of analogy rather than one of reduction. Berkeley's incipient idealism does not lead him to the conclusion that everything is language any more than Burke's incipient materialism leads him to the conclusion that everything is sensation. Over and over again empiricism shows us sensation verging on language and language merging into sensation.

Ruskin maintains this tradition, both in his optical constructivism and in his oscillation between visual and verbal models. For Ruskin the two hardest things for a painter to capture are visual depth of field and nature's writing, even though both are on the surface, as it were. What distinguishes Ruskin is that for all his optical constructivism he attributes ineffable, almost mystical characteristics to visual sensations of spatial depth. In this he prefigures the phenomenology of William James and the gestalt school, according to which sensations of depth are innate and available directly through visual experience. And as we saw in Chapter 1, the phenomenological position is rightly interpreted by intellectual historians as a rejection of an empiricist tradition that stretches from Locke and Berkeley up to Ruskin. Once the naturalness of our sensations of depth has been conceded, we no longer have a fully empiricist philosophy. From one point of view, then, empiricism ceased to exist before the enterprise of academic literary criticism even began.

We saw in the Introduction that literary theory tends to characterize empiricism as a philosophical paradigm crippled by its schematic reliance on optical models of observation and experience. We have also seen just how problematic this characterization is for the texts of classical empiricism. But what of empiricist literary criticism, specifically? The writers we have examined in this book are not primarily literary critics. Burke cites literary examples for the most part to demonstrate how literary writers agree with his theories of psychology and sense perception, not to make claims concerning the qualities of literary writing or the nature of literary language. Hazlitt is interested more in Wordsworth and Coleridge as philosophers and cultural figures than he is with the qualities of their verse. And for Ruskin, poetry is more an ideal to be invoked than an object of study. What empiricist writers do provide, though, is a vocabulary (the figures of reflection, surface, and depth), a dramatic scene (the blind restored to sight), and an analogy (between language and visual inference), all of which haunt the practice of modern literary criticism.

Empiricist literary criticism—or more properly the literary criticism inspired by empiricism—begins with I. A. Richards. Though it is in his work with C. K. Ogden on *The Meaning of Meaning* (1923) that Richards first worked out the positivist conception of emotive value that underpins so much American formalist literary criticism, it is *Principles of Literary Criticism* (1925) that articulates most fully and systematically an empiricist theory of literary response. Richards's work involves four axioms that are empiricist in the most general and received sense. First, literary works record and transmit "experiences" (notably experiences that have been "judged" to be most "valuable").[2] Second, the circuit of

---

[2] Richards, *Principles of Literary Criticism*, 32–33. See also his definition of a "poem" in terms of "experience" (225–27).

communication or affect that links the experience of the writer and that of the reader may be analyzed scientifically in terms of its "causes" and "consequences."[3] Third, literary response is simply a special case of the more general human processes of adaptation and habit formation.[4] Fourth, rhetorical language is assumed to provide the chief obstacle to any clear apprehension of the creative and critical processes, since it tends to hypostatize *processes*, representing them as objects, qualities, or states. "All our natural turns of speech are misleading," writes Richards, "especially those we use in discussing works of art" (20). This suspicious attitude is reinforced by a rather conventional alignment of figurative language with emotion: words, according to Richards, are used either "symbolically [and] scientifically" or "figuratively and emotionally" (131).

Distilling this set of principles even further, Richards's critics have claimed to discern in his work three fundamental presuppositions: that sensory perception is the simplest form of experience, that complex experiences are somehow reducible or analogous to sensation, and that language is essentially adequate to represent such experience. But these three propositions are not entirely characteristic either of Richards or of empiricism more generally. Although Richards does exhibit a certain naive positivism with regard to linguistic reference (and here, one might argue, he is *least* classically empiricist), he exhibits a typically empiricist reluctance to let sensory perception become the privileged ground of experience.

Let us turn first to a particularly subtle and even sympathetic criticism of Richards, Paul de Man's "The Dead-End of Formalist Criticism."[5] Though Richards's account of critical understanding "appears to be governed by common sense," writes de Man, it "implies in fact, some highly questionable ontological presuppositions, the most basic of which is, no doubt, the notion that language, poetic or otherwise, can *say* any experience, of whatever kind, even a simple perception. Neither the statement 'I see a cat' nor, for that matter, Baudelaire's poem '*Le Chat*' con-

---

[3] Ibid., 82–83.

[4] The general thesis is outlined on 85–91, the more specific thesis on 112–13 and 132–33. Richards's empiricism here is inflected by his Coleridgean organicism, which stresses harmony, reconciliation, and balance as the principles guiding the mind in its development of habits (e.g., 109). As we shall see, such organicism is not integral to classical empiricist accounts of habit modification, which tend to stress *economy* rather than harmony.

[5] See de Man, *Blindness and Insight*, 229–45.

tains wholly the experience of this perception" (232). De Man's qualifier "even a simple perception" is deceptive, for it implies that Richards's theory rests its authority on the assumption that sensory perception is the simplest and most straightforward kind of communicable experience. According to de Man, if it turns out to be the case that "even a simple perception" cannot be translated into language without residue or distortion, then the confidence with which Richards characterizes the far more complex transactions of literary response must be all that much more problematic. But does visual perception really play the foundational role for Richards that de Man implies? Though Richards's remarks concerning *signification* are indeed reductive in the way de Man suggests, we shall see that these remarks are embedded in a much more extended, complicated, and even ambiguous account of the total literary response.

Richards's theory of signification is symbolic rather than semiotic. Words are learned by association with objects that they come to replace; the experience of the word becomes the experience of the object. Richards does not address the theoretical-historical question of whether the bond between signifier and signified was originally motivated or arbitrary, but it is clear from his remarks that he considers language to function in ordinary practice by a kind of natural synecodoche or metonymy:

> A sign is something which has once been a member of a context or configuration that worked in the mind as a whole. When it reappears its effects are as though the rest of the context were present. (90)

> The process of learning to use words is not difficult to analyse. On a number of occasions the word is heard in connection with objects of a certain kind. Later the word is heard in the absence of any such object. In accordance with one of the few fundamental laws known about mental process, something then happens in the mind which is like what would happen if such an object were actually present and engaging the attention. The word has become a *sign* of an object of that kind. (127)

Here Richards clearly assumes, as de Man quite rightly points out, an undisturbed "continuity between experience and language," an assumption sustained by the mistaken belief that "the experience of [an] object" is identical with "the experience of the consciousness of the object" (244).[6] But if Richards is confident in the powers of language to commu-

---

[6] In another essay from the same volume, "The Rhetoric of Temporality," de Man further criticizes the "illusion" of a continuity between experience and language, casting the

nicate experience, he remains resistant to the notion that experience is modeled on perception.

For Richards, no experience is more misleadingly expressed in language than perception (and, correlatively, no verbal expressions are more misleading than those that report on visual sensation). In his discussion of the visual arts he expresses distrust of even so simple a report as that contained in the verb "to see":

> In analysing the experiences of the visual arts the first essential is to avoid the word "see," a term which is treacherous in its ambiguity. If we say that we see a picture we may mean either that we see the pigment-covered surface, or that we see the image on the retina cast by this surface, or that we see certain planes or volumes in what is called the "picture-space." These senses are completely distinct. (148)

At the very least this suggests that Richards finds the vocabulary of sensory perception to be inadequate for describing aesthetic experience. In fact Richards, as we shall see, never equates experience with perception. Despite his visual rhetoric, Richards disavows the alleged simplicity, intensity, or communicability of visual experience. His literary aesthetic is consistently antipictorial. In the chapter "The Analysis of a Poem" he writes:

> Too much importance has always been attached to the sensory qualities of images. (119)

> The value of the visual image in the experience [of reading a poem] is not pictorial. (122)

> What is required will be found if we turn our attention from the sensory qualities of the imagery to the more fundamental qualities upon which its efficacy in modifying the rest of the experience depends. (122–23)

When Richards does discuss the role of "imagery," he uses the term to cover a wide spectrum of phenomena ranging from the "visual sensations of the printed words" to "images . . . of things words stand for" and

---

issue explicitly in terms of "empiricism." De Man posits an inevitable disjunction between an "empirical self" (214), immersed in an "empirical world" (213), and a linguistic self, self-consciously "determined by an authentic experience of temporality"—an experience that is nonorganic and nonempirical (222).

including such diverse experiences as "the auditory image—the sound of the words in the mind's ear—and the image of articulation—the feel in the lips, mouth, and throat, of what the words would be like to speak" (118–21). Thus *image* and *imagery* are always somewhat ambiguous, even metaphoric terms for Richards.

Richards's famous chapter "The Analysis of a Poem" divides the process of literary response into "six distinct kinds of events" (117), several of them containing further divisions and distinctions. Though the rhetorical apparatus of the account (its diagrams, numbered categories, materialist vocabulary, etc.) certainly give it a positivist cast, Richards stresses at almost every point the intrinsically ambiguous, converging, and overlapping categories that constitute the total spectrum of literary response, ranging from the minimal activity of optically scanning a printed page to the more complex processes of reference, association, and emotion.

According to Richards's account of reading a poem, verbal signs generate two separate trains of response: one material and sensory (which Richards designates as "formal"), the other semantic (a category that includes emotions and attitudes as well as references and associations). What makes Richards's theory distinctively empiricist, however, is the way in which these trains of response converge. According to Richards, externally stimulated sensations (in this case, of printed words) lead to the incipient motions that he calls "images" (acoustic or articulatory); while other externally stimulated responses (in this case the meanings of words) lead to the incipient actions he calls "attitudes." But images and attitudes share the characteristic of being imperceptible dispositions toward movement, and an analogy is thus established between them: "This incipient activity [attitude] stands to overt action much as an image stands to a sensation" (108).

The consequences of this analogy are profound. Sensory and intellectual processes are mutually illustrated, if not mutually constituted. This is something quite different from the metaphoric modeling of intellectual processes upon perception, a trope that runs deep through all Western philosophy. Traditional Western philosophical discourse privileges intellectual over sensory phenomena and literal over figurative usages, even as it paradoxically aligns the body with the literal and the soul with the figurative. Yet while metaphysical philosophy must repress this paradox, empiricism can in a sense celebrate it. Richards's analysis conforms to an empiricist tradition that, as we have seen, tends to describe language (and in particular, reading and listening) in increasingly material terms while describing sensation in increasingly discursive terms (as the reading of "signs," "analogies," "metaphors"). Accordingly, Richards's definition of "imagery"—and later of the "imagination" (239–53)—eludes the schematic distinction between the verbal and the visual and avoids the reduction of experience to perception.

The course taken by Richardsian-inspired criticism in the twentieth century is a complex story of its own, one that has been polemically narrated in different ways by de Man, Fredric Jameson, and others.[7] There is no doubt that Richards's work plays a privileged role in the development of Anglo-American formalist criticism, or any doubt that "the philosophical and ideological roots" of Richards's approach lie "in the long tradition of British empiricism" (*The Prison-House of Language*, 4).[8] But literary criticism has responded ambiguously and sporadically at best to the distinctive concerns and complexities of empiricist philosophy and aesthetics. Empiricism has become less a developing intellectual tradition than a slogan or dogma, and this is unfortunate, since empiricism has much to say about the reciprocal relations of language and perception and about the rhetoric in which we frame our claims about those relations. Ruskin's work admittedly represents an impasse in the rhetorical conditions of empiricism—one that it may require considerable self-criticism (and considerable demystification of the figures "reflection," "surface," and "depth") to surpass. But empiricism's concentration on the rhetoric of perception remains a model for such meditation; a model whose full possibilities have not yet been exhausted.

Rethinking empiricism and rewriting its history cannot resolve the contradictory uses to which its rhetoric is put in contemporary critical theory. For in the empiricist tradition, criticism—figured as "reflection"— is both an active and a passive process, involving both a concentration on

---

[7] See particularly de Man, "Form and Intent in the New American Criticism" and "The Dead-End of Formalist Criticism," both in *Blindness and Insight*; and Jameson, *The Prison-House of Language*, chap. 1, passim.

[8] Cf. de Man's remark in "The Dead-End of Formalist Criticism": "It has been said that all of American formalist criticism originates in the works of the English linguist and psychologist I. A. Richards. As a historical statement such an assertion is questionable, for the mutual relations of American and English criticism are rendered more complex by the existence of purely native strands on both sides; but it is certainly true that Richards's theories have found fertile terrain in the United States, and that all American works of formalist criticism accord him a special status" (231).

the material constraints of signification and a concentration on "ideas" signified; at once the easy, natural, customary way to proceed and the strenuous, unnatural, philosophical way. I have not attempted here to tell a story about the real, literal origins of "reflection"—to uncover the sensory figure lurking in the philosophical metaphor—since the "recovery" of literal meanings from abstract philosophical metaphors is a project that empiricism constantly critiques. But the figure's complexity is important because it exemplifies the contradictory claims that empiricism makes concerning its own literal and figurative meanings, a contradiction that haunts even as it enriches the rhetoric of literary criticism.

As literary critics we are still highly conditioned by empiricism—nowhere so much as in the use we still make of "surface," "depth," and "reflection" in our own critical vocabulary, and in the wide range of reference we would like those figures to have. My focus here has been chiefly on the way in which empiricist texts use the figures of reflection, surface, and depth to dramatize the complex analogy linking our conception of the "sensory" to our conception of the "linguistic"—a constantly recurring and endlessly circular analogy that does not permit of any simple division between perception and signification. According to empiricism, the question of whether perception is conditioned by signification or signification by perception cannot be decided at the level of principle, though it is a question that can—and must—be asked constantly in practice.

APPENDIX

Empiricism among the Isms

CLASSICAL EMPIRICISM is frequently lumped together with a number of twentieth-century philosophical movements, among them realism, positivism (logical or otherwise), analytic philosophy, phenomenalism, and phenomenology.[1] How does it differ from these? To begin with realism: "realism" in twentieth-century philosophy bears little or no relation to what critics and historians of literature intend by the term "literary realism." Philosophical realism in this century is associated primarily with the epistemological and ethical positions developed by G. E. Moore. As an epistemological position, realism is a commonsense defense of the existence of material objects independent of any particular experience we have of them.[2] As a moral position, realism claims that ethical values can be directly intuited and known—that the ethical dimension of a situation can be assessed as rationally, directly, and noninferentially as can the "facts." And realism holds that the "sense" and the "truth" of moral judgments are not ascertained in a way categorically distinct from our assessment of "facts" about the empirical world.[3] In these respects, realism certainly clashes with modern empiricism, which holds tightly to the "fact"/"value" distinction. But such realism also clashes with traditional empiricism because the latter holds that there is very little about the world that can be directly or noninferentially known (even though, according to empiricism, there are good reasons for not rejecting the commonsense view of the world embodied in our ordinary habits, expectations, and figures of speech).

---

[1] See, e.g., Jameson, *The Prison-House of Language.* In just a few pages, Jameson manages to group together "Anglo-American empiricism," Locke, Wittgenstein, symbolic logic, atomism, "Basic English, common language philosophy, and semantics as an organized discipline" (23–24, 31–33).

[2] See G. E. Moore, "A Defence of Common Sense" and "Proof of an External World" in *Philosophical Papers* (London: George Allen and Unwin, 1959).

[3] See Sabina Lovibond, *Realism and Imagination in Ethics* (Minneapolis: University of Minnesota Press, 1983), 1–26.

Logical positivism (or "logical empiricism"), which may be considered one impulse within Anglo-American *analytic* philosophy, differs significantly from traditional empiricism. Logical positivism is verificationist, it is interested in "propositions" rather than in "objects," and it is concerned primarily with establishing criteria for the "meaningfulness" of those propositions.[4] Yet as Michael Williams writes, "'meaning' is now a technical notion in a way that it never was for Hume."[5] As Williams, Ian Hacking, and Richard Rorty have pointed out repeatedly, modern analytic philosophy has become obsessed with "pure" or "technical" theories of "language" and "meaning" bearing little relation to the pragmatic concerns that characterize traditional empiricism. We might speculate that some of this has to do with the difference between an older empiricism modeled on, and informed by, the natural sciences, and a modern one modeled on, and informed by, mathematics and logic. This might also explain the difference in feel between a Locke or a Berkeley and the J. S. Mill who is by many accounts the last true empiricist in the mainstream philosophical tradition. Mill, I believe, already points the way toward modern empiricism and analytic philosophy, and has more in common with A. J. Ayer and Karl Popper than with the interests that link Locke, Berkeley, Burke, Hazlitt, and Ruskin.

Both the analytic tradition of "phenomenalism" and the Husserlian tradition of phenomenology consider themselves to be extensions and critiques of empiricism. Like empiricism, phenomenology is interested primarily in the world as it is *experienced*; and like the empiricist, the phenomenologist sees a corollary between the dynamics of optical perception and those by which we discover the broader "dimensions" of any given experience (interpersonal, social, ethical, political, historical). Yet whereas empiricism sees visual three-dimensionality or "depth" as an *inference* from experience, phenomenology sees "depth" in all its senses and manifestations as an immanent and directly intuited quality.[6] In this sense, then, phenomenology follows William James and the gestalt psychologists in revising the constructivist optical theory of classical empiri-

---

[4] The two best general accounts of logical positivism are Oswald Hanfling, *Logical Positivism* (New York: Columbia University Press, 1981); and Leszek Kolakowski, *The Alienation of Reason: A History of Positivist Thought*, trans. Norbert Guterman (Garden City, N.Y.: Doubleday, 1968), chap. 8.

[5] See Williams, "Hume's Criterion of Significance," 276.

[6] See Maurice Merleau-Ponty, *Phenomenology of Perception*, trans. Colin Smith (London: Routledge and Kegan Paul, 1962), chaps. 1–2, especially pp. 23–25.

cism. Moreover, phenomenology departs from British empiricism to the extent that it draws its definitions of "judgment" and "reflection" from the Kantian transcendental analytic that it aspires to critique, rather than from the Lockean notion of reflection.

Phenomenalism, as a branch of analytic philosophy, holds that we have immediate awareness only of "sensa" rather than material objects. We have access to our impressions of things rather than things themselves. This does not mean that we cannot intelligently talk about things as they "really" are; but it does mean that "reality" is a *logical construction* of out of *sensa*, rather than being a mere collection of, or reading-off from, sense data.[7] A "collection," according to Jonathan Bennett, is merely cumulative; a "logical construction" involves at the very least an implicit sorting out of "counterfactual conditionals."[8] The tendency of phenomenalism, as of analytic philosophy in general, is to analyze philosophical propositions and to expose them as improperly or misleadingly constructed statements about sense data. Though traditional empiricism often uses sense perception and introspection as criteria for correcting or excising specific philosophic terms (e.g., *substance*, *essence*), empiricism is not concerned primarily with correcting the form of propositions.

ᐧ As opposed to realism, empiricism holds that processes of inference and judgment necessarily intervene between us and our impressions; as opposed to logical positivism and phenomenalism, empiricism holds our judgments to be cumulative, ad hoc, and contingent rather than "logically constructed"; as opposed to phenomenology, empiricism holds that "depth"—whether in the restricted sense of an optical third dimension or in the extended sense of "character," "intention," or "meaning"—must be constructed from "surface" impressions.

---

[7] The significance of this distinction, particularly as it pertains to a critique of traditional empiricism, is outlined by Bennett, *Locke, Berkeley, Hume*, 63–68, 135–39.

[8] See ibid., 135–37. Roger Scruton suggests that the concept of "logical construction" from sense data is in fact the distinguishing feature of modern empiricism (and of its revision of traditional empiricism), starting with Bertrand Russell. See Scruton, *From Descartes to Wittgenstein: A Short History of Modern Philosophy* (New York: Harper and Row, 1982), 278–79.

Works Cited

Aarsleff, Hans. *From Locke to Saussure: Essays on the Study of Language and Intellectual History*. Minneapolis: University of Minnesota Press, 1982.

Abrams, M. H. *The Mirror and the Lamp: Romantic Theory and the Critical Tradition*. Oxford: Oxford University Press, 1953.

Addison, Joseph, and Richard Steele. *Selections from the "Tatler" and the "Spectator."* Ed. with intro. and notes by Angus Ross. Harmondsworth: Penguin, 1982.

Aristotle. *Poetics*. Trans. W. Ingram Bywater. In *The Rhetoric and Poetics of Aristotle*. Intro. Edward P. J. Corbett. New York: Modern Library, 1954.

——. *Rhetoric*. Trans. W. Rhys Roberts. In *The Rhetoric and Poetics of Aristotle*, intro. Edward P. J. Corbett. New York: Modern Library, 1954.

Bacon, Francis. *The Advancement of Learning and New Atlantis*. With a preface by Thomas Case. London: Oxford University Press, 1969.

Ball, Patricia M. *The Science of Aspects: The Changing Role of Fact in the Work of Coleridge, Ruskin and Hopkins*. London: Athlone Press, 1971.

Belsey, Catherine. *Critical Practice*. London: Methuen, 1980.

Bennett, Jonathan. *Locke, Berkeley, Hume: Central Themes*. Oxford: Clarendon Press, 1971.

Berkeley, George. *Alciphron: Or, the Minute Philosopher*. In *The Works of George Berkeley*, 3 vols., ed. Alexander Campbell Fraser. Vol. 2. Oxford: Clarendon Press, 1871.

——. *An Essay towards a New Theory of Vision*. In *The Works of George Berkeley*, ed. Alexander Campbell Fraser. Vol. 1. Oxford: Clarendon Press, 1871.

——. *Three Dialogues between Hylas and Philonous*. In *The Works of George Berkeley*, ed. Alexander Campbell Fraser. Vol. 1. Oxford: Clarendon Press, 1871.

——. *A Treatise Concerning the Principles of Human Knowledge*. In *The Works of George Berkeley*, ed. Alexander Campbell Fraser. Vol. 1. Oxford: Clarendon Press, 1871.

——. *A Treatise Concerning the Principles of Human Knowledge*. With critical essays. Ed. Colin M. Turbayne. Indianapolis: Bobbs-Merrill, 1970.

Booth, Wayne. *Modern Dogma and the Rhetoric of Assent*. Chicago: University of Chicago Press, 1974.

Borges, Jorge Luis. *Labyrinths: Selected Stories and Other Writings*. Ed. Donald A. Yates and James E. Irby. Preface by André Maurois. New York: New Directions, 1962; reprint, 1964.

Boyle, Robert. *Occasional Reflections upon Several Subjects. With a Discourse about Such Kinds of Thoughts* (1669). Oxford, 1848.

Bromwich, David. *Hazlitt: The Mind of a Critic*. New York: Oxford University Press, 1983.

Burke, Edmund. *A Philosophical Enquiry into the Origin of Our Ideas of the Sublime and Beautiful*. Ed. with an intro. by James T. Boulton. Notre Dame, Ind.: Notre Dame University Press, 1968.

Burke, Kenneth. *A Grammar of Motives*. Berkeley and Los Angeles: University of California Press, 1945; reprint, 1969.

Caruth, Cathy. *Empirical Truths and Critical Fictions: Locke, Wordsworth, Kant, Freud*. Baltimore: Johns Hopkins University Press, 1991.

Cassirer, Ernst. *The Philosophy of the Enlightenment* (1932). Trans. Fritz C. A. Koelln and James P. Pettegrove. Boston: Beacon Press, 1951.

———. *The Platonic Renaissance in England*. Trans. J. P. Pettegrove. Austin: University of Texas Press, 1953.

Cohen, Murray. *Sensible Words: Linguistic Practice in England 1640–1785*. Baltimore: Johns Hopkins University Press, 1977.

Cohen, Ralph. *The Art of Discrimination: Thomson's "The Seasons" and the Language of Criticism*. Berkeley and Los Angeles: University of California Press, 1964.

Coleridge, Samuel Taylor. *Biographia Literaria*. 2 vols. Ed. John T. Shawcross. Oxford: Clarendon Press, 1907.

Collingwood, R. G. *The Principles of Art*. Oxford: Clarendon Press, 1938.

De Man, Paul. *Allegories of Reading: Figural Language in Rousseau, Nietzsche, Rilke, and Proust*. New Haven: Yale University Press, 1979.

———. *Blindness and Insight: Essays in the Rhetoric of Contemporary Criticism*. Rev. 2d ed. Intro. Wlad Godzich. Theory and History of Literature, vol. 7. Minneapolis: University of Minnesota Press, 1971; reprint, 1983.

———. "The Epistemology of Metaphor." *Critical Inquiry* 5 (Autumn 1978): 13–30.

Derrida, Jacques. *Of Grammatology*. Trans. Gayatri Chakravorty Spivak. Baltimore: Johns Hopkins University Press, 1976.

———. "Plato's Pharmacy." In *Dissemination*, trans. Barbara Johnson, 61–171. Chicago: University of Chicago Press, 1981.

———. "White Mythology: Metaphor in the Text of Philosophy." Trans. Alan Bass. In *Margins of Philosophy*, 207–72. Chicago: University of Chicago Press, 1982.

Fellows, Jay. *The Failing Distance: The Autobiographical Impulse in John Ruskin*. Baltimore: Johns Hopkins University Press, 1975.

———. *Ruskin's Maze: Mastery and Madness in His Art.* Princeton: Princeton University Press, 1981.

Fielding, Henry. "An Essay on the Knowledge of the Character of Men" (1743). In *Miscellanies by Henry Fielding, Esq.,* vol. 1. Ed. Henry Knight Miller. Oxford: Wesleyan University Press, 1972.

Firth, Roderick. "Sense-Data and the Percept Theory." In *Perceiving, Sensing, and Knowing: A Book of Readings from Twentieth-Century Sources in the Philosophy of Perception,* ed. and intro. Robert J. Swartz. Berkeley and Los Angeles: University of California Press, 1965.

Foucault, Michel. *The Order of Things: An Archaeology of the Human Sciences.* A translation of *Lets Mots et les choses* (1966). New York: Random House, 1973.

Fry, Roger. *Cézanne: A Study of His Development.* New York: Macmillan, 1927.

———. *French, Flemish, and British Art.* New York: Coward-McCann, 1951.

Frye, Northrop. *The Secular Scripture: A Study of the Structure of Romance.* Cambridge: Harvard University Press, 1976.

———. *A Study of English Romanticism.* New York: Random House, 1968.

Gasché, Rodolphe. *The Tain of the Mirror: Derrida and the Philosophy of Reflection.* Cambridge: Harvard University Press, 1986.

Glanvill, Joseph. *A Seasonable Recommendation, and Defence of Reason in the Affairs of Religion.* London, 1670.

———. "The Vanity of Dogmatizing: Or Confidence in Opinions." In *The Vanity of Dogmatizing: The Three "Versions,"* intro. Stephen Medcalf. Sussex: Harvester Press, 1970.

Gombrich, E. H. *Art and Illusion: A Study in the Psychology of Pictorial Representation.* Princeton: Princeton University Press, Bollingen series 35, no. 5, 1960; reprint, 1969.

Goodman, Nelson. *Ways of Worldmaking.* Indianapolis: Hackett, 1978.

Hacking, Ian. *The Emergence of Probability: A Philosophical Study of Early Ideas about Probability, Induction, and Statistical Reference.* Cambridge: Cambridge University Press, 1975.

———. *Why Does Language Matter to Philosophy?* Cambridge: Cambridge University Press, 1975.

Hagstrum, Jean H. *Samuel Johnson's Literary Criticism.* Chicago: University of Chicago Press, 1952; reprint, 1967.

———. *The Sister Arts: The Tradition of Literary Pictorialism and English Poetry from Dryden to Gray.* Chicago: University of Chicago Press, 1958.

Hanfling, Oswald. *Logical Positivism.* New York: Columbia University Press, 1981.

Hartley, David. *Observations on Man, His Frame, His Duty, and His Ex-*

pectations (1748). 2 parts. 6th ed., corrected and revised. London, 1834.

Hazlitt, William. *The Complete Works of William Hazlitt*. Centenary edition. 21 vols. Ed. P. P. Howe, after the edition of A. R. Waller and Arnold Glover. London: J. M. Dent, 1930–34.

Helsinger, Elizabeth K. *Ruskin and the Art of the Beholder*. Cambridge: Harvard University Press, 1982.

Hersey, George L. "Ruskin as an Optical Thinker." In *The Ruskin Polygon: Essays on the Imagination of Johhn Ruskin*, ed. Faith M. Holland and John Dixon Hunt. Manchester: Manchester University Press, 1982.

Hewison, Robert. *John Ruskin: The Argument of the Eye*. London: Thames and Hudson, 1976.

Hipple, Walter. *The Beautiful, The Sublime, and the Picturesque in Eighteenth-Century British Aesthetic Theory*. Carbondale: Southern Illinois University Press, 1957.

Hirsch, E. D., Jr. *The Aims of Interpretation*. Chicago: University of Chicago Press, 1976.

———. *Validity in Interpretation*. New Haven: Yale University Press, 1967.

Hobbes, Thomas. *Leviathan: Or the Matter, Forme, and Power of a Commonwealth Ecclesiastical and Civil* (1651). Ed. and intro. Michael Oakeshott. Oxford: Basil Blackwell, 1946.

Holland, Faith M., and John Dixon Hunt, eds. *The Ruskin Polygon: Essays on the Imagination of John Ruskin*. Manchester: Manchester University Press, 1982.

Howell, Wilbur Samuel. *Eighteenth-Century British Logic and Rhetoric*. Princeton: Princeton University Press, 1971.

———. *Logic and Rhetoric in England, 1500–1700*. New York: Russell and Russell, 1961.

Hume, David. *Essays, Moral, Political, and Literary*. London, 1742.

———. *A Treatise of Human Nature* (1739–40). Ed. with an analytical index by L. A. Selby-Bigge. 2d ed. with text revised and variant readings by P. H. Nidditch. Oxford: Clarendon Press, 1888; reprint, 1978.

Iser, Wolfgang. *Laurence Sterne: Tristram Shandy*. Trans. David Henry Wilson. Landmarks of world literature series. Cambridge: Cambridge University Press, 1988.

James, William. *The Principles of Psychology* (1890). 2 vols. New York: Dover, 1950.

Jameson, Fredric. *Marxism and Form: Twentieth-Century Dialectical Theories of Literature*. Princeton: Princeton University Press, 1971.

———. *The Prison-House of Language: A Critical Account of Structuralism and Russian Formalism*. Princeton: Princeton University Press, 1972.

Johnson, Samuel. "The Rambler." In *The Yale Edition of the Works of Sam-*

uel Johnson, vol. 4, ed. W. J. Bate and Albrecht B. Strauss. New Haven: Yale University Press, 1969.

Kant, Immanuel. *Critique of Aesthetic Judgement*. In *The Critique of Judgement*, trans. with analytical indexes by James Creed Meredith. Oxford: Clarendon Press, 1928; reprint, 1952.

——. *Critique of Pure Reason*. Trans. Norman Kemp Smith. New York: St. Martin's Press, 1929; reprint, 1965.

Kay, Carol. *Political Constructions: Defoe, Richardson, and Sterne in Relation to Hobbes, Hume, and Burke*. Ithaca: Cornell University Press, 1988.

Kolakowski, Leszek. *The Alienation of Reason: A History of Positivist Thought*. Trans. Norbert Guterman. Garden City, N.Y.: Doubleday, 1968.

Kroll, Richard W. F. *The Material Word: Literate Culture in the Restoration and Early Eighteenth Century*. Baltimore: Johns Hopkins University Press, 1991.

Kuhn, Thomas S. *The Structure of Scientific Revolutions*. 2d ed., enlarged. Vol. 2, no. 2 of the International Encyclopedia of Unified Science. Chicago: University of Chicago Press, 1962; reprint, 1970.

Kuklick, Bruce. "Seven Thinkers and How They Grew: Descartes, Spinoza, Leibniz; Locke, Berkeley, Hume; Kant." In *Philosophy and History: Essays on the Historiography of Philosophy*, ed. Richard Rorty et al., 125–39. Cambridge: Cambridge University Press, 1984.

Lamy, Bernard. *The Art of Speaking: Written in French by Messiurs du Port Royal in purSuance of a Former Treatife, Intituled, The Art of Thinking. Rendred into English*. London, 1676.

Land, Stephen K. *From Signs to Propositions: The Concept of Form in Eighteenth-Century Semantic Theory*. London: Longman, 1974.

Landow, George P. *The Aesthetic and Critical Theories of John Ruskin*. Princeton: Princeton University Press, 1971.

Lewis, Wyndham. *Time and Western Man*. Boston: Beacon Press, 1957.

Lipking, Lawrence. *The Ordering of the Arts in Eighteenth-Century England*. Princeton: Princeton University Press, 1970.

Locke, John. *An Essay Concerning Human Understanding* (1690). Ed. Peter H. Nidditch. Oxford: Clarendon Press, 1975.

Longinus. *On the Sublime*. Ed. A. O. Prickard. Oxford: Clarendon Press, 1906.

Lovibond, Sabina. *Realism and Imagination in Ethics*. Minneapolis: University of Minnesota Press, 1983.

Lukács, Georg. "Reification and the Consciousness of the Proletariat." In *History and Class Consciousness: Studies in Marxist Dialectics*, trans. Rodney Livingstone, 83–222. Cambridge: MIT Press, 1971.

McKeon, Michael. *The Origins of the English Novel, 1600–1740.* Baltimore: Johns Hopkins University Press, 1986.

MacLean, Kenneth. *John Locke and English Literature of the Eighteenth Century.* New Haven: Yale University Press, 1936.

Marshall, David. *The Figure of Theater: Shaftesbury, Defoe, Adam Smith, and George Eliot.* New York: Columbia University Press, 1986.

Mandelbaum, Maurice. *Philosophy, Science, and Sense Perception: Historical and Critical Studies.* Baltimore: Johns Hopkins University Press, 1964.

Merleau-Ponty, Maurice. *Phenomenology of Perception.* Trans. Colin Smith. London: Routledge and Kegan Paul, 1962.

Miller, Perry. *Errand into the Wilderness.* Cambridge: Harvard University Press, 1956.

Mitchell, W.J.T. *Iconology: Image, Text, Ideology.* Chicago: University of Chicago Press, 1986.

Monk, Samuel H. *The Sublime: A Study of Critical Theories in Eighteenth-Century England.* New York: Modern Language Association, 1935.

Moore, George Edward. *Philosophical Papers.* London: George Allen and Unwin, 1959.

Morgan, Michael J. *Molyneux's Question: Vision, Touch, and the Philosophy of Perception.* Cambridge: Cambridge University Press, 1977.

Newton, Isaac. *Opticks: Or a Treatise of the Reflections, Refractions, Inflections, and Colours of Light.* Based on the 4th ed. (London, 1730). New York: Dover, 1952.

Nicolson, Marjorie Hope. *Mountain Gloom and Mountain Glory: The Development of the Aesthetics of the Infinite* (1959). New York: Norton, 1963.

———. *Newton Demands the Muse: Newton's "Opticks" and the Eighteenth-Century Poets.* Princeton: Princeton University Press, 1946.

Nuttall, A. D. *A Common Sky: Philosophy and the Literary Imagination.* Berkeley and Los Angeles: University of California Press, 1974.

Park, Roy. *Hazlitt and the Spirit of the Age: Abstraction and Critical Theory.* Oxford: Clarendon Press, 1971.

Plato. *Phaedrus.* Trans. with an intro. and commentary by R. Hackforth. Cambridge: Cambridge University Press, 1952.

———. *Republic.* Trans., intro., and notes by Francis MacDonald Cornford. Oxford: Oxford University Press, 1941.

Popper, Karl L. *Conjectures and Refutations: The Growth of Scientific Knowledge.* London: Routledge and Kegan Paul, 1963; reprint, 1969.

Quine, Willard Van Orman. "Two Dogmas of Empiricism." In *From A Logical Point of View.* Cambridge: Harvard University Press, 1953.

Quintilian. *Institutio Oratoria.* 4 vols. Trans. H. F Butler. London: William Heinemann, 1920–22.

Richards, I. A. *Principles of Literary Criticism.* New York: Harcourt Brace Jovanovich, 1925.

Richetti, John. *Philosophical Writing: Locke, Berkeley, Hume.* Cambridge: Harvard University Press, 1983.

Rorty, Richard. "The Historiography of Philosophy: Four Genres." In *Philosophy and History: Essays on the Historiography of Philosophy*, ed. Richard Rorty et al., 49–75. Cambridge: Cambridge University Press, 1984.

——. *Philosophy and the Mirror of Nature.* Princeton: Princeton University Press, 1979.

——, J. B. Schneewind, and Quentin Skinner, eds. *Philosophy and History: Essays on the Historiography of Philosophy.* Cambridge: Cambridge University Press, 1984.

Ruskin, John. *The Works of John Ruskin.* 39 vols. Ed. E. T. Cook and Alexander Wedderburn. London: George Allen, 1903–12.

Russell, Bertrand. *History of Western Philosophy.* London: George Allen and Unwin, 1946.

Sawyer, Paul L. *Ruskin's Poetic Argument: The Design of the Major Works.* Ithaca: Cornell University Press, 1985.

Scott, Joan W. "The Evidence of Experience." *Critical Inquiry* 17 (Summer 1991): 773–97.

Scruton, Roger. *From Descartes to Wittgenstein: A Short History of Modern Philosophy.* New York: Harper and Row, 1981; reprint, 1982.

Shaftesbury, Anthony, earl of. *Characteristics of Men, Manners, Opinions, Times, etc.* (1711). 2 Vols. Ed. and intro. John M. Robertson. Vol. 2. London: Grant Richards, 1900.

Smith, Barbara Herrnstein. *Contingencies of Value: Alternative Perspectives for Critical Theory.* Cambridge: Harvard University Press, 1988.

Spear, Jeffrey L. *Dreams of an English Eden: Ruskin and His Tradition in Social Criticism.* New York: Columbia University Press, 1984.

Steinkraus, Warren, ed. *New Studies in Berkeley's Philosophy.* New York: Holt, Rinehart, and Winston, 1966.

Traugott, John. *Tristram Shandy's World: Sterne's Philosophical Rhetoric.* Berkeley and Los Angeles: University of California Press, 1954.

Turbayne, Colin Murray. "Berkeley's Metaphysical Grammar." In George Berkeley, *A Treatise Concerning the Principles of Human Knowledge*, with Critical Essays, ed. Colin M. Turbayne. Indianapolis: Bobbs-Merrill, 1970.

——. "Berkeley's Two Concepts of Mind." In George Berkeley, *A Treatise*

Concerning the Principles of Human Knowledge, with Critical Essays, ed. Colin M. Turbayne. Indianapolis: Bobbs-Merrill, 1970.

———. *The Myth of Metaphor*. Rev. ed. Forewords by Morse Peckham and Rolf Eberle. Columbia: University of South Carolina Press, 1962; reprint, 1970.

———. "The Origin of Berkeley's Paradoxes." In *New Studies in Berkeley's Philosophy*, ed. Warren Steinkraus. New York: Holt, Rinehart, and Winston, 1966.

Tuveson, Ernest Lee. *The Imagination as a Means of Grace: Locke and the Aesthetics of Romanticism*. Berkeley and Los Angeles: University of California Press, 1960.

Watt, Ian. *Conrad in the Nineteenth Century*. Berkeley and Los Angeles: University of California Press, 1979.

———. *The Rise of the Novel: Studies in Defoe, Richardson, and Fielding*. Harmondsworth: Penguin, 1972.

Weiskel, Thomas. *The Romantic Sublime: Studies in the Structure and Psychology of Transcendence*. Baltimore: Johns Hopkins University Press, 1976.

Wellek, René. *A History of Modern Criticism: 1750–1950*. 7 Vols. New Haven: Yale University Press, 1955–86.

Wihl, Gary. *Ruskin and the Rhetoric of Infallibility*. Yale Studies in English, no. 194. New Haven: Yale University Press, 1985.

Williams, Michael. *Groundless Belief: An Essay on the Possibility of Epistemology*. Oxford: Basil Blackwell, 1977.

———. "Hume's Criterion of Significance." *Canadian Journal of Philosophy* 15 (June 1985): 273–304.

Wimsatt, W. K., Jr. *Day of the Leopards: Essays in Defense of Poems*. New Haven: Yale University Press, 1976.

———. *Philosophic Words: A Study of Style and Meaning in the "Rambler" and "Dictionary" of Samuel Johnson*. New Haven: Yale University Press, 1948.

———. *The Verbal Icon: Studies in the Meaning of Poetry*. Lexington: University Press of Kentucky, 1954.

———, and Cleanth Brooks. *Literary Criticism: A Short History*. New York: Knopf, 1959.

Wittgenstein, Ludwig. *Philosophical Investigations*. Trans. G.E.M. Anscombe. Oxford: Basil Blackwell, 1953; reprint, 1968.

Wordsworth, William. *The Prelude* (1850). In *Poetical Works*, ed. Thomas Hutchinson and rev. Ernest de Selincourt. Oxford: Oxford University Press, 1969.

Yolton, John. *John Locke and the Way of Ideas*. Oxford: Clarendon Press, 1968.

Index

Aarsleff, Hans, 5 n. 10, 6 n. 13, 11, 42 n. 28, 186 n. 15
Abrams, M. H., 8, 73 n. 35
Abstraction, 182–86, 193–95, 197–202
Addison, Joseph, 8 n. 18, 138 n. 5, 150–51
Analogy: linguistic, 3–4, 12–13, 25, 40–44, 50–60, 90–91, 94, 97–105, 237; optical, 2–5, 12–13, 32, 50–60, 98, 128–30, 163–64, 237; of the senses, 131–64
Antipictorialism, 9, 13, 32, 162, 241

Bacon, Francis, 77 n. 38
Ball, Patricia M., 206 n. 3, 225 n. 19
Beauty, contrasted with sublimity, 131–64
Belsey, Catherine, 1–3
Bennett, Jonathan, 247
Berkeley, George, 12–13, 15–16, 22, 26–40, 81 n. 40, 93–130, 131–34, 148–50, 163–64, 166, 183–84, 198, 209–10, 236–38
Boulton, James T., 137 n. 4, 139 n. 8, 141 n. 12, 150
Boyle, Robert, 61–63, 64 n. 26
Bromwich, David, 11, 174 n. 4, 183, 184 n. 13, 185 n. 14, 197 n. 18
Burke, Edmund, 16, 31–33, 35, 70, 129–30, 131–64, 170, 177 n. 5, 198, 207, 216 n. 12, 235, 238

Cartesianism, 9, 13 n. 26
Caruth, Cathy, 3 n. 7, 6 n. 13, 11
Cassirer, Ernst, 8 n. 18, 76 n. 36
Character, Hazlitt's discussion of, 166–67, 174–82, 201–2
Chiaroscuro, 209–14, 219
Cohen, Murray, 86 n. 44
Coleridge, Samuel Taylor, 174, 177–78

De Man, Paul, 2 n. 6, 38–39, 46–51, 232 n. 22, 239–43
Derrida, Jacques, 41 n. 27, 45–46
Descartes, René, 60 n. 15
Du Bos, Abbé, 185–86

Etymology, 41–48, 114–15
Experimental method, 6–7

Fellows, Jay, 207 n. 4, 218 n. 14, 218 n. 15
Fielding, Henry, 147 n. 17, 179 n. 8
Foucault, Michel, 9 n. 20, 13 n. 26, 42 n. 28, 54 n. 3
Frye, Northrop, 149

Gasché, Rodolphe, 60 n. 15
Glanvill, Joseph, 63 n. 25
Gombrich, E. H., 7 n. 16, 21 n. 6, 22

Hacking, Ian, 5–6, 13 n. 26, 246
Hagstrum, Jean, 8 n. 18, 73 n. 35, 76 n. 37
Hartley, David, 139–40
Hazlitt, William, 16, 33–35, 95, 164, 165–203, 207, 219–20, 236–38
Helsinger, Elizabeth K., 205 n. 1, 221, 225 n. 20
Hertz, Neil, 152 n. 22, 160–61
Hobbes, Thomas, 73, 80 n. 39
Hume, David, 24 n. 12, 32, 52, 104 n. 18, 137 n. 4, 150, 158 n. 26, 159 n. 27, 193 n. 17

Immaterialism, Berkeley's doctrine of, 95–97, 106, 115–19, 123–26, 132

James, William, 21, 24 n. 12, 36–37, 105 n. 20, 237, 246
Jameson, Fredric, 1 n. 3, 15, 243, 245
Johnson, Samuel, 8 n. 17, 30 n. 16

Index

Kant, Immanuel, 21; on the sublime, 69 n. 30, 70, 118–19
Kay, Carol, 10
Kroll, Richard W. F., 10–11, 42 n. 28

Lamy, Bernard, 42–44, 69 n. 29
Land, Stephen K., 8 n. 18, 42 n. 29
Landow, George P., 205 n. 1, 217 n. 13
Language: analogies with, 3–4, 12–13, 25, 40–44, 50–60, 90–91, 94, 97–105, 237; origins of, 38–50, 114–15; transparency of, 1–3, 94
Locke, John, 3–6, 8–12, 15–16, 24–34, 38–50, 51–92, 94–99, 117–18, 128–30, 131–34, 138 n. 5, 158–59, 163–64, 182–84, 198, 236–38
Longinus, 141 n. 14, 143 n. 15
Lukács, Georg, 1 n. 3

Mabbott, J. D., 112 n. 30
McKeon, Michael, 10
Marshall, David, 8 n. 18, 115 n. 33
Metaphor: and analogy, 55, 66–71, 90–91, 102–3, 121–24; and cognition, 39–46, 66–71; and metonymy, 122–24; origins of, 38–50, 114–15; and synecdoche, 67; visual signs as, 26–32
Mitchell, W. J. T., 9 n. 19, 162 n. 31
Molyneux Question, 3, 15, 19–38, 52–53, 120–22
Moore, G. E., 245
Morgan, Michael J., 20 n. 4, 25 n. 13

Newton, Isaac, 61 n. 17, 142, 197–99
Nicolson, Marjorie Hope, 20 n. 4, 61 n. 17

Optics, analogies drawn from, 2–5, 12–13, 32, 50–60, 98, 128–30, 163–64, 237

Phenomenalism, 95, 245–47
Pictorialism, 9
Popper, Karl L., 6–7, 34 n. 19, 35 n. 20, 166–67
Positivism, 1, 245–47

Quintilian, 102 n. 16, 103 n. 17

Rationalism, 11
Realism, 245–47
Richards, I. A., 16–17, 21 n. 6, 36–38, 238–43
Richetti, John, 10, 46–50, 55, 58 n. 9, 70 n. 31, 71 n. 32, 88 n. 45, 98–99, 108, 113 n. 31, 115 n. 33, 121 n. 39, 124 n. 42
Romanticism, 8, 11, 165, 232 n. 22
Rorty, Richard, 5 n. 10, 6 n. 12, 9 n. 20, 19 n. 1, 20 n. 2, 56, 60 n. 15, 73 n. 35, 246
Royal Society, 61
Ruskin, John, 16–17, 19, 21–24, 35–38, 202–3, 204–34, 235–38

Sawyer, Paul L., 205–6, 220–21
Shaftesbury, Earl of, 58 n. 10, 61, 62 n. 20, 63 n. 23, 116–18
Skepticism, 4–5, 66–67, 94–95
Sterne, Laurence, 8 n. 17
Sublime: and cognitive failure, 70–71, 118–19, 138, 141–44; contrasted with beauty, 131–64

Turbayne, Colin Murray, 38, 98–99, 100 n. 11, 107–8
Turner, J. M. W., 205, 214–16, 223, 225–27
Tuveson, Ernest Lee, 8 n. 17, 8 n. 18, 73 n. 35

Verificationism, 6–7

Watt, Ian, 8, 22
Weiskel, Thomas, 141 n. 14, 152 n. 22, 154 n. 23
Wihl, Gary, 205 n. 1, 207 n. 4, 220–21
Williams, Michael, 5–6, 246
Wimsatt, W. K., 6–7, 8 n. 17, 62 n. 21, 63 n. 24
Wittgenstein, Ludwig, 60, 193 n. 17
Wordsworth, William: cited by Ruskin, 231–32; Hazlitt's discussion of, 165–74, 201; on reflections, 158